Published in Scotland by

BERNARD STOCKS
3 Lindsay Road, East Kilbride
Lanarkshire G74 4HZ

© September 2000

Layout and Design by
TRON PUBLISHING (UK) LTD
Glasgow

Cover Design by
NEIL SHAND
Cover photographs courtesy of The Daily Record and Sunday Mail

Printed in Scotland by
BELL & BAIN
Glasgow

Typeset in Univers

the winners

BERNARD STOCKS

Introduction

For over thirty years I have been hoping that a book like this would come on to the market. Eventually I realised that the only way to make it happen would be to do it myself, so herein lies the result of nearly three years of intensive research.

I feel that this book is necessary, before any more information is lost for all time. As you will see, some has already gone, and more will follow soon. Old newspapers are crumbling and won't be around for much longer. Though most have been microfilmed the film is often difficult and sometimes impossible to read. Old cups have been melted down to form new trophies, or have simply disappeared into thin air. And of course nobody thought to record the details of the engraving beforehand.

I have verified as much as I can, but a lot of the information has been so difficult to obtain that double-checking has not been possible. If anyone, therefore, should spot any errors please let me know. Similarly, if anyone can fill in any of the gaps in Sections 1 and 2, expand on the competitions in Section 3 or supply details of any competitions not covered, I would be delighted to hear from them. I'm planning an update in four or five years' time.

Where 'No Competition' has been shown, this is taken either from a direct statement to that effect in the press, or the fact that no results of league or cup fixtures have appeared for that competition season. In the latter case the check was made from a minimum of three newspapers.

I think I have included everyone who has given help in the acknowledements section that follows, but if I have inadvertently missed anyone out please accept my sincere apologies. I would like to give particular thanks to the staff at the many libraries I visited, especially those at Dundee Central Library, where they ferried well over 100 heavy bound volumes from basement to second floor and back for my use. Thanks also to the various Clubs that I visited, both Senior and Junior, for their hospitality and helpfulness. It has been a privilege to get a glimpse behind the scenes and see the sheer hard work that goes into running a football club. In particular, I am full of admiration for the Junior club officials, who work just as hard as their Senior counterparts but entirely without recompense. Last, but by no means least, thanks to my good friend Stewart Davidson, who not only supplied a good deal of the information herein but also kept my morale high with his encouragement and enthusiasm for the project.

Finally, I would like to dedicate this book to the memory of all those clubs no longer with us, from the successful ones who feature in these pages, such as St. Bernards, Third Lanark, Denbeath Star, Strathclyde, Burnbank Athletic, Stobswell et al, to those such as North Fife, Monifieth Tayside and Mount Ellen United who only flitted briefly on to the scene and never won anything. Each and every one is part of the rich tapestry that is Scottish Football history.

Bernard Stocks
August 2000

Sources & Acknowledgements

Books and Periodicals

A Bathgate History - Ian Anderson
Fifeshire Football Memories - David Allan
Forfar West End Centenary Brochure
A Game of Two Halves - John Byrne
Historic Saints of Edinburgh - George Campbell
History of the Highland Football League - Bill McAllister
The Juniors - David McGlone & Bill McClure
Non-League - Bob Barton
One Hundred Years of Football - Duncan Buchanan
Scottish Football Historian
Scottish Football League - The First 100 Years - Bob Crampsey
Scottish Non-League Review - Stewart Davidson
The Scottish Qualifying Cup - Stewart Davidson
Senior Non-League Football in South West Scotland - Malcolm Pagan
Renfrewshire F.A. Cup - The First 50 Years - Stewart Davidson

Newspapers

Sunday Post, Sunday Mail, Glasgow Herald, The Scotsman, Courier &
Advertiser, Evening Telegraph (Dundee), Evening News (Edinburgh),
The Bulletin, Sporting Post (Dundee), Scottish Referee, Perthshire Advertiser,
Forfar Despatch, Arbroath Herald, Dunfermline Press, Fife Free Press,
Fifeshire Advertiser, West Lothian Courier, West Lothian Gazette, East Lothian
Courier, Paisley Daily Express, Greenock Telegraph, Hamilton Advertiser,
Airdrie Advertiser, Stirling Journal, Falkirk Herald, Clydebank Post, Lennox
Herald, St Andrews Citizen, Central Fife Times, Evening Express (Aberdeen),
Northern Scot, Banffshire Herald, Banffshire Journal, Elgin Courant.

Libraries

Central Library, Aberdeen
Central Library, Dundee
Central Library, Edinburgh
Elgin Heritage Centre
The Mitchell Library, Glasgow
The National Library of Scotland
West Lothian Libraries HQ
Public Libraries at: Airdrie, Arbroath, Clydebank, Dumbarton, Dunfermline,
East Kilbride, Falkirk, Greenock, Haddington, Hamilton, Paisley, Perth,
St Andrews, Stirling, Woodside (Aberdeen)

Individual & Other Sources

Angus Press Ltd, Craig 'o Loch Road, Forfar
Auchinleck Talbot F.C.
G. Bennett - Vice President, Newtongrange Star F.C.
James Bolton, Chirnside
J. Derrick Brown - Secretary, Fife F.A.
John Byrne - Historian, Arthurlie F.C.
Richard Cairns - Kilmarnock F.C. Programme Editor
Stewart Davidson, Paisley
Dunfermline Press Ltd, Pitreavie Industrial Estate, Dunfermline
Hugh Ferguson - Secretary, Musselburgh Athletic F.C.
John Ferguson - Secretary & Historian, Kilsyth Rangers F.C.
Kenny Ferguson - Secretary, Brechin City F.C.
William C. Hardie - Ex-Secretary, Scottish Second XI Cup Committee
E.S. Gorrie - Former Editor, The (Dundee) Sporting Post
Jim Hendry - Ex-Commercial Manager, Falkirk F.C.
Jim Hutton, Cumbernauld
Simon Keates - Tron Publishing Ltd
D. Lapsley - Secretary, Bo'ness United F.C.
Linlithgow Rose F.C.
The Royal Bar, Harthill
Jim McAllister - Historian, Dumbarton F.C.
Arthur MacDonald - Ex-Secretary, East Regional J.F.A.
Peter McGauley - Secretary, Whitehill Welfare F.C.
Jock McKay - Assistant Secretary, North Caledonian F.A.
Robin Marwick - Historian, Albion Rovers F.C.
Douglas Mitchell - Historian, Carnoustie Panmure F.C.
Elaine Mearns - Secretary, Harthill Royal F.C.
Albert Moffat - President, Petershill F.C.
Albert Oswald - Secretary, Tayport F.C.
Ron Ross - Secretary, Fife Region Junior F.A.
The Scottish Football League
Duncan Simpson - Statistician, Dunfermline Athletic F.C.
John Simpson - Sports Editor, Alloa Advertiser
Scott Struthers - Secretary, Hamilton Academical F.C.
Brian Sweeney - The Daily Record and Sunday Mail
E. Tappenden - Airdrieonians F.C.
Tranent Juniors F.C.
Robert Weldon - Secretary, Oakley United F.C.
Social Club Committee, Whitburn F.C.
Magnus Wylie - Secretary, Jeanfield Swifts F.C.

Aberdeenshire Charity Cup

1887-88	Orion	1891-92	Aberdeen	1895-96	Victoria United
1888-89	*Cup Withheld*	1892-93	Orion	1896-97	Orion
1889-90	Victoria United	1893-94	Victoria United	1897-98	Aberdeen
1890-91	Victoria United	1894-95	Orion	1898-99	Orion

Aberdeenshire Cup

1887-88	Aberdeen	1925-26	Aberdeen	1965-66	Deveronvale
1888-89	Aberdeen	1926-27	Aberdeen	1966-67	Keith
1889-90	Aberdeen	1927-28	Aberdeen	1967-68	Peterhead
1890-91	Orion	1928-29	Aberdeen	1968-69	Peterhead
1891-92	Victoria United	1929-30	Aberdeen	1969-70	Peterhead
1892-93	Victoria United	1930-31	Aberdeen	1970-71	Peterhead
1893-94	Victoria United	1931-32	Aberdeen	1971-72	Peterhead
1894-95	Orion	1932-33	Aberdeen	1972-73	Fraserburgh
1895-96	Victoria United	1933-34	Aberdeen	1973-74	Keith
1896-97	Orion	1934-35	Peterhead	1974-75	Peterhead
1897-98	Aberdeen	1935-36	Peterhead	1975-76	Fraserburgh
1898-99	Orion	1936-37	Buckie Thistle	1976-77	Peterhead
1899-00	Victoria United	1937-38	Fraserburgh	1977-78	Keith
1900-01	Orion	1938-39	Buckie Thistle	1978-79	Peterhead
1901-02	Aberdeen	1939-45	*No competition*	1979-80	Keith
1902-03	Victoria United	1945-46	Buckie Thistle	1980-81	Aberdeen 'A'
1903-04	Aberdeen	1946-47	Peterhead	1981-82	Aberdeen 'A'
1904-05	Aberdeen	1947-48	Deveronvale	1982-83	Aberdeen 'A'
1905-06	Peterhead	1948-49	Peterhead	1983-84	Peterhead
1906-07	Aberdeen	1949-50	Peterhead	1984-85	Buckie Thistle
1907-08	Aberdeen	1950-51	Deveronvale	1985-86	Huntly
1908-09	Aberdeen	1951-52	Deveronvale	1986-87	Buckie Thistle
1909-10	Aberdeen	1952-53	Buckie Thistle	1987-88	Aberdeen 'A'
1910-11	Fraserburgh	1953-54	Buckie Thistle	1988-89	Peterhead
1911-12	Aberdeen	1954-55	Buckie Thistle	1989-90	Aberdeen 'A'
1912-13	Aberdeen	1955-56	Fraserburgh	1990-91	Aberdeen 'A'
1913-14	Aberdeen	1956-57	Buckie Thistle	1991-92	Huntly
1914-15	Aberdeen	1957-58	Keith	1992-93	Aberdeen 'A'
1915-19	*No competition*	1958-59	Peterhead	1993-94	Huntly
1919-20	Aberdeen	1959-60	Keith	1994-95	Deveronvale
1920-21	Aberdeen University	1960-61	Huntly	1995-96	Huntly
1921-22	Aberdeen	1961-62	Deveronvale	1996-97	Fraserburgh
1922-23	Aberdeen	1962-63	Peterhead	1997-98	Aberdeen 'A'
1923-24	Aberdeen	1963-64	Fraserburgh	1998-99	Peterhead
1924-25	Aberdeen	1964-65	Peterhead	1999-00	Huntly

Summary of Wins: *22 - Aberdeen; 20 - Peterhead; 8 - Aberdeen 'A', Buckie Thistle; - Fraserburgh; 6 - Deveronvale, Huntly, Keith, Victoria United; 5 - Orion; 1 - Aberdeen University.*

Aberdeenshire Shield

1991-92	Fraserburgh	1994-95	Deveronvale	1997-98	Keith
1992-93	Buckie Thistle	1995-96	Fraserburgh	1998-99	Peterhead
1993-94	Fraserburgh	1996-97	Fraserburgh	1999-00	Fraserburgh

Airdrie Charity Cup

1885-86 Airdrieonians	1889-90 Carfin Shamrock	*1893-94 No Competition*
1886-87 Airdrieonians	1890-91 Royal Albert	1894-95 Airdrieonians
1887-88 Airdrieonians	1891-92 Albion Rovers	
1888-89 No Competition	1892-93 Motherwell	

Alex Jack Trophy
(For member clubs of the East of Scotland F.A.)

1988-89 Kelso United	1992-93 Manor Thistle	1996-97 Edinburgh Athletic
1989-90 Berwick Rangers 'A'	1993-94 Craigroyston	1997-98 Tollcross United
1990-91 Easthouses Lily	1994-95 Preston Athletic	1998-99 Easthouses Lily
1991-92 Edinburgh City	1995-96 Manor Thistle	1999-00 Peebles Rovers

Annandale Cup

1900-01 Dumfries	1902-03 Nithsdale Wanderers	*1904-05 Not Completed*
1901-02 Maxwelltown Volunteers	1903-04 Dumfries	

Atholl Cup
(For member clubs of the Perthshire Senior F.A)

1887-88 Vale of Atholl	1900-01 St. Johnstone	1913-14 Stanley
1888-89 Vale of Atholl	1901-02 Scone	*1914-19 No Competition*
1889-90 Vale of Atholl	1902-03 Vale of Atholl	1919-20 Vale of Atholl
1890-91 Vale of Atholl	1903-04 Vale of Atholl	1920-21 Blairgowrie Amateurs
1891-92 Vale of Atholl 'A'	1904-05 Vale of Atholl	1921-22 Blairgowrie Amateurs
1892-93 Vale of Atholl	1905-06 St. Johnstone	1922-23 Vale of Atholl
1893-94 Our Boys Blairgowrie	1906-07 St. Johnstone	1923-24 Breadalbane
1894-95 Breadalbane	1907-08 St. Johnstone	1924-25 Breadalbane
1895-96 Vale of Atholl	1908-09 Our Boys Blairgowrie	1925-26 Vale of Atholl
1896-97 Vale of Atholl	1909-10 Our Boys Blairgowrie	1926-27 Breadalbane
1897-98 Vale of Atholl	1910-11 Scone	1927-28 Vale of Atholl
1898-99 Fair City Athletic	1911-12 Scone	1928-29 Vale of Atholl
1899-00 St. Johnstone	1912-13 Breadalbane	

Summary: *16 - Vale of Atholl; 5 - Breadalbane, St. Johnstone; 3 - Our Boys Blairgowrie, Scone; 2 - Blairgowrie Amateurs; 1 - Fair City Athletic, Stanley, Vale of Atholl 'A'.*

Ayr Charity Cup

1884-85 Ayr F.C.	1904-05 Ayr F.C.	1923-24 Ayr United
1885-86 Ayr F.C.	1905-06 Annbank	1924-25 Queens Park
1886-87 Ayr F.C.	1906-07 Ayr Parkhouse	1925-26 Ayr United
1887-88 Kilmarnock	1907-08 Beith	1926-27 Ayr United
1888-89 Kilbirnie	1908-09 Annbank	1927-28 Kilmarnock
1889-90 Annbank	*1909-10 Not Completed*	1928-29 Ayr United
1890-91 Ayr F.C.	*1910-11 No Competition*	1929-30 Ayr United
1891-92 Annbank	1911-12 Ayr United	1930-31 Ayr United
1892-93 Ayr F.C.	1912-13 Ayr United	1931-32 Ayr United
1893-94 Ayr Parkhouse	1913-14 Ayr United	1932-33 Ayr United
1894-95 Ayr Parkhouse	1914-15 Ayr United	1933-34 Kilmarnock
1895-96 Ayr Parkhouse	1915-16 Ayr United	1934-35 Kilmarnock
1896-97 Ayr Parkhouse	*1916-17 No Competition*	1935-36 Ayr United
1897-98 Ayr Parkhouse	1917-18 Queens Park	1936-37 Kilmarnock
1898-99 Ayr Parkhouse	1918-19 Ayr United	1937-38 Ayr United
1899-00 Annbank	1919-20 Queens Park	*1938-51 No Competition*
1900-01 Ayr F.C.	1920-21 Ayr United	1951-52 Ayr United
1901-02 Ayr F.C.	1921-22 Queens Park	
1902-04 No Competition	1922-23 Queens Park	

Summary; *18 - Ayr United; 8 - Ayr F.C.; 7 - Ayr Parkhouse; 5 - Annbank, Kilmarnock, Queen's Park; 1 - Beith, Kilbirnie.*

Ayrshire Combination

93-94	Annbank	1895-96	Ayr F.C.
94-95	Ayr F.C.	1896-97	Ayr F.C.

Ayrshire Cup (Senior)

77-78	Mauchline	1914-15	Stevenston United	1961-62	Kilmarnock
78-79	Kilmarnock Athletic	*1915-19*	*No Competition*	*1962-64*	*No Competition*
79-80	Beith	1919-20	Stevenston United	1964-65	Ayr United
80-81	Lugar Boswell	1920-21	Kilmarnock	1965-66	Kilmarnock
81-82	Kilmarnock Portland	1921-22	Kilmarnock	*1966-68*	*No Competition*
82-83	Kilmarnock Athletic	1922-23	Kilmarnock	1968-69	Ayr United
83-84	Kilmarnock	1923-24	Beith	1969-70	Ayr United
84-85	Kilmarnock	1924-25	Galston	1970-71	Ayr United
85-86	Kilmarnock	1925-26	Ayr United	1971-72	Kilmarnock
86-87	Hurlford	1926-27	Beith	1972-73	Kilmarnock
87-88	Kilbirnie	1927-28	Kilmarnock	1973-74	Kilmarnock
88-89	Hurlford	1928-29	Ayr United	1974-75	Ayr United
89-90	Annbank	1929-30	Kilmarnock	1975-76	Ayr United
90-91	Kilmarnock	1930-31	Kilmarnock	1976-77	Ayr United
91-92	Annbank	*1931-32*	*Not Completed*	1977-78	Ayr United
92-93	Annbank	1932-33	Ayr United	1978-79	Kilmarnock
93-94	Hurlford	*1933-34*	*No Competition*	1979-80	Ayr United
94-95	Annbank	1934-35	Kilmarnock	1980-81	Kilmarnock
95-96	Kilmarnock	1935-36	Ayr United	1981-82	Kilmarnock
96-97	Kilmarnock Athletic	*1936-37*	*Not Completed*	1982-83	Kilmarnock
97-98	Kilmarnock	1937-38	Ayr United	1983-84	Kilmarnock
98-99	Kilmarnock	1938-39	Ayr United	1984-85	Kilmarnock
99-00	Kilmarnock	*1939-46*	*No Competition*	1985-86	Ayr United
00-01	Ayr F.C.	1946-47	Kilmarnock	1986-87	Kilmarnock
01-02	Ayr Parkhouse	*1947-49*	*No Competition*	1987-88	Ayr United
02-03	Galston	1949-50	Ayr United	1988-89	Ayr United
03-04	Galston	1950-51	Kilmarnock	1989-90	Kilmarnock
04-05	Ayr F.C.	1951-52	Kilmarnock	1990-91	Ayr United
05-06	Ayr F.C.	1952-53	Kilmarnock	1991-92	Kilmarnock
06-07	Hurlford	1953-54	Kilmarnock	1992-93	Kilmarnock
07-08	Galston	1954-55	Kilmarnock	1993-94	Kilmarnock
08-09	Hurlford	1955-56	Kilmarnock	1994-95	Ayr United
09-10	Ayr F.C.	1956-57	Kilmarnock	1995-96	Kilmarnock
10-11	Hurlford	1957-58	Ayr United	1996-97	Ayr United
11-12	Ayr United	1958-59	Ayr United	1997-98	Kilmarnock
12-13	Galston	1959-60	Kilmarnock		
13-14	Galston	1960-61	Ayr United		

SUMMARY: *42 - Kilmarnock; 26 - Ayr United; 6 - Galston, Hurlford; 4 - Annbank, Ayr F.C.; - Beith, Kilmarnock Athletic; 2 - Stevenston United; 1 - Ayr Parkhouse, Kilbirnie, Kilmarnock Portland, Lugar Boswell, Mauchline.*

Ayrshire Qualifying Cup
(Formerly Ayrshire 2nd XI & Ayrshire Consolation Cup)

87-88	2nd Ayr	1900-01	Kilwinning Eglinton	1913-14	Hurlford
88-89	2nd Kilbirnie	1901-02	Kilwinning Eglinton	1914-15	Hurlford
89-90	2nd Kilmarnock	1902-03	Beith	*1915-19*	*No Competition*
90-91	2nd Annbank	1903-04	Annbank	*1919-20*	*Not Completed*
91-92	2nd Hurlford	1904-05	Annbank	*1920-21*	*No Competition*
92-93	2nd Kilmarnock	1905-06	Hurlford	1921-22	Stevenston United
93-94	*Not Completed*	1906-07	Kilmarnock 'A'	1922-23	Kilmarnock 'A'
94-95	2nd Ayr	1907-08	Galston	1923-24	Ayr United 'A'
95-96	2nd Lanemark	1908-09	Galston	1924-25	Galston
96-97	2nd Ayr Parkhouse	1909-10	Hurlford	1925-26	Kilmarnock 'A'
97-98	Ayr Parkhouse	1910-11	Hurlford	1926-27	Beith
98-99	Annbank	1911-12	Annbank		
99-00	Annbank	1912-13	Galston		

SUMMARY OVERLEAF

the winners

Summary *5 - Annbank, Hurlford; 4 - Galston; 3 - Kilmarnock 'A'; 2 - Beith, Kilwinning Eglinton, 2nd Ayr, 2nd Kilmarnock; 1 - Ayr Parkhouse, Ayr United 'A', Stevenston United, 2nd Annbank, 2nd Ayr Parkhouse, 2nd Hurlford, 2nd Kilbirnie, 2nd Lanemark.*

Birks Cup
(For member clubs of the Perthshire (Senior) F.A.)

1925-26	Breadalbane	1926-27	Vale of Atholl	1927-28	Vale of Atholl

Blenheim Cup
(Played for intermittently between St. Bernards and Leith Athletic)

1913-14	St. Bernards	1923-24	Leith Athletic	*1929-33*	*No Competition*
1914-15	Leith Athletic	*1924-25*	*No Competition*	1933-34	Leith Athletic
1915-16	St. Bernards	1925-26	Leith Athletic	1934-35	St. Bernards
1916-20	*No Competition*	1926-27	Leith Athletic	1935-36	St. Bernards
1920-21	St. Bernards	1927-28	Leith Athletic		
1921-23	*No Competition*	1928-29	St. Bernards		

Border Cup (1)

1873-74	Selkirk	1876-77	Peebles Rovers	1879-80	Selkirk
1874-75	Duns	1877-78	Selkirk		
1875-76	Selkirk	1878-79	Selkirk		

Border Cup (2)
(Full name - Scottish Border Counties Football Association Challenge Cup. Originally for East of Scotland League teams in the Borders, now played for by local amateur teams.)

1890-91	Selkirk	1909-10	Vale of Leithen	1932-33	Vale of Leithen
1891-92	Duns	1910-11	Berwick Rangers	1933-34	Vale of Leithen
1892-93	Selkirk	1911-12	Coldstream	1934-35	Duns
1893-94	Peebles	1912-13	Vale of Leithen	1935-36	Chirnside United
1894-95	Selkirk	1913-14	Gala Fairydean	1936-37	Jedforest Artisans
1895-96	Selkirk	*1914-19*	*No Competition*	1937-38	Duns
1896-97	Selkirk	1919-20	Peebles Rovers	1938-39	Selkirk
1897-98	Peebles	1920-21	Vale of Leithen	*1939-45*	*No Competition*
1898-99	Vale of Leithen	1921-22	Coldstream	1945-46	
1899-00	Vale of Leithen	1922-23	Coldstream	1946-47	Gala Fairydean
1900-01	Vale of Leithen	1923-24	Selkirk	1947-48	
1901-02	Vale of Leithen	1924-25	Coldstream	1948-49	
1902-03	Vale of Leithen	1925-26	Vale of Leithen	1949-50	
1903-04	Selkirk	1926-27	Civil Service Strollers	1950-51	Peebles Rovers
1904-05	Peebles Rovers	1927-28	Berwick Rangers	1951-52	Peebles Rovers
1905-06	Selkirk	1928-29	Berwick Rangers	1952-53	Peebles Rovers
1906-07	Berwick Rangers	1929-30	Berwick Rangers	1953-54	
1907-08	Peebles Rovers	1930-31	Selkirk	1954-55	
1908-09	Berwick Rangers	1931-32	Selkirk	1955-56	Gala Fairydean

Cafolla Cup
(See under Wigtownshire & Kirkcudbrightshire Cup)

Candida Casa Cup

1910-11	Newton Stewart	1911-12	Whithorn	1912-13	Newton Stewart

Central League (Senior)

1896-97	Cowdenbeath	*1898-09*	*No Competition*	1910-11	Dunfermline Athletic
1897-98	*Not Completed*	1909-10	Bo'ness	1911-12	Dunfermline Athletic

| 12-13 | Alloa | 1914-15 | Armadale | 1919-20 | Bo'ness |
| 13-14 | Armadale | *1915-19* | *No Competition* | 1920-21 | Bo'ness |

Chic Allan Memorial Cup
(For member clubs of the North Caledonian F.A.)

74-75	Golspie Sutherland	1983-84	Fort William	1992-93	Balintore
75-76	Golspie Sutherland	1984-85	Fort William	1993-94	Clachnacuddin
76-77	Bunillidh Thistle	1985-86	Tain St. Duthus	1994-95	Inverness Caledonian Th.
77-78	Dingwall Thistle	1986-87	Bunillidh Thistle	1995-96	Fearn Thistle
78-79	Dingwall Thistle	1987-88	Wick Academy	1996-97	Balintore
79-80	Dingwall Thistle	1988-89	Invergordon	1997-98	Balintore
80-81	Alness	1989-90	Balintore	1998-99	Inverness Caledonian Th.
81-82	Wick Academy	1990-91	Inverness Thistle	1999-00	Golspie Sutherland
82-83	Bunillidh Thistle	1991-92	Balintore		

Summary *5 - Balintore; 3 - Bunillidh Thistle, Dingwall Thistle, Golspie Sutherland; 2 - Fort William, Inverness Caledonian Thistle, Wick Academy; 1 - Alness, Clachnacuddin, Fearn Thistle, Invergordon, Inverness Thistle, Tain St. Duthus.*

Churchill Cup
(For member clubs of the South of Scotland F.A.)

81-82	Newton Stewart/5th KRV	1886-87	Mid-Annandale	1891-92	Mid-Annandale
82-83	Vale o' Nith	1887-88	Moffat	1892-93	Queen of the South W.
83-84	5th KRV	1888-89	5th KRV	1893-94	5th KRV
84-85	Queen of the South Wand.	1889-90	Moffat	1894-95	5th KRV
85-86	Queen of the South Wand.	1890-91	5th KRV		

City Cup
(See under East of Scotland (City) Cup)

Clackmannanshire Charity Cup (Senior)

87-88	Alloa	1890-91	Clackmannan	1893-94	Clackmannan
88-89	Alloa	1891-92	Clackmannan	1894-95	Alloa
89-90	Alloa	1892-93	Alva	1895-96	Alloa

Coatbridge Express Cup
(See under Lanarkshire Express Cup)

Cree Lodge Cup
(For member clubs of the South of Scotland F.A.)

21-22	Newton Stewart	*1939-46*	*No Competition*	1965-66	Stranraer 'A'
22-23	Whithorn	1946-47	Wigtown & Bladnoch	*1966-71*	*No Competition*
23-24	Newton Stewart	*1947-48*	*No Competition*	1971-72	St. Cuthbert Wanderers
24-25	Tarff Rovers	1948-49	Newton Stewart	*1972-74*	*No Competition*
25-26	Stranraer	1949-50	Stranraer 'A'	1974-75	Stranraer 'A'
26-27	Kirkcudbright	*1950-53*	*No Competition*	*1975-80*	*No Competition*
27-28	Stranraer	1953-54	Stranraer 'A'	1980-81	Dalbeattie Star
28-29	Newton Stewart	*1954-55*	*No Competition*	*1981-82*	*No Competition*
29-30	Newton Stewart	1955-56	Stranraer 'A'	1982-83	Annan Athletic
30-31	*No Competition*	*1956-57*	*No Competition*	*1983-84*	*No Competition*
31-32	*No Competition*	1957-58	Greystone Rovers	1984-85	Dalbeattie Star
32-33	Wigtown	*1958-59*	*No Competition*	*1985-86*	*No Competition*
33-34	Stranraer	1959-60	Stranraer 'A'	1986-87	St. Cuthbert Wanderers
34-35	Wigtown	1960-61	Threave Rovers	*1987-88*	*No Competition*
35-36	*No Competition*	1961-62	Newton Stewart	1988-89	St. Cuthbert Wanderers
36-37	Creetown	*1962-63*	*No Competition*	*1989-90*	*No Competition*
37-38	*No Competition*	1963-64	Newton Stewart	1990-91	Annan Athletic
38-39	St. Cuthbert Wanderers	*1964-65*	*No Competition*	*1991-92*	*No Competition*

CONTINUED OVERLEAF

1992-93	Threave Rovers	1995-96	Annan Athletic	1998-99	Tarff Rovers
1993-94	Annan Athletic	1996-97	Threave Rovers	1999-00	Tarff Rovers
1994-95	Annan Athletic	1997-98	Tarff Rovers		

Summary *7 - Newton Stewart; 6 - Stranraer 'A'; 5 - Annan Athletic; 4 - St. Cuthbert Wanderers, Tarff Rovers; 3 - Stranraer, Threave Rovers; 2 - Dalbeattie Star, Wigtown; 1 - Creetown, Greystone Rovers, Kirkcudbright, Whithorn, Wigtown & Bladnoch.*

Dewar Shield

(Competed for by Scottish League Clubs in east and central Scotland. Not played every year and occasionally one tournament would run over more than one season. The following is believed to be the complete list of winners.)

1898-99	King's Park	1913-14	Falkirk	1939-40	Aberdeen
1899-00	Dunblane	1914-15	Aberdeen	1945-46	Aberdeen
1900-01	Dundee	1926-27	Aberdeen	1949-50	Aberdeen
1901-02	Stenhousemuir	1927-28	Falkirk	1953-54	Buckie Thistle
1902-03	Dundee	1928-29	Aberdeen	1955-56	Stirling Albion
1903-04	Dundee Wanderers	1929-30	East Stirlingshire	1956-57	Stirling Albion
1904-05	Dundee	1930-31	Aberdeen	1958-59	St. Johnstone
1905-06	Falkirk	1931-32	Aberdeen	1959-60	St. Johnstone
1906-07	Aberdeen	1932-33	Aberdeen	1966-67	St. Johnstone
1907-08	St. Johnstone	1933-34	Aberdeen	1967-68	Dundee United
1908-09	Aberdeen	1934-35	St. Johnstone	1970-71	Dundee United
1909-10	Falkirk	1935-36	Aberdeen	1971-72	Dundee
1910-11	St. Johnstone	1936-37	Aberdeen	1972-73	Dundee
1911-12	St. Johnstone	1937-38	Arbroath	1982-83	St. Johnstone
1912-13	Aberdeen	1938-39	Falkirk		

Summary: *15 - Aberdeen; 8 - St. Johnstone; 5 - Dundee, Falkirk; 2 - Dundee United, Stirling Albion 1 - Arbroath, Buckie Thistle, Dunblane, Dundee Wanderers, East Stirlingshire, King's Park, Stenhousemuir.*

Drybrough Cup

1971-72	Aberdeen	1974-75	Celtic	1979-80	Rangers
1972-73	Hibernian	*1975-79*	*No Competition*	1980-81	Aberdeen
1973-74	Hibernian	1978-79	Rangers		

Dumfries & Galloway Cup

1898-99	6th G.R.V.	1906-07	Newton Stewart	1924-25	St. Cuthbert Wanderers
1899-00	Dumfries	1907-08	Maxwelltown Volunteers	1925-26	St. Cuthbert Wanderers
1900-01	Dumfries	1908-09	St. Cuthbert Wanderers	1926-27	St. Cuthbert Wanderers
1901-02	Douglas Wanderers	*1909-10*	*No Competition*	1927-28	Dalbeattie Star
1902-03	Maxwelltown Volunteers	*1910-11*	*Cup Withheld*	1928-29	Dalbeattie Star
1903-04	Maxwelltown Volunteers	1911-12	Dalbeattie Star	1929-30	St. Cuthbert Wanderers
1904-05	Dumfries	*1912-23*	*No Competition*	1930-31	Dalbeattie Star
1905-06	Dumfries	1923-24	Stranraer		

Dunbartonshire Charity Cup

1915-16	Clydebank	1919-20	Dumbarton	*1923-24*	*No Competition*
1916-17	Dumbarton	1920-21	Vale of Leven	1924-25	Clydebank
1917-18	Dumbarton	1921-22	Dumbarton		
1918-19	Dumbarton Harp	1922-23	Dumbarton		

Dunbartonshire Cup

1884-85	Dumbarton	1890-91	Dumbarton	1896-97	Vale of Leven
1885-86	Vale of Leven	1891-92	Dumbarton	1897-98	Dumbarton
1886-87	Renton	1892-93	Dumbarton	1898-99	Dumbarton
1887-88	Vale of Leven	1893-94	Dumbarton	1899-00	Vale of Leven
1888-89	Dumbarton	1894-95	Dumbarton	1900-01	Vale of Leven
1889-90	Dumbarton	1895-96	Renton	1901-02	Vale of Leven

902-04	No Competition	1915-16	Clydebank	1927-28	Clydebank
904-05	Vale of Leven	1916-17	Clydebank	1928-29	Clydebank
905-06	Vale of Leven	1917-18	Clydebank	1929-30	Dumbarton
906-07	Vale of Leven	1918-19	Clydebank	1930-31	Dumbarton
907-08	Renton	1919-20	Clydebank	1931-32	Dumbarton
908-09	Dumbaton	1920-21	Dumbarton	1932-33	Dumbarton
909-10	Dumbarton Harp	1921-22	Dumbarton	1933-34	Vale Ocoba
910-11	Vale of Leven	1922-23	Dumbarton	1934-35	Vale Ocoba
911-12	Dumbarton Harp	1923-24	Clydebank	1935-36	Dumbarton
912-13	Dumbarton Harp	1924-25	Helensburgh	1936-37	Dumbarton
913-14	Renton	1925-26	Dumbarton	1937-39	No Competition
914-15	Dumbarton	1926-27	Helensburgh	1939-40	Dumbarton

Summary: *23 - Dumbarton; 10 - Vale of Leven; 8 - Clydebank; 4 - Renton; 3 - Dumbarton Harp; - Helensburgh, Vale Ocoba.*

Dundee Charity Cup

(Dundee Burns Charity Cup until 1892)

890-91	Our Boys	1895-96	Wanderers	1886-87	Wanderers
891-92	East End	1883-84	Harp	1887-88	Wanderers
892-93	East End	1884-85	Harp	1888-89	Cup Withheld
893-95	No Competition	1885-86	Harp	1889-90	East End

Dunedin Cup

(Played for initially by the four Edinburgh Clubs plus Falkirk and Raith Rovers. Leith Athletic and St. Bernards dropped out after the first few years.)

909-10	St. Bernards	1918-20	No Competition	1927-28	Hearts
910-11	Hearts	1920-21	Hearts	1928-29	Hearts
911-12	Hearts	1921-22	Hibernian	1929-30	Hibernian
912-13	Hearts	1922-23	Falkirk	1930-31	Hearts
913-14	Falkirk	1923-24	Raith Rovers	1931-32	Hearts
914-15	Hearts	1924-25	Hearts	1932-33	Hearts
915-17	No Competition	1925-26	Hearts		
917-18	Falkirk	1926-27	Hearts		

Summary: *13 - Hearts; 3 - Falkirk; 2 - Hibernian; 1 - Raith Rovers, St. Bernards.*

Dunfermline Charity Cup

(See under Fifeshire Charity Cup)

Dunfermline Cottage Hospital Cup

896-97	Dunfermline Athletic	1898-99	Cowdenbeath	1900-02	No Competition
897-98	No Competition	1899-00	Cowdenbeath	1902-03	Lochgelly United

Eastern League

903-04	Bo'ness	1915-16	Armadale	1918-19	No Competition
904-05	East Fife	1916-17	Cowdenbeath	1919-20	Dundee Hibernians
905-15	No Competition	1917-18	Cowdenbeath		

East of Scotland (City) Cup

903-04	Hearts	1912-13	Cup withheld	1925-26	St. Bernards
904-05	Hearts	1913-14	Leith Athletic	1926-27	Leith Athletic
905-06	Hearts	1914-19	No Competition	1927-28	St. Bernards
906-07	Hearts	1919-20	St. Bernards	1928-29	Leith Athletic
907-08	Hearts	1920-21	St. Bernards	1929-30	Murrayfield Amateurs
908-09	St. Bernards	1921-22	Leith Athletic	1930-31	No Competition
909-10	Broxburn	1922-23	Peebles Rovers	1931-32	St. Bernards
910-11	Hearts	1923-24	Leith Athletic	1932-33	St. Bernards
911-12	St. Bernards	1924-25	St. Bernards	1933-34	No Competition

CONTINUED OVERLEAF

1934-35	St. Bernards	1962-63	Berwick Rangers	1981-82	Berwick Rangers
1935-36	Leith Athletic	1963-64	Hawick Royal Albert	1982-83	Berwick Rangers
1936-37	Leith Athletic	1964-65	Berwick Rangers	1983-84	Berwick Rangers
1937-38	St. Bernards	1965-66	Berwick Rangers	1984-85	Berwick Rangers
1938-46	*No Competition*	1966-67	Berwick Rangers	1985-86	Meadowbank Thistle
1946-47	Selkirk	1967-68	Berwick Rangers	1986-87	Berwick Rangers
1947-48	Edinburgh City	1968-69	Berwick Rangers	1987-88	Gala Fairydean
1948-49	Chirnside United	1969-70	Berwick Rangers	1988-89	Meadowbank Thistle
1949-50	Peebles Rovers	1970-71	Berwick Rangers	1989-90	Meadowbank Thistle
1950-51	Eyemouth United	1971-72	Berwick Rangers	1990-91	Berwick Rangers
1951-52	Berwick Rangers	1972-73	Berwick Rangers	1991-92	Vale of Leithen
1952-54	*No Competition*	1973-74	Berwick Rangers	1992-93	Berwick Rangers
1954-55	Peebles Rovers	1974-75	Berwick Rangers	1993-94	Whitehill Welfare
1955-57	*No Competition*	1975-76	Berwick Rangers	1994-95	Meadowbank Thistle
1957-58	Eyemouth United	1976-77	Berwick Rangers	1995-96	Berwick Rangers
1958-59	Duns	1977-78	Berwick Rangers	1996-97	Livingston
1959-60	Berwick Rangers	1978-79	Berwick Rangers	1997-98	Spartans
1960-61	Gala Fairydean	1979-80	Berwick Rangers	1998-99	Whitehill Welfare
1961-62	Berwick Rangers	1980-81	Meadowbank Thistle	1999-00	Whitehill Welfare

Summary: *28 - Berwick Rangers; 11 - St. Bernards; 7 - Leith Athletic; 6 - Hearts, Meadowbank/Livingston; 3 - Peebles Rovers, Whitehill Welfare; 2 - Eyemouth United, Gala Fairydean; 1 - Broxburn, Chirnside United, Duns, Edinburgh City, Hawick Royal Albert, Murrayfield Amateurs, Selkirk, Spartans, Vale of Leithen.*

East of Scotland Consolation Cup

1883-84	Bo'ness	1897-98	Raith Rovers	1911-12	Vale of Leithen
1884-85	Durhamtown Rangers	1898-99	Cowdenbeath	1912-13	Berwick Rangers
1885-86	Bo'ness	1899-00	Lochgelly United	1913-14	Berwick Rangers
1886-87	Bo'ness	1900-01	Cowdenbeath	*1914-19*	*No Competition*
1887-88	Leith Harp	1901-02	Bo'ness	1919-20	Edinburgh Civil Service
1888-89	Bo'ness	1902-03	Edinburgh Adventurers	1920-21	Leith Athletic
1889-90	Bo'ness	1903-04	Black Watch	1921-22	Berwick Rangers
1890-91	Polton Vale	1904-05	Broxburn	1922-23	Vale of Leithen
1891-92	Lassodie	1905-06	Berwick Rangers	1923-24	Coldstream
1892-93	Polton Vale	1906-07	Broxburn Athletic	1924-25	Leith Amateurs
1893-94	Penicuik Athletic	1907-08	Uphall	1925-26	Coldstream
1894-95	Lochgelly United	1908-09	Peebles Rovers	1926-27	Berwick Rangers
1895-96	Penicuik Athletic	*1909-10*	*Cup Withheld*	1927-28	Leith Amateurs
1896-97	Cowdenbeath	1910-11	Armadale	1928-29	Peebles Rovers

Summary: *6 - Bo'ness; 5 - Berwick Rangers; 3 - Cowdenbeath; 2 - Coldstream, Leith Amateurs, Leith Athletic, Lochgelly United, Peebles Rovers, Penicuik Athletic, Polton Vale, Vale of Leithen; 1 - Armadale, Black Watch, Broxburn, Broxburn Athletic, Durhamtown Rangers, Edinburgh Adventurers, Edinburgh Civil Service, Lassodie, Leith Harp, Raith Rovers, Uphall.*

East of Scotland League - Premier Division

1927-28	Berwick Rangers	1948-49	Hibernian 'B'	1964-65	Gala Fairydean
1928-29	Peebles Rovers	1949-50	Hearts 'B'	1965-66	Gala Fairydean
1929-30	Bathgate	1950-51	Hibernian 'B'	1966-67	Hawick Royal Albert
1930-31	Bathgate	1951-52	Hibernian 'B'	1967-68	Hawick Royal Albert
1931-32	Penicuik Athletic	1952-53	Hibernian 'B'	1968-69	Gala Fairydean
1932-33	Peebles Rovers	*1953-54*	*Not Completed*	1969-70	Cowdenbeath 'A'
1933-34	Peebles Rovers	1954-55	Eyemouth United	1970-71	Eyemouth United
1934-35	Peebles Rovers	1955-56	Eyemouth United	1971-72	Spartans
1935-36	Peebles Rovers	1956-57	Eyemouth United	1972-73	Civil Service Strollers
1936-37	Jedburgh Artisans	*1957-58*	*Not Completed*	1973-74	Hawick Royal Albert
1937-38	Penicuik Athletic	*1958-59*	*Not Completed*	1974-75	Selkirk
1938-39	Bo'ness	*1959-60*	*Not Completed*	1975-76	Selkirk
1939-45	*No Competition*	1960-61	Gala Fairydean	1976-77	Selkirk
1945-46	Peebles Rovers	1961-62	Gala Fairydean	1977-78	Vale of Leithen
1946-47	Berwick Rangers	*1962-63*	*Not Completed*	1978-79	Vale of Leithen
1947-48	Hibernian 'B'	1963-64	Gala Fairydean	1979-80	Whitehill Welfare

80-81	Whitehill Welfare	1987-88	Whitehill Welfare	1994-95	Whitehill Welfare
81-82	Whitehill Welfare	1988-89	Gala Fairydean	1995-96	Whitehill Welfare
82-83	Whitehill Welfare	1989-90	Annan Athletic	1996-97	Spartans
83-84	Spartans	1990-91	Gala Fairydean	1997-98	Whitehill Welfare
84-85	Whitehill Welfare	1991-92	Easthouses Lily	1998-99	Whitehill Welfare
85-86	Whitehill Welfare	1992-93	Whitehill Welfare	1999-00	Annan Athletic
86-87	Vale of Leithen	1993-94	Whitehill Welfare		

Summary: *13 - Whitehill Welfare; 8 - Gala Fairydean; 6 - Peebles Rovers; 5 - Hibernian 'B'; Eyemouth United; 3 - Hawick Royal Albert, Selkirk, Spartans, Vale of Leithen; 2 - Annan Athletic, Bathgate, Berwick Rangers, Penicuik Athletic; 1 -Bo'ness, Cowdenbeath 'A', Easthouses Lily, Hearts 'B', Jedburgh Artisans.*

East of Scotland League - Division One

87-88	Annan Athletic	1992-93	Civil Service Strollers	1997-98	Peebles Rovers
88-89	Peebles Rovers	1993-94	Tollcross United	1998-99	Easthouses Lily
89-90	Coldstream	1994-95	Pencaitland	1999-00	Threave Rovers
90-91	Easthouses Lily	1995-96	Edinburgh City		
91-92	Manor Thistle	1996-97	Lothian Thistle		

East of Scotland League Cup

87-88	Whitehill Welfare	1992-93	Edinburgh City	1997-98	Whitehill Welfare
88-89	Whitehill Welfare	1993-94	Gala Fairydean	1998-99	Whitehill Welfare
89-90	Berwick Rangers 'A'	1994-95	Whitehill Welfare	1999-00	Annan Athletic
90-91	Whitehill Welfare	1995-96	Whitehill Welfare		
91-92	Whitehill Welfare	1996-97	Whitehill Welfare		

East of Scotland Qualifying Cup

97-98	Raith Rovers	1931-32	Penicuik Athletic	1969-70	Gala Fairydean
98-99	West Calder	1932-33	Berwick Rangers	1970-71	Gala Fairydean
99-00	Cowdenbeath	1933-34	Berwick Rangers	1971-72	Eyemouth United
00-01	Raith Rovers	1934-35	Chirnside United	1972-73	Edinburgh University
01-02	Raith Rovers	1935-36	Duns	1973-74	Selkirk
02-03	Cowdenbeath	1936-37	Duns	1974-75	Hawick Royal Albert
03-04	Bathgate	1937-38	Peebles Rovers	1975-76	Selkirk
04-05	Bo'ness	1938-39	Berwick Rangers	1976-77	Edinburgh University
05-06	Bo'ness	*1939-46*	*No Competition*	1977-78	Hawick Royal Albert
06-07	Bathgate	1946-47	Gala Fairydean	1978-79	Vale of Leithen
07-08	West Lothian Albion	1947-48	Coldstream	1979-80	Civil Service Strollers
08-09	Broxburn	1948-49	Vale of Leithen	1980-81	Whitehill Welfare
09-10	Broxburn	1949-50	Peebles Rovers	1981-82	Vale of Leithen
10-11	Broxburn	1950-51	Peebles Rovers	1982-83	Postal United
11-12	Peebles Rovers	1951-52	Duns	1983-84	Spartans
12-13	Armadale	1952-53	Peebles Rovers	1984-85	Whitehill Welfare
13-14	Peebles Rovers	1953-54	Eyemouth United	1985-86	Whitehill Welfare
14-15	Peebles Rovers	1954-55	Peebles Rovers	1986-87	Gala Fairydean
15-18	*No Competition*	1955-56	Eyemouth United	1987-88	Gala Fairydean
18-19	Vale of Leithen	1956-57	Eyemouth United	1988-89	Civil Service Strollers
19-20	Vale of Leithen	1957-58	Murrayfield Amateurs	1989-90	Spartans
20-21	Edinburgh Civil Service	1958-59	Eyemouth United	1990-91	Gala Fairydean
21-22	Peebles Rovers	1959-60	Duns	1991-92	Whitehill Welfare
22-23	Peebles Rovers	1960-61	Duns	1992-93	Manor Thistle
23-24	Berwick Rangers	1961-62	Gala Fairydean	1993-94	Whitehill Welfare
24-25	Vale of Leithen	1962-63	Peebles Rovers	1994-95	Gala Fairydean
25-26	Corstorphine	1963-64	Ferranti Thistle	1995-96	Spartans
26-27	Gala Fairydean	1964-65	Hawick Royal Albert	1996-97	Lothian Thistle
27-28	Berwick Rangers	1965-66	Gala Fairydean	1997-98	Spartans
28-29	Murrayfield Amateurs	1966-67	Coldstream	1998-99	Whitehill Welfare
29-30	Murrayfield Amateurs	1967-68	Kelso United	1999-00	Whitehill Welfare
30-31	Murrayfield Amateurs	1968-69	Hawick Royal Albert		

SUMMARY OVERLEAF

Summary: *11 - Peebles Rovers; 10 - Gala Fairydean; 7 - Whitehill Welfare; 6 - Vale of Leithen; 5 - Berwick Rangers, Duns, Eyemouth United; 4 - Hawick Royal Albert, Murrayfield Amateurs, Spartans; 3 - Broxburn, Raith Rovers; 2 - Bathgate, Bo'ness, Civil Service Strollers, Coldstream, Cowdenbeath, Edinburgh University, Selkirk; 1 - Armadale, Chirnside United, Corstorphine, Edinbur, Civil Service, Ferranti Thistle, Kelso United, Lothian Thistle, Manor Thistle, Penicuik Athletic, Postal United, West Calder, West Lothian Albion.*

Edinburgh & District League

1930-31	Murrayfield Amateurs	1932-33	Murrayfield Amateurs	1934-35	Rosyth Dockyard
1931-32	Bathgate	1933-34	Penicuik Athletic		

East of Scotland Shield
(Edinburgh Challenge Cup until 1891)

1875-76	3rd Eastern R.V.	1918-19	Hearts	1960-61	Hibernian
1876-77	Thistle	1919-20	Hearts	1961-62	Hearts
1877-78	Hearts	1920-21	Hibernian	1962-63	Hibernian
1878-79	Hibernian	1921-22	Hearts	1963-64	Hearts
1879-80	Hibernian	1922-23	Hibernian	1964-65	Hearts
1880-81	Hibernian	1923-24	Hibernian	1965-66	Hearts
1881-82	Hibernian	1924-25	Hibernian	1966-67	Hearts
1882-83	University	1925-26	Hibernian	1967-68	Hibernian
1883-84	Hibernian	1926-27	Hearts	1968-69	Hearts
1884-85	Hibernian	1927-28	Hibernian	1969-70	Hearts
1885-86	Hibernian	1928-29	Hibernian	1970-71	Hibernian
1886-87	Hearts	1929-30	Hearts	*1971-72*	*Not Completed*
1887-88	Mossend Swifts	1930-31	Hearts	*1972-73*	*No Competition*
1888-89	Hearts	1931-32	Hearts	1973-74	Hearts
1889-90	Hearts	1932-33	Hearts	1974-75	Hearts
1890-91	Hearts	1933-34	Hearts	1975-76	Hearts
1891-92	Hearts	1934-35	Hibernian	1976-77	Hibernian
1892-93	Hearts	1935-36	Hearts	1977-78	Hibernian
1893-94	Hearts	1936-37	Hearts	*1978-79*	*No Competition*
1894-95	Bo'ness	1937-38	Hibernian	1979-80	Hibernian
1895-96	Mossend Swifts	1938-39	Hibernian	1980-81	Berwick Rangers
1896-97	St. Bernards	1939-40	Hearts	1981-82	Hearts
1897-98	Hearts	*1940-41*	*No Competition*	1982-83	Hibernian
1898-99	Hearts	1941-42	Hearts	1983-84	Berwick Rangers
1899-00	Hibernian	1942-43	Hibernian	*1984-85*	*No Competition*
1900-01	Raith Rovers	1943-44	Hearts	1985-86	Hearts
1901-02	Hearts	1944-45	Hibernian	1986-87	Hibernian
1902-03	Hibernian	1945-46	Hearts	1987-88	Hearts
1903-04	Hearts	1946-47	Hibernian	1988-89	Hearts
1904-05	Hibernian	1947-48	Hearts	1989-90	Hibernian
1905-06	Hibernian	1948-49	Hibernian	1990-91	Hibernian
1906-07	Hearts	1949-50	Hearts	1991-92	Hibernian
1907-08	Hibernian	1950-51	Hibernian	1992-93	Hearts
1908-09	Hibernian	1951-52	Hibernian	1993-94	Hibernian
1909-10	Hearts	1952-53	Hibernian	1994-95	Hearts
1910-11	Hibernian	1953-54	Hearts	1995-96	Hibernian
1911-12	Hibernian	1954-55	Hearts	*1996-97*	*No Competition*
1912-13	Hibernian	1955-56	Hearts	1997-98	Hearts
1913-14	Hearts	1956-57	Hibernian	1998-99	Hearts
1914-15	Hearts	1957-58	Hearts	*1999-00*	*Held over*
1915-17	*No Competition*	1958-59	Hibernian		
1917-18	Hibernian	1959-60	Hibernian		

Summary: *55 - Hearts; 51 - Hibernian; 2 - Berwick Rangers, Mossend Swifts, St. Bernards/3rd Eastern R.V.; 1 - Bo'ness, Raith Rovers, Thistle, University.*

Falkirk & District Charity Cup

1884-85	East Stirlingshire	1886-87	East Stirlingshire	1888-89	Camelon
1885-86	East Stirlingshire	1887-88	East Stirlingshire	1889-90	Falkirk

| 390-91 | East Stirlingshire | 1892-93 | Stenhousemuir | 1894-95 | Stenhousemuir |
| 391-92 | Falkirk | 1893-94 | Falkirk | 1895-96 | East Stirlingshire |

Falkirk Infirmary Shield
(Formerly the Falkirk Cottage Hospital Shield)

889-90	East Stirlingshire	1906-07	Falkirk	1924-25	East Stirlingshire
390-91	East Stirlingshire	1907-08	Falkirk	1925-26	Falkirk
391-92	Falkirk	1908-09	Falkirk	1926-27	East Stirlingshire
392-93	Falkirk	1909-10	Falkirk	1927-28	Falkirk
393-94	Falkirk	1910-11	Falkirk	1928-29	East Stirlingshire
394-95	Falkirk	1911-12	Stenhousemuir	1929-30	Falkirk
395-96	Stenhousemuir	1912-13	Falkirk	1930-31	Falkirk
396-97	Stenhousemuir	1913-14	Falkirk	1931-32	East Stirlingshire
397-98	Stenhousemuir	1914-15	Falkirk	1932-33	Falkirk
898-99	*No Competition*	*1915-16*	*No Competition*	1933-34	Falkirk
399-00	East Stirlingshire	1916-17	Falkirk	1934-35	Falkirk
900-01	*No Competition*	*1917-19*	*No Competition*	1935-36	Falkirk
901-02	Falkirk	1919-20	Falkirk	1936-37	Falkirk
902-03	Camelon	1920-21	Falkirk	1937-38	Falkirk
903-04	East Stirlingshire	1921-22	Falkirk	1938-39	Falkirk
904-05	Falkirk	1922-23	Falkirk	1939-40	Stenhousemuir
905-06	Falkirk	1923-24	Falkirk		

Summary: *32 - Falkirk; 8 - East Stirlingshire; 5 - Stenhousemuir; 1 - Camelon.*

Fife Cup

882-83	Dunfermline	1920-21	Raith Rovers	1965-66	Dun'line A./Raith Rovers
883-84	Dunfermline	1921-22	Raith Rovers	1966-67	Raith Rovers
884-85	Cowdenbeath	1922-23	Raith Rovers	1967-68	Raith Rovers
885-86	Alloa	1923-24	Cowdenbeath	1968-69	Raith Rovers
886-87	Dunfermline Athletic	1924-25	Raith Rovers	1969-70	Dunfermline Athletic
887-88	Lassodie	1925-26	Cowdenbeath	1970-71	Cowdenbeath
888-89	Cowdenbeath	1926-27	Dunfermline Athletic	1971-72	Raith Rovers
889-90	Cowdenbeath	1927-28	Cowdenbeath	1972-73	Dunfermline Athletic
890-91	Cowdenbeath	1928-29	Cowdenbeath	1973-74	East Fife
891-92	Raith Rovers	1929-30	Raith Rovers	1974-75	Dunfermline Athletic
892-93	Cowdenbeath	1930-31	East Fife	1975-76	Raith Rovers
893-94	Raith Rovers	1931-32	East Fife	1976-77	Dunfermline Athletic
894-95	Clackmannan	1932-33	East Fife	1977-78	East Fife
895-96	Clackmannan	1933-34	Dunfermline Athletic	1978-79	East Fife
896-97	Dunfermline Athletic	1934-35	Cowdenbeath	1979-80	Dunfermline Athletic
897-98	Raith Rovers	1935-36	East Fife	1980-81	Raith Rovers
898-00	*No Competition*	1936-37	East Fife	1981-82	Dunfermline Athletic
900-01	Hearts of Beath	*1937-46*	*No Competition*	1982-83	Dunfermline Athletic
901-02	Cowdenbeath	1946-47	Dunfermline Athletic	1983-84	Cowdenbeath
902-03	Hearts of Beath	*1947-48*	*No Competition*	1984-85	East Fife
903-04	Cowdenbeath	1948-49	Raith Rovers	1985-86	East Fife
904-05	Cowdenbeath	1949-50	East Fife	1986-87	Raith Rovers
905-06	Raith Rovers	1950-51	Raith Rovers	1987-88	Cowdenbeath
906-07	Kirkcaldy United	1951-52	Dunfermline Athletic	1988-89	Cowdenbeath
907-08	East Fife	1952-53	East Fife/Raith Rovers	1989-90	Raith Rovers
908-09	Raith Rovers	1953-54	East Fife	1990-91	Raith Rovers
909-10	Cowdenbeath	1954-55	East Fife/Raith Rovers	1991-92	Dunfermline Athletic
910-11	Dunfermline Athletic	1955-56	Raith Rovers	1992-93	Raith Rovers
911-12	Dunfermline Athletic	1956-57	Dun'line A./Raith Rovers	1993-94	Raith Rovers
912-13	Kirkcaldy United	1957-58	Dunfermline Athletic	1994-95	Raith Rovers
913-14	Dunfermline Athletic	1958-59	Dunfermline Athletic	1995-96	Cowdenbeath
914-15	Raith Rovers	1959-60	East Fife	1996-97	Dunfermline Athletic
915-16	Cowdenbeath	1960-61	Dunfermline Athletic	1997-98	Raith Rovers
916-17	Cowdenbeath	1961-62	Raith Rovers	1998-99	Raith Rovers
917-18	Dunfermline Athletic	1962-63	Dunfermline Athletic	1999-00	Raith Rovers
918-19	*No Competition*	1963-64	Dunfermline Athletic		
919-20	Dunfermline Athletic	1964-65	Dunfermline Athletic		

SUMMARY OVERLEAF

the winners

Summary: *34 - Raith Rovers (incl. 4 shared); 28 - Dunfermline Athletic (incl. 2 shared); 21 - Cowdenbeath; 16 - East Fife (incl. 2 shared); 2 - Clackmannan, Dunfermline, Hearts of Beath, Kirkcaldy United; 1 - Alloa, Lassodie.*

Fifeshire Charity Cup

(Formerly the Dunfermline Charity Cup)

1887-88	Cowdenbeath	1891-92	Dunfermline Athletic	1924-25	East Fife
1888-89	Cowdenbeath	1898-99	Cowdenbeath	1926-27	Cowdenbeath
1889-90	Lassodie	1899-00	Cowdenbeath		
1890-91	Raith Rovers	1923-24	Cowdenbeath		

Football Times Cup

(For member clubs of the North Caledonian F.A.)

1923-24	Citadel	1953-54	Inverness Caledonian	1977-78	Muir of Ord
1924-25	Inverness Thistle	1954-55	Inverness Caledonian	1978-79	Wick Academy
1925-26	Inverness Thistle	1955-56	Clachnacuddin	1979-80	Muir of Ord
1926-27	Nelson	1956-57	Clachnacuddin	1980-81	Tain St. Duthus
1927-28	Dingwall Victoria United	1957-58	Nairn County	1981-82	Tain St. Duthus
1928-29	Nelson	1958-59	Ross County	1982-83	Balintore
1929-30	Inverness Caledonian	1959-60	Inverness Thistle	1983-84	Fort William
1930-31	I.D.A.	1960-61	Ross County	1984-85	Dingwall Thistle
1931-32	Clachnacuddin	*1961-62*	*Not Completed*	1985-86	Muir of Ord
1932-33	Muir of Ord	1962-63	Clachnacuddin	1986-87	Bunillidh Thistle
1933-34	Nelson	1963-64	Inverness Caledonian	1987-88	Invergordon
1934-35	Inverness Thistle	1964-65	Ross County	1988-89	Balintore
1935-36	Inverness Caledonian	1965-66	Ross County	1989-90	Invergordon
1936-37	Nelson	1966-67	Avoch Rovers	1990-91	Invergordon
1937-38	*No Competition*	1967-68	Black Rock Rovers	1991-92	Clachnacuddin
1938-39	Inverness Caledonian	1968-69	Golspie Sutherland	1992-93	Clachnacuddin
1939-46	*No Competition*	1969-70	Inverness Caledonian	1993-94	Ross County
1946-47	Ross County	1970-71	Easter Ross	1994-95	Clachnacuddin
1947-48	Inverness Caledonian	1971-72	Dingwall Thistle	1995-96	Ross County
1948-49	Ross County	1972-73	Wick Academy	1996-97	Ross County
1949-50	Inverness Caledonian	1973-74	Brora Rangers	1997-98	Balintore
1950-51	Clachnacuddin	1974-75	Invergordon	1998-99	Inverness Cal. Th.
1951-52	Inverness Caledonian	1975-76	Dingwall Thistle	1999-00	Invergordon
1952-53	Inverness Thistle	1976-77	Invergordon		

Summary: *10 - Inverness Caledonian; 9 - Ross County; 8 - Clachnacuddin; 6 - Invergordon; 5 - Inverness Thistle; 4 - Muir of Ord, Nelson; 3 - Balintore, Dingwall Thistle; 2 - Tain St. Duthus, Wick Academy; 1 - Avoch Rovers, Black Rock Rovers, Brora Rangers, Bunillidh Thistle, Citadel, Dingwall Victoria United, Easter Ross, Fort William, Golspie Sutherland, I.D.A., Inverness Caledonian Thistle, Nairn County.*

Forfarshire Charity Cup

1887-88	Forfar Athletic	1890-91	Forfar Athletic	1893-94	Forfar Athletic
1888-89	Arbroath	1891-92	Forfar Athletic	*1894-97*	*No Competition*
1889-90	Forfar Athletic	1892-93	Montrose	1897-98	Montrose

Forfarshire Cup

1883-84	Arbroath	1893-94	Dundee	1903-04	Dundee Wanderers
1884-85	Harp	1894-95	Dundee	1904-05	Dundee
1885-86	Harp	1895-96	Arbroath	1905-06	Forfar Athletic
1886-87	Harp	1896-97	Arbroath	1906-07	Arbroath
1887-88	Arbroath	1897-98	Dundee Wanderers	1907-08	Forfar Athletic
1888-89	Arbroath	1898-99	Arbroath	1908-09	Dundee
1889-90	Our Boys	1899-00	Arbroath	1909-10	Brechin City
1890-91	Our Boys	1900-01	Dundee	1910-11	Dundee Hibernian
1891-92	Montrose	1901-02	Dundee Wanderers	1911-12	Dundee
1892-93	Arbroath	1902-03	Dundee	1912-13	Dundee

913-14	Arbroath	1947-48	Dundee United	1974-75	Dundee United
914-15	Dundee Hibernian	1948-49	Dundee	1975-76	Dundee United
915-16	Montrose	1949-50	Dundee	1976-77	Dundee United
916-19	*No Competition*	1950-51	Dundee United	1977-78	*Not Completed*
919-20	Dundee Hibernian	1951-52	Montrose	1978-79	Forfar Athletic
920-21	Arbroath	1952-53	Brechin City	1979-80	Dundee United
921-22	Montrose	1953-54	Dundee United	*1980-81*	*Not Completed*
922-23	Dundee	1954-55	Dundee	*1981-82*	*Not Completed*
923-24	Arbroath	1955-56	Dundee	*1982-83*	*Not Completed*
924-25	Dundee	*1956-57*	*Not Completed*	1983-84	Forfar Athletic
925-28	*No Competition*	1957-58	Arbroath	1984-85	Dundee United
928-29	Dundee United	1958-59	Brechin City	1985-86	Dundee
929-30	Dundee United	1959-60	Dundee	1986-87	Dundee United
930-31	Forfar Athletic	1960-61	Dundee United	1987-88	Dundee United
931-32	Montrose	1961-62	Montrose	1988-89	Dundee
932-33	Montrose	1962-63	Dundee United	1989-90	Dundee
933-34	Arbroath	1963-64	Not Completed	1990-91	Forfar Athletic
934-35	Dundee	1964-65	Dundee United	1991-92	Montrose
935-36	Arbroath	1965-66	Dundee	1992-93	St. Johnstone
936-37	Arbroath	1966-67	Dundee	1993-94	
937-38	Dundee	*1967-68*	*Not Completed*	1994-95	Forfar Athletic
938-39	Arbroath	1968-69	Dundee United	1995-96	Forfar Athletic
939-40	Arbroath	*1969-70*	*Not Completed*	1996-97	Brechin City
940-44	*No Competition*	1970-71	Dundee	1997-98	
944-45	Dundee	1971-72	Dundee United	1998-99	St. Johnstone
945-46	Dundee	1972-73	Not Completed	*1999-00*	*Held Over*
946-47	Dundee	1973-74	Montrose		

ummary: *26 - Dundee; 20 - Dundee United/Dundee Hibernian; 18 - Arbroath; 9 - Montrose; - Forfar Athletic; 4 - Brechin City; 3 - Dundee Wanderers, Harp; 2 - Our Boys, St. Johnstone.*

Gardeners Cup

Charity Cup for Linlithgowshire senior clubs, presented by the local Ancient Order of Free ardeners. Played for intermittently: this is believed to be the complete list of winners)

885-86	Armadale	1910-11	Broxburn	*1917-21*	*No Competition*
886-96	*No Competition*	1911-12	Broxburn	1921-22	Bathgate
896-97	Armadale Volunteers	1912-13	Broxburn United	1922-23	Armadale
897-07	*No Competition*	1913-14	Armadale	1923-24	Bathgate
907-08	Bathgate	1914-15	Broxburn United	1924-25	Broxburn United
908-09	West Lothian Albion	*1915-16*	*Not Completed*	1925-26	Armadale
909-10	Broxburn	1916-17	Armadale		

Glasgow Charity Cup

876-77	Queen's Park	1895-96	Celtic	1914-15	Celtic
877-78	Queen's Park	1896-97	Rangers	1915-16	Celtic
878-79	Rangers	1897-98	Third Lanark	1916-17	Celtic
879-80	Queen's Park	1898-99	Celtic	1917-18	Celtic
880-81	Queen's Park	1899-00	Rangers	1918-19	Rangers
881-82	Vale of Leven	1900-01	Third Lanark	1919-20	Celtic
882-83	Queen's Park	1901-02	Hibernian	1920-21	Celtic
883-84	Queen's Park	1902-03	Celtic	1921-22	Rangers
884-85	Queen's Park	1903-04	Rangers	1922-23	Rangers
885-86	Renton	1904-05	Celtic	1923-24	Celtic
886-87	Renton	1905-06	Rangers	1924-25	Rangers
887-88	Renton	1906-07	Rangers	1925-26	Celtic
888-89	Renton	1907-08	Celtic	1926-27	Partick Thistle
889-90	Third Lanark	1908-09	Rangers	1927-28	Rangers
890-91	Queen's Park	1909-10	Clyde	1928-29	Rangers
891-92	Celtic	1910-11	Rangers	1929-30	Rangers
892-93	Celtic	1911-12	Celtic	1930-31	Rangers
893-94	Celtic	1912-13	Celtic	1931-32	Rangers
894-95	Celtic	1913-14	Celtic	1932-33	Rangers

CONTINUED OVERLEAF

1933-34	Rangers	1943-44	Rangers	1953-54	Third Lanark
1934-35	Partick Thistle	1944-45	Rangers	1954-55	Rangers
1935-36	Celtic	1945-46	Rangers	1955-56	Third Lanark
1936-37	Celtic	1946-47	Rangers	1956-57	Rangers
1937-38	Celtic	1947-48	Rangers	1957-58	Clyde
1938-39	Rangers	1948-49	Partick Thistle	1958-59	Celtic
1939-40	Rangers	1949-50	Celtic	1959-60	Rangers
1940-41	Rangers	1950-51	Rangers	1960-61	Celtic
1941-42	Rangers	1951-52	Clyde		
1942-43	Celtic	1952-53	Celtic		

Summary: *32 - Rangers; 28 - Celtic; 8 - Queen's Park; 5 - Third Lanark; 4 - Renton; 3 - Clyde, Partick Thistle; 1 - Hibernian, Vale of Leven.*

Glasgow Cup

1887-88	Cambuslang	1921-22	Rangers	1955-56	Celtic
1888-89	Queen's Park	1922-23	Rangers	1956-57	Rangers
1889-90	Queen's Park	1923-24	Rangers	1957-58	Rangers
1890-91	Celtic	1924-25	Rangers	1958-59	Clyde
1891-92	Celtic	1925-26	Clyde	1959-60	Rangers
1892-93	Rangers	1926-27	Celtic	1960-61	Partick Thistle
1893-94	Rangers	1927-28	Celtic	1961-62	Celtic
1894-95	Celtic	1928-29	Celtic	1962-63	Third Lanark
1895-96	Celtic	1929-30	Rangers	1963-64	Celtic
1896-97	Rangers	1930-31	Celtic	1964-65	Celtic
1897-98	Rangers	1931-32	Rangers	*1965-66*	*No Competition*
1898-99	Queen's Park	1932-33	Rangers	1966-67	Celtic
1899-00	Rangers	1933-34	Rangers	1967-68	Celtic
1900-01	Rangers	1934-35	Partick Thistle	1968-69	Rangers
1901-02	Rangers	1935-36	Rangers	1969-70	Celtic
1902-03	Third Lanark	1936-37	Rangers	1970-71	Rangers
1903-04	Third Lanark	1937-38	Rangers	*1971-74*	*No Competition*
1904-05	Celtic	1938-39	Celtic	1974-75	Rangers/Celtic
1905-06	Celtic	1939-40	Rangers	1975-76	Rangers
1906-07	Celtic	1940-41	Celtic	*1976-77*	*Not Completed*
1907-08	Celtic	1941-42	Rangers	*1977-78*	*No Competition*
1908-09	Third Lanark	1942-43	Rangers	1978-79	Rangers
1909-10	Celtic	1943-44	Rangers	1979-80	Not Completed
1910-11	Rangers	1944-45	Rangers	1980-81	Partick Thistle
1911-12	Rangers	1945-46	Queen's Park	1981-82	Celtic
1912-13	Rangers	1946-47	Clyde	1982-83	Rangers
1913-14	Rangers	1947-48	Rangers	*1983-84*	*No Competition*
1914-15	Clyde	1948-49	Celtic	1984-85	Rangers
1915-16	Celtic	1949-50	Rangers	1985-86	Rangers
1916-17	Celtic	1950-51	Partick Thistle	1986-87	Rangers
1917-18	Rangers	1951-52	Clyde	*1987-88*	*Not Completed*
1918-19	Rangers	1952-53	Partick Thistle	1988-89	Partick Thistle
1919-20	Celtic	1953-54	Rangers	1989-90	Celtic
1920-21	Celtic	1954-55	Partick Thistle		

Summary: *41 - Rangers*; 30 - Celtic*; 7 - Partick Thistle; 5 - Clyde; 4 - Queen's Park, Third Lanark; 1 - Cambuslang.   * includes 1 shared.*

Greenock & District Charity Cup

1884-85	Morton	1888-89	Morton	1892-93	Partick Thistle
1885-86	Morton	1889-90	Dumbarton	1893-94	Morton
1886-87	Morton	1890-91	Dumbarton		
1887-88	Dumbarton Athletic	1891-92	Morton		

Haig Gordon Memorial Trophy
(For member clubs of the South of Scotland F.A.)

1964-65	Tarff Rovers	1966-67	Threave Rovers	1968-69	Threave Rovers
1965-66	Tarff Rovers	1967-68	Stranraer 'A'	1969-70	St. Cuthbert Wanderers

1970-71	Stranraer 'A'	1980-81	Threave Rovers	1990-91	Wigtown & Bladnoch
1971-72	Stranraer 'A'	1981-82	Wigtown & Bladnoch	1991-92	Maxwelltown HSFP
1972-73	St. Cuthbert Wanderers	1982-83	Dalbeattie Star	1992-93	Annan Athletic
1973-74	Threave Rovers	1983-84	Annan Athletic	1993-94	Annan Athletic
1974-75	Stranraer 'A'	1984-85	Stranraer ' A'	*1994-95*	*No Competition*
1975-76	Stranraer 'A'	1985-86	Annan Athletic	1995-96	Annan Athletic
1976-77	Stranraer 'A'	*1986-87*	*No Competition*	1996-97	Stranraer Athletic
1977-78	Dalbeattie Star	1987-88	Annan Athletic	1997-98	St. Cuthbert Wanderers
1978-79	*No Competition*	1988-89	Dalbeattie Star	1998-99	Tarff Rovers
1979-80	Threave Rovers	1989-90	Threave Rovers	1999-00	Tarff Rovers

Summary: 7 - Stranraer 'A'; 6 - Annan Athletic, Threave Rovers; 4 - St. Cuthbert Wanderers, Tarff Rovers; 3 - Dalbeattie Star; 2 - Wigtown & Bladnoch; 1 - Maxwelltown HSFP, Stranraer Athletic.

Highland League

1893-94	Inverness Thistle	1929-30	Huntly	1968-69	Elgin City
1894-95	Clachnacuddin	1930-31	Inverness Caledonian	1969-70	Elgin City
1895-96	Inverness Caledonian	1931-32	Elgin City	1970-71	Inverness Caledonian
1896-97	Clachnacuddin	1932-33	Fraserburgh	1971-72	Inverness Thistle
1897-98	Clachnacuddin	1933-34	Buckie Thistle	1972-73	Inverness Thistle
1898-99	Inverness Caledonian	1934-35	Elgin City	1973-74	Elgin City
1899-00	Inverness Caledonian	1935-36	Inverness Thistle	1974-75	Clachnacuddin
1900-01	Clachnacuddin	1936-37	Buckie Thistle	1975-76	Nairn County
1901-02	Inverness Caledonian	1937-38	Fraserburgh	1976-77	Inverness Caledonian
1902-03	Clachnacuddin	1938-39	Clachnacuddin	1977-78	Inverness Caledonian
1903-04	Clachnacuddin	*1939-46*	*No Competition*	1978-79	Keith
1904-05	Clachnacuddin	1946-47	Peterhead	1979-80	Keith
1905-06	Clachnacuddin	1947-48	Clachnacuddin	1980-81	Keith
1906-07	Inverness Thistle	1948-49	Peterhead	1981-82	Inverness Caledonian
1907-08	Clachnacuddin	1949-50	Peterhead	1982-83	Inverness Caledonian
1908-09	Inverness Citadel	1950-51	Inverness Caledonian	1983-84	Inverness Caledonian
1909-10	Inverness Thistle	1951-52	Inverness Caledonian	1984-85	Keith
1910-11	Inverness Caledonian	1952-53	Elgin City	1985-86	Forres Mechanics
1911-12	Clachnacuddin	1953-54	Buckie Thistle	1986-87	Inverness Thistle
1912-13	Aberdeen 'A'	*1954-55*	*Not Completed*	1987-88	Inverness Caledonian
1913-14	Inverness Caledonian	1955-56	Elgin City	1988-89	Peterhead
1914-15	*Not Completed*	1956-57	Buckie Thistle	1989-90	Elgin City
1915-19	*No Competition*	1957-58	Buckie Thistle	1990-91	Ross County
1919-20	Buckie Thistle	1958-59	Rothes	1991-92	Ross County
1920-21	Clachnacuddin	1959-60	Elgin City	1992-93	Elgin City#
1921-22	Clachnacuddin	1960-61	Elgin City	1993-94	Huntly
1922-23	Clachnacuddin	1961-62	Keith	1994-95	Huntly
1923-24	Clachnacuddin	1962-63	Elgin City	1995-96	Huntly
1924-25	Aberdeen 'A'	1963-64	Inverness Caledonian	1996-97	Huntly
1925-26	Inverness Caledonian	1964-65	Elgin City	1997-98	Huntly
1926-27	Buckie Thistle	1965-66	Elgin City	1998-99	Peterhead
1927-28	Buckie Thistle	1966-67	Ross County	1999-00	Keith
1928-29	Inverness Thistle	1967-68	Elgin City		

= CHAMPIONSHIP WITHHELD

Summary: 18 - Inverness Caledonian; 17 - Clachnacuddin; 15 - Elgin City; 8 - Buckie Thistle, Inverness Thistle; 6 - Huntly, Keith; 5 -Peterhead; 3 - Ross County; 2 - Aberdeen 'A', Fraserburgh; 1 - Forres Mechanics, Inverness Citadel, Nairn County, Rothes.

Highland League Cup

1946-47	Forres Mechanics	1954-55	Forres Mechanics	1962-63	Peterhead
1947-48	Clachnacuddin	1955-56	Buckie Thistle	1963-64	Nairn County
1948-49	Huntly	1956-57	Buckie Thistle	1964-65	Keith
1949-50	Ross County	1957-58	Buckie Thistle	1965-66	Peterhead
1950-51	Clachnacuddin	1958-59	Fraserburgh	1966-67	Elgin City
1951-52	Huntly	1959-60	Elgin City	1967-68	Peterhead
1952-53	Inverness Caledonian	1960-61	Buckie Thistle	1968-69	Ross County
1953-54	Buckie Thistle	1961-62	Lossiemouth	1969-70	Inverness Caledonian

CONTINUED OVERLEAF

1970-71	Inverness Thistle	1980-81	Peterhead	1990-91	Elgin City
1971-72	Inverness Caledonian	1981-82	Clachnacuddin	1991-92	Ross County
1972-73	Inverness Thistle	1982-83	Elgin City	1992-93	Huntly
1973-74	Keith	1983-84	Keith	1993-94	Huntly
1974-75	Keith	1984-85	Buckie Thistle	1994-95	Cove Rangers
1975-76	Keith	1985-86	Keith	1995-96	Huntly
1976-77	Inverness Caledonian	1986-87	Inverness Caledonian	1996-97	Lossiemouth
1977-78	Inverness Caledonian	1987-88	Inverness Thistle	1997-98	Elgin City
1978-79	Ross County	1988-89	Keith	1998-99	Forres Mechanics
1979-80	Buckie Thistle	1989-90	Peterhead	1999-00	Cove Rangers

Summary: *7 - Buckie Thistle, Keith; 6 - Inverness Caledonian; 5 - Elgin City, Huntly, Peterhead; 4 - Ross County; 3 - Clachnacuddin, Forres Mechanics, Inverness Thistle; 2 - Cove Rangers, Lossiemouth; 1 - Fraserburgh, Nairn County.*

Inverness Cup

1895-96	Inverness Caledonian	1926-27	Inverness Thistle	1973-74	Inverness Thistle
1896-97	Inverness Caledonian	1927-28	Inverness Thistle	*1974-75*	*No Competition*
1897-98	Clachnacuddin	1928-29	Clachnacuddin	1975-76	Inverness Thistle
1898-99	Inverness Caledonian	1929-30	Clachnacuddin	1976-77	Nairn County
1899-00	Inverness Caledonian	1930-31	Ross County	1977-78	Inverness Caledonian
1900-01	Clachnacuddin	1931-32	Inverness Citadel	1978-79	Ross County
1901-02	Inverness Caledonian	1932-33	Inverness Thistle	1979-80	Ross County
1902-03	Inverness Citadel	1933-34	Inverness Thistle	1980-81	Inverness Thistle
1903-04	Clachnacuddin	1934-35	Inverness Thistle	1981-82	Inverness Thistle
1904-05	Clachnacuddin	1935-36	Inverness Thistle	1982-83	Inverness Caledonian
1905-06	Inverness Thistle	1936-37	Clachnacuddin	1983-84	Inverness Thistle
1906-07	Clachnacuddin	1937-38	Elgin City	1984-85	Inverness Caledonian
1907-08	Inverness Caledonian	1938-39	Inverness Thistle	1985-86	Forres Mechanics
1908-09	Inverness Thistle	*1939-51*	*No Competition*	1986-87	Inverness Caledonian
1909-10	Clachnacuddin	1951-52	Clachnacuddin	1987-88	Inverness Thistle
1910-11	Inverness Caledonian	1952-53	Clachnacuddin	1988-89	Inverness Caledonian
1911-12	Inverness Caledonian	1953-54	Inverness Thistle	1989-90	Forres Mechanics
1912-13	Inverness Caledonian	*1954-59*	*No Competition*	1990-91	Inverness Thistle
1913-14	Inverness Caledonian	1959-60	Ross County	1991-92	Ross County
1914-19	*No Competition*	*1960-63*	*No Competition*	1992-93	Ross County
1919-20	Clachnacuddin	1963-64	Inverness Caledonian	1993-94	Inverness Thistle
1920-21	Inverness Caledonian	1964-65	Ross County	1994-95	Brora Rangers
1921-22	Clachnacuddin	*1965-66*	*No Competition*	1995-96	Inverness Caledonian T
1922-23	Inverness Caledonian	1966-67	Ross County	1996-97	Inverness Caledonian T
1923-24	Clachnacuddin	*1967-70*	*No Competition*	1997-98	Inverness Cal. Thistle 'A
1924-25	Inverness Thistle	1970-71	Elgin City	1998-99	Inverness Caledonian T
1925-26	Inverness Caledonian	*1971-73*	*No Competition*	1999-00	Inverness Caledonian T

Summary: *19 - Inverness Caledonian, Inverness Thistle; 14 - Clachnacuddin; 8 - Ross County; 4 - Inverness Caledonian Thistle; 2 - Elgin City, Forres Mechanics, Inverness Citadel; 1 - Brora Rangers, Inverness Caledonian Thistle 'A', Nairn County.*

Johnstone-Currie Cup

1946-47	St. Andrew's	1948-49	LMS Rovers
1947-48	St. Andrew's	1949-50	Annan Athletic

Kilmarnock Charity Cup

1880-81	*Not Completed*	1889-90	Hurlford	1898-99	Kilmarnock
1881-82	Kilmarnock Portland	1890-91	Annbank	1899-00	Kilmarnock
1882-83	Kilmarnock Athletic	1891-92	Kilmarnock	1900-01	Kilmarnock
1883-84	Kilmarnock	1892-93	Annbank	1901-02	Kilwinning Eglinton
1884-85	Ayr F.C.	1893-94	Kilmarnock	*1902-13*	*No Competition*
1885-86	Kilmarnock	1894-95	Ayr Parkhouse	1913-14	Kilmarnock
1886-87	Ayr F.C.	1895-96	Kilmarnock	1914-27	No Competition
1887-88	Hurlford	1896-97	Ayr Parkhouse	1928	Kilmarnock
1888-89	Kilbirnie	1897-98	Kilmarnock	1929	Kilmarnock

30	Ayr United	1934	Ayr United	1938	*No Competition*
31	Kilmarnock	1935	Kilmarnock	1939	Kilmarnock
32	Kilmarnock	1936	Ayr United		
33	Ayr United	1937	Ayr United		

summary: *16 - Kilmarnock; 5 - Ayr United; 2 - Annbank, Ayr F.C., Ayr Parkhouse, Hurlford; Kilbirnie, Kilmarnock Athletic, Kilmarnock Portland, Kilwinning Eglinton.*

King Cup

87-88	Mossend Swifts	1926-27	Berwick Rangers	1966-67	Hawick Royal Albert
88-89	Mossend Swifts	1927-28	Civil Service Strollers	1967-68	Coldstream
89-90	Broxburn	1928-29	Berwick Rangers	1968-69	Gala Fairydean
90-91	Armadale	1929-30	Gala Fairydean	1969-70	Hearts Colts
91-92	Raith Rovers	1930-31	Bathgate	1970-71	Hearts Colts
92-93	Bathgate Rovers	1931-32	Penicuik Athletic	1971-72	Gala Fairydean
93-94	Bo'ness	1932-33	Penicuik Athletic	1972-73	Hibernian Colts
94-95	Cowdenbeath	1933-34	Berwick Rangers	1973-74	Spartans
95-96	Polton Vale	1934-35	Clerwood Amateurs	1974-75	Selkirk
96-97	Mossend Swifts	1935-36	Duns	1975-76	Selkirk
97-98	St. Bernards	1936-37	Penicuik Athletic	1976-77	Edinburgh University
98-99	Cowdenbeath	1937-38	Vale of Leithen	1977-78	Spartans
99-00	Raith Rovers	1938-39	Penicuik Athletic	*1978-79*	*No Competition*
00-01	Cowdenbeath	1939-40	Duns	1979-80	Kelso United
01-02	Raith Rovers	*1940-46*	*No Competition*	1980-81	Berwick Rangers 'A'
02-03	Lochgelly United	1946-47	Gala Fairydean	1981-82	Hawick Royal Albert
03-04	Hearts of Beath	1947-48	Hibernian 'B'	1982-83	Whitehill Welfare
04-05	Bathgate	1948-49	Hibernian 'B'	1983-84	Hawick Royal Albert
05-06	Bathgate	1949-50	Hearts 'B'	1984-85	Postal United
06-07	Broxburn	1950-51	Hearts 'B'	1985-86	Vale of Leithen
07-08	West Lothian Albion	1951-52	Hearts 'B'	1986-87	Vale of Leithen
08-09	Peebles Rovers	1952-53	Peebles Rovers	1987-88	Spartans
09-10	Berwick Rangers	1953-54	Peebles Rovers	1988-89	Gala Fairydean
10-11	West Calder Swifts	*1954-55*	*Not Completed*	1989-90	Berwick Rangers 'A'
11-12	Gala Fairydean	1955-56	Vale of Leithen	1990-91	Civil Service Strollers
12-13	Gala Fairydean	*1956-57*	*Not Completed*	1991-92	Vale of Leithen
13-14	*No Competition*	1957-58	Duns	1992-93	Whitehill Welfare
14-15	Gala Fairydean	1958-59	Eyemouth United	1993-94	Whitehill Welfare
15-20	*No Competition*	1959-60	Vale of Leithen	1994-95	Whitehill Welfare
20-21	Bo'ness	1960-61	Gala Fairydean	1995-96	Whitehill Welfare
21-22	Edinburgh Civil Service	1961-62	Peebles Rovers	1996-97	Craigroyston
22-23	Vale of Leithen	1962-63	Peebles Rovers	1997-98	Whitehill Welfare
23-24	Leith Athletic	1963-64	Duns	1998-99	Edinburgh City
24-25	Berwick Rangers	1964-65	Gala Fairydean	1999-00	Edinburgh City
25-26	Civil Service Strollers	1965-66	Gala Fairydean		

summary: *11 - Gala Fairydean; 7 - Berwick Rangers, Vale of Leithen; 6 - Whitehill Welfare; Hearts 'B'/Colts, Peebles Rovers; 4 - Duns, Penicuik Athletic; 3 - Bathgate, Civil Service Strollers, Cowdenbeath, Hawick Royal Albert, Hibernian 'B'/Colts, Mossend Swifts, Raith Rovers, Spartans; Bo'ness, Broxburn, Edinburgh City, Selkirk; 1 - Armadale, Bathgate Rovers, Clerwood Amateurs, Coldstream, Craigroyston, Edinburgh Civil Service, Edinburgh University, Eyemouth United, Hearts of Beath, Kelso United, Leith Athletic, Lochgelly United, Polton Vale, Postal United, St. Bernards, West Calder Swifts, West Lothian Albion*

Kirkcaldy Cottage Hospital Cup

| 96-97 | Raith Rovers | 1898-99 | Raith Rovers | 1902-03 | Raith Rovers |
| 97-98 | Raith Rovers | 1901-02 | Buckhaven | | |

Lanarkshire Cup

79-80	Stonelaw	1883-84	Cambuslang	1887-88	Airdrieonians
80-81	Thistle	1884-85	Cambuslang	1888-89	Royal Albert
81-82	Shotts	1885-86	Airdrieonians	1889-90	Royal Albert
82-83	West Benhar	1886-87	Airdrieonians	1890-91	Airdrieonians

CONTINUED OVERLEAF

1891-92	Airdrieonians	1924-25	Airdrieonians	1964-65	Airdrieonians
1892-93	Wishaw Thistle	*1925-26*	*Cup withheld*	1965-66	Airdrieonians
1893-94	Royal Albert	1926-27	Motherwell	1966-67	Airdrieonians
1894-95	Motherwell	1927-28	Motherwell	1967-68	Motherwell
1895-96	Royal Albert	1928-29	Motherwell	1968-69	Motherwell
1896-97	Airdrieonians	1929-30	Motherwell	1969-70	Airdrieonians
1897-98	Airdrieonians	1930-31	Airdrieonians	1970-71	Airdrieonians
1898-99	Motherwell	1931-32	Motherwell	*1971-72*	*Not Completed*
1899-00	Albion Rovers	*1932-33*	*Not Completed*	1972-73	Motherwell
1900-01	Motherwell	1933-34	Hamilton Academical	1973-74	Albion Rovers
1901-02	Hamilton Academical	1934-35	Airdrieonians	1974-75	Albion Rovers
1902-03	Airdrieonians	1935-36	Airdrieonians	1975-76	Airdrieonians
1903-04	Airdrieonians	*1936-37*	*Not Completed*	1976-77	Motherwell
1904-05	Hamilton Academical	1937-38	Airdrieonians	*1977-78*	*Not Completed*
1905-06	Hamilton Academical	1938-39	Hamilton Academical	*1978-79*	*Not Completed*
1906-07	Motherwell	1939-40	Motherwell	1979-80	Airdrieonians
1907-08	Motherwell	*1940-48*	*No Competition*	1980-81	Motherwell
1908-09	Airdrieonians	1948-49	Albion Rovers	1981-82	Albion Rovers
1909-10	Hamilton A/Wishaw Th.	1949-50	Motherwell	1982-83	Motherwell
1910-11	Airdrieonians	1950-51	Albion Rovers	1983-84	Airdrieonians
1911-12	Motherwell	1951-52	Hamilton Academical	1984-85	Motherwell
1912-13	Airdrieonians	1952-53	Motherwell	1985-86	Hamilton Academical
1913-14	Airdrieonians	1953-54	Motherwell	1986-87	Albion Rovers
1914-15	Airdrieonians	1954-55	Motherwell	1987-88	Airdrieonians
1915-16	Wishaw Thistle	*1955-56*	*Not Completed*	1988-89	Motherwell
1916-17	Wishaw Thistle	1956-57	Motherwell	1989-90	Motherwell
1917-18	Airdrieonians	1957-58	Motherwell	1990-91	Motherwell
1918-19	Airdrieonians	1958-59	Motherwell	*1991-92*	*Not Completed*
1919-20	Hamilton Academical	1959-60	Motherwell	1992-93	Airdrieonians
1920-21	Albion Rovers	1960-61	Motherwell	*1993-94*	*Not Completed*
1921-22	Airdrieonians	1961-62	Motherwell	*1994-95*	*No Competition*
1922-23	Airdrieonians	1962-63	Airdrieonians	1995-96	Airdrieonians
1923-24	Hamilton Academical	1963-64	Motherwell		

Summary: *35 - Airdrieonians; 33 - Motherwell; 10 - Hamilton Academical *; 8 - Albion Rovers; 4 - Royal Albert, Wishaw Thistle *; 2 - Cambuslang; 1 - Shotts, Stonelaw, Thistle, West Benhar. * = one shared.*

Lanarkshire Express Cup

(Formerly the Coatbridge Express Cup and the Lanarkshire Consolation Cup)

1889-90	Carfin Shamrock	1898-99	Wishaw Thistle	1915-16	Wishaw Thistle
1890-91	Burnbank Swifts	1899-00	Dykehead	*1916-20*	*No Competition*
1891-92	Royal Albert	*1900-09*	*No Competition*	1920-21	Motherwell
1892-93	Motherwell	1909-10	Airdrieonians	1921-22	Albion Rovers
1893-94	Albion Rovers	1910-11	Airdrieonians	1922-23	Airdrieonians
1894-95	Royal Albert	1911-12	Airdrieonians	*1923-24*	*Not Completed*
1895-96	Airdrieonians	1912-13	Albion Rovers	1924-25	Motherwell
1896-97	Hamilton Academical	1913-14	Shotts	1925-26	Motherwell
1897-98	Longriggend	1914-15	Motherwell		

Summary: *5 - Airdrieonians, Motherwell,: 3 - Albion Rovers; 2 - Royal Albert, Wishaw Thistle; 1 - Burnbank Swifts, Carfin Shamrock, Dykehead, Hamilton Academical, Longriggend, Shotts.*

Law-Galloway Cup

(For member clubs of the South of Scotland F.A.)

1889-90	Stranraer	1895-96	Douglas Wanderers	1901-02	Douglas Wanderers
1890-91	Newton Stewart Athletic	1896-97	6th G.R.V.	1902-03	Douglas Wanderers
1891-92	Newton Stewart Athletic	1897-98	Newton Stewart Athletic	1903-04	St. Cuthbert Wanderers
1892-93	Newton Stewart Athletic	1898-99	Newton Stewart Athletic	1904-05	Douglas Wanderers
1893-94	St. Cuthbert Wanderers	1899-00	Newton Stewart Athletic	1905-06	Stranraer
1894-95	St. Cuthbert Wanderers	1900-01	6th G.R.V.	1906-07	Douglas Wanderers

Linlithgowshire Cup

4-85	Mossend Swifts	1898-99	Bo'ness	1912-13	Armadale
5-86	Armadale	1899-00	Bo'ness	1913-14	Broxburn United
6-87	Armadale	1900-01	Bo'ness	1914-15	Broxburn United
7-88	Bo'ness	1901-02	Bo'ness	1915-16	Armadale
8-89	Bo'ness	1902-03	Broxburn	1916-17	Armadale
9-90	Broxburn	1903-04	Broxburn	*1917-19*	*No Competition*
0-91	Armadale	1904-05	Bathgate	1919-20	Bathgate
1-92	Bathgate Rovers	1905-06	Bathgate	1920-21	Bo'ness
2-93	Broxburn	1906-07	Bo'ness	1921-22	Armadale
3-94	Broxburn Shamrock	1907-08	Broxburn	1922-23	Broxburn United
4-95	Bathgate	1908-09	Bo'ness	1923-24	Broxburn United
5-96	Bo'ness	1909-10	Bo'ness	1924-25	Bo'ness
6-97	Armadale Volunteers	1910-11	Bo'ness	1925-26	Bo'ness
7-98	Bo'ness	1911-12	Bathgate		

mmary: *14 - Bo'ness; 7 - Armadale; 6 - Bathgate; 5 - Broxburn; 4 - Broxburn United; Armadale Volunteers, Bathgate Rovers, Broxburn Shamrock, Mossend Swifts*

Linlithgowshire Second XI Cup

5-86	Bo'ness	1889-90	Champfleurie	1893-94	Bo'ness
6-87	Armadale	1890-91	Bathgate Rovers	1894-95	Bathgate
7-88	Bo'ness	1891-92	Broxburn		
8-89	Armadale	1892-93	Bo'ness		

MacNicol Trophy

(Formerly The Supplementary Cup)

)TE: *Since 1974-75 this trophy has not been competed for, but awarded to the club th the best disciplinary record. For member clubs of the North Caledonian F.A.*

9-50	Ross County	1958-59	Inverness Thistle	1967-68	Ross County
0-51	Loco Rangers	1959-60	Nairn County	1968-69	Invergordon
1-52	Loco Rangers	1960-61	Clachnacuddin	1969-70	Brora Rangers
2-53	R.A.F. Dalcross	1961-62	Not Completed	1970-71	Ross County
3-54	Elgin City	1962-63	Clachnacuddin	1971-72	Ross County
4-55	Nairn County	1963-64	Dingwall Thistle	1972-73	Bunillidh Thistle
5-56	Clachnacuddin	1964-65	Inverness Caledonian	1973-74	Wick Academy
6-57	Nairn County	1965-66	Ross County		
7-58	Ross County	1966-67	Avoch Rovers		

mmary: *6 - Ross County; 3 - Clachnacuddin, Nairn County; 2 - Loco Rangers; 1 - Avoch Rovers, ora Rangers, Bunillidh Thistle, Dingwall Thistle, Elgin City, Invergordon, Inverness Caledonian, erness Thistle, R.A.F. Dalcross, Wick Academy.*

Midland League

1-92	Raith Rovers	1894-95	Falkirk	*1897-08*	*No Competition*
2-93	King's Park	1895-96	Stenhousemuir	1908-09	Falkirk 'A'
3-94	East Stirlingshire	1896-97	Clackmannan	*1909-10*	*Not Completed*

Mitchell Cup

(Wartime competition for Scottish League clubs)

1-42	Aberdeen	1943-44	Rangers
2-43	Aberdeen	1944-45	Aberdeen

Morris Newton Cup
(For member clubs of the North Caledonian F.A.)

1979-80	Alness	1986-87	Muir of Ord	1993-94	Bonar Bridge
1980-81	Dingwall Thistle	1987-88	Ross County	1994-95	Clachnacuddin
1981-82	Balintore	1988-89	Ross County	1995-96	Fearn Thistle
1982-83	Balintore	1989-90	Invergordon	1996-97	Balintore
1983-84	Fort William	1990-91	Tain St. Duthus	1997-98	Invergordon
1984-85	Fort William	1991-92	Tain St. Duthus	1998-99	Balintore
1985-86	Balintore	1992-93	Golspie Sutherland	1999-00	Alness United

Summary: *5 - Balintore; 2 - Fort William, Invergordon, Ross County, Tain St. Duthus; 1 - Alness, Alness United, Bonar Bridge, Clachnacuddin, Dingwall Thistle, Fearn Thistle, Golspie Sutherland, Muir of Ord.*

Ness Cup
(For member clubs of the North Caledonian F.A.)

1955-56	Inverness Caledonian	1964-65	Inverness Caledonian	1974-75	Golspie Sutherland
1956-57	Clachnacuddin	1965-66	Ross County	1975-76	Golspie Sutherland
1957-58	Nairn County	1966-67	Avoch Rovers	1976-77	Invergordon
1958-59	*Not Completed*	1967-68	Brora Rangers	1977-78	Alness
1959-60	Inverness Thistle	*1968-69*	*Not Completed*	1978-79	Tain St. Duthus
1960-61	Ross County	*1969-71*	*No Competition*	*1979-80*	*No Competition*
1961-62	*Not Completed*	1971-72	Golspie Sutherland	1980-81	Tain St. Duthus
1962-63	*No Competition*	1972-73	Invergordon	1981-82	Dingwall Thistle
1963-64	Dingwall Thistle	1973-74	Bunillidh Thistle		

Summary: *3 - Golspie Sutherland; 2 - Dingwall Thistle, Invergordon, Inverness Caledonian, Ross County, Tain St. Duthus; 1 - Alness, Avoch Rovers, Brora Rangers, Bunillidh Thistle, Clachnacuddin, Inverness Thistle, Nairn County.*

North Caledonian League

1896-97	Inverness Celtic	1929-30	Clachnacuddin	1964-65	Avoch Rovers
1897-98	Inverness Citadel	1930-31	Inverness Thistle	1965-66	Ross County
1898-99	Nelson	1931-32	Clachnacuddin	1966-67	Brora Rangers
1899-00	Nelson	1932-33	I.D.A.	1967-68	Brora Rangers
1900-01	Inverness Thistle	1933-34	I.D.A.	1968-69	Dingwall Thistle
1901-02	Inverness Citadel	1934-35	Inverness Thistle	1969-70	Inverness Caledonian
1902-03	Inverness Citadel	1935-36	Nairn County	1970-71	Dingwall Thistle
1903-04	Clachnacuddin	1936-37	Clachnacuddin	1971-72	Dingwall Thistle
1904-05	Clachnacuddin	*1937-38*	*No Competition*	1972-73	Alness
1905-06	Nelson	1938-39	H.L.I.	1973-74	Alness
1906-07	Nelson	*1939-46*	*No Competition*	1974-75	Golspie Sutherland
1907-08	Nelson	1946-47	Invergordon	1975-76	Golspie Sutherland
1908-09	Nelson	1947-48	Inverness Thistle	1976-77	Invergordon
1909-10	Clachnacuddin	1948-49	Inverness Caledonian	1977-78	Dingwall Thistle
1910-11	Inverness Citadel	1949-50	Clachnacuddin	1978-79	Wick Academy
1911-12	Nelson	1950-51	Clachnacuddin	1979-80	Wick Academy
1912-13	Nelson	1951-52	Inverness Caledonian	1980-81	Wick Academy
1913-14	Albert	1952-53	Inverness Caledonian	1981-82	Wick Academy
1914-19	*No Competition*	1953-54	Elgin City	1982-83	Bunillidh Thistle
1919-20	Dingwall Victoria United	1954-55	Nairn County/Buckie Th.	1983-84	Muir of Ord
1920-21	Nelson	1955-56	Clachnacuddin	1984-85	Fort William
1921-22	Inverness Citadel	1956-57	Clachnacuddin	1985-86	Muir of Ord
1922-23	Inverness Caledonian	1957-58	Clachnacuddin	1986-87	Wick Academy
1923-24	Fortrose Union	1958-59	Inverness Thistle	1987-88	Invergordon
1924-25	Catch-my-pal	1959-60	Inverness Thistle	1988-89	Bunillidh Thistle
1925-26	Nelson	*1960-61*	*Not Completed*	1989-90	Balintore
1926-27	Clachnacuddin	*1961-62*	*Not Completed*	1990-91	Balintore
1927-28	Dingwall Victoria United	1962-63	Inverness Thistle	1991-92	Clachnacuddin
1928-29	Inverness Thistle	1963-64	Clachnacuddin	1992-93	Golspie Sutherland

3-94	Halkirk United	1996-97	Ross County	1999-00	Thurso
4-95	Inverness Caledonian Th.	1997-98	Inverness Caledonian Th.		
5-96	Fearn Thistle	1998-99	Golspie Sutherland		

nmary: 14 - Clachnacuddin; 10 - Nelson; 8 - Inverness Thistle; 5 - Inverness Caledonian, erness Citadel, Wick Academy; 4 - Dingwall Thistle, Golspie Sutherland; 3 - Invergordon; Alness, Balintore, Brora Rangers, Bunillidh Thistle, Dingwall Victoria United, I.D.A., Inverness edonian Thistle, Muir of Ord, Nairn County*, Ross County; 1 - Albert, Avoch Rovers, Buckie stle*, Catch-my-pal, Elgin City, Fearn Thistle, Fortrose Union, Fort William, Halkirk United, H.L.I., erness Celtic, Thurso. * includes one shared.

North Caledonian Cup

7-88	Crusaders	1926-27	Camerons	1967-68	Muir of Ord
3-89	Camerons	1927-28	Dingwall Victoria United	1968-69	Golspie Sutherland
9-90	Union	1928-29	Nelson	1969-70	Ross County
0-91	Inverness Thistle	1929-30	Clachnacuddin	1970-71	Inverness Caledonian
1-92	Crown Strollers	1930-31	Inverness Thistle	1971-72	Bunillidh Thistle
2-93	Inverness Caledonian	1931-32	Inverness Thistle	1972-73	Ross County
3-94	Inverness Thistle	1932-33	Nelson	1973-74	Alness
4-95	Inverness Caledonian	1933-34	Muir of Ord	1974-75	Golspie Sutherland
5-96	Inverness Caledonian	1934-35	Muir of Ord	1975-76	Golspie Sutherland
6-97	Inverness Citadel	1935-36	Nelson	1976-77	Dingwall Thistle
7-98	Inverness Citadel	1936-37	Clachnacuddin	1977-78	Bonar Bridge
8-99	Heatherly	*1937-38*	*No Competition*	1978-79	Tain St. Duthus
9-00	Inverness Caledonian	1938-39	H.L.I.	1979-80	Wick Academy
0-01	Inverness Thistle	*1939-46*	*No Competition*	1980-81	Wick Academy
1-02	Clachnacuddin	1946-47	Ross County	1981-82	Bunillidh Thistle
2-03	Dingwall Victoria United	1947-48	Inverness Caledonian	1982-83	Muir of Ord
3-04	Dingwall Victoria United	1948-49	Inverness Caledonian	1983-84	Tain St. Duthus
4-05	Inverness Caledonian	1949-50	Clachnacuddin	1984-85	Balintore
5-06	Inverness Caledonian	1950-51	Ross County	1985-86	Wick Academy
6-07	Inverness Caledonian	1951-52	Loco Rangers	1986-87	Tain St. Duthus
7-08	Nelson	1952-53	Nelson	1987-88	Invergordon
8-09	Clachnacuddin	1953-54	Nairn County	1988-89	Inverness Caledonian
9-10	Inverness Thistle	1954-55	Inverness Caledonian	1989-90	Tain St. Duthus
0-11	Grantown	1955-56	Clachnacuddin	1990-91	Inverness Caledonian
1-12	Bishopmill	1956-57	Clachnacuddin	1991-92	Clachnacuddin
2-13	*No Competition*	1957-58	Clachnacuddin	1992-93	Ross County
3-14	Albert	1958-59	Ross County	1993-94	Bonar Bridge
4-19	*No Competition*	1959-60	Inverness Caledonian	1994-95	Clachnacuddin
9-20	Clachnacuddin	1960-61	Clachnacuddin	1995-96	Fearn Thistle
0-21	Inverness Citadel	*1961-62*	*Not Completed*	1996-97	Balintore
1-22	Inverness Caledonian	1962-63	Clachnacuddin	1997-98	Balintore
2-23	Clachnacuddin	1963-64	Clachnacuddin	1998-99	Inverness Caledonian Th.
3-24	Fortrose Union	1964-65	Brora Rangers	1999-00	Alness United
4-25	Tain St. Duthus	1965-66	Inverness Caledonian		
5-26	Inverness Thistle	1966-67	Black Rock Rovers		

nmary: 16 - Inverness Caledonian; 15 - Clachnacuddin; 7 - Inverness Thistle; 6 - Ross County; Nelson, Tain St. Duthus; 4 - Muir of Ord; 3 - Balintore, Dingwall Victoria United, Golspie herland, Inverness Citadel, Wick Academy; 2 - Bonar Bridge, Bunillidh Thistle, Camerons; Albert, Alness, Alness United, Bishopmill, Black Rock Rovers, Brora Rangers, Crown Strollers, saders, Dingwall Thistle, Fearn Thistle, Fortrose Union, Grantown, Heatherly, H.L.I., Invergordon, erness Caledonian Thistle, Loco Rangers, Nairn County, Union.

North-Eastern Cup

2-83	Petershill	1887-88	Tollcross	1892-93	Clyde
3-84	Cowlairs	1888-89	Celtic	*1893-94*	*Not Completed*
4-85	Cowlairs	1889-90	Celtic	1894-95	Clyde
5-86	Northern	1890-91	Clyde		
6-87	Cowlairs	1891-92	Northern		

North-Eastern Supplementary Cup
(Wartime competition for Scottish League clubs)

1941-42	Aberdeen	1942-43	Aberdeen	1943-44	Rangers

North-Eastern League
(Wartime competition for Scottish League Clubs)
(Eastern League 1939-40; 'B' Division 1945-46)

1939-40	Falkirk	1942-43	Aberdeen*	1944-45	Dundee*
1940-41	*No Competition*		Aberdeen*		Aberdeen*
1941-42	Rangers*	1943-44	Raith Rovers*	1945-46	Dundee
	Aberdeen*		Aberdeen*		

* Played in two series each season.

Northern League

1891-92	East End/Our Boys	1900-01	Dundee 'A'	1909-10	Dundee 'A'
1892-93	Arbroath	1901-02	Raith Rovers	1910-11	Aberdeen 'A'
1893-94	*Not Completed*	1902-03	Dundee 'A'	*1911-12*	*Not Completed*
1894-95	*No Competition*	1903-04	Montrose	1912-13	Brechin City
1895-96	Forfar Athletic	1904-05	Dundee 'A'	*1913-14*	*Not Completed*
1896-97	Orion	1905-06	Aberdeen	1914-15	Forfar Athletic
1897-98	Victoria United	1906-07	Kirkcaldy United	*1915-19*	*No Competition*
1898-99	Orion	1907-08	Brechin City	1919-20	Montrose
1899-00	Dundee Wanderers	1908-09	Dundee 'A'		

North of Scotland Cup

1888-89	Crown	1927-28	Inverness Caledonian	1966-67	Forres Mechanics
1889-90	Inverness Caledonian	1928-29	Inverness Citadel	1967-68	Elgin City
1890-91	Camerons	1929-30	Ross County	1968-69	Elgin City
1891-92	Inverness Caledonian	1930-31	Inverness Thistle	1969-70	Ross County
1892-93	Inverness Thistle	1931-32	Inverness Citadel	1970-71	Elgin City
1893-94	Inverness Thistle	1932-33	Inverness Citadel	1971-72	Ross County
1894-95	Clachnacuddin	1933-34	Inverness Caledonian	1972-73	Elgin City
1895-96	Clachnacuddin	1934-35	Inverness Thistle	1973-74	Inverness Caledonian
1896-97	Inverness Caledonian	1935-36	Forres Mechanics	1974-75	Inverness Caledonian
1897-98	Clachnacuddin	1936-37	Elgin City	1975-76	Elgin City
1898-99	Elgin City	1937-38	Clachnacuddin	1976-77	Inverness Caledonian
1899-00	Clachnacuddin	1938-39	Inverness Thistle	1977-78	Inverness Thistle
1900-01	Inverness Citadel	1939-40	Clachnacuddin	1978-79	Rothes
1901-02	Inverness Caledonian	*1940-45*	*No Competition*	1979-80	Clachnacuddin
1902-03	Clachnacuddin	1945-46	Inverness Thistle	1980-81	Brora Rangers
1903-04	Clachnacuddin	1946-47	Clachnacuddin	1981-82	Inverness Caledonian
1904-05	Inverness Citadel	1947-48	Clachnacuddin	1982-83	Elgin City
1905-06	Clachnacuddin	1948-49	Clachnacuddin	1983-84	Inverness Caledonian
1906-07	Clachnacuddin	1949-50	Clachnacuddin	1984-85	Inverness Thistle
1907-08	Forres Mechanics	1950-51	Inverness Caledonian	1985-86	Inverness Caledonian
1908-09	Inverness Citadel	1951-52	Inverness Caledonian	1986-87	Forres Mechanics
1909-10	Inverness Citadel	1952-53	Inverness Thistle	1987-88	Inverness Thistle
1910-11	Inverness Caledonian	1953-54	Clachnacuddin	1988-89	Elgin City
1911-12	Inverness Caledonian	1954-55	Elgin City	1989-90	Elgin City
1912-13	Inverness Thistle	1955-56	Elgin City	1990-91	Brora Rangers
1913-14	Inverness Caledonian	1956-57	Nairn County	1991-92	Ross County
1914-19	*No Competition*	1957-58	Forres Mechanics	1992-93	Clachnacuddin
1919-20	Clachnacuddin	1958-59	Rothes	1993-94	Inverness Caledonian
1920-21	Clachnacuddin	1959-60	Inverness Thistle	1994-95	Lossiemouth
1921-22	Inverness Caledonian	1960-61	Elgin City	1995-96	Lossiemouth
1922-23	Clachnacuddin	1961-62	Elgin City	1996-97	Lossiemouth
1923-24	Elgin City	1962-63	Nairn County	1997-98	Elgin City
1924-25	Inverness Caledonian	1963-64	Nairn County	1998-99	Elgin City
1925-26	Inverness Caledonian	1964-65	Clachnacuddin	1999-00	Inverness Caledonian
1926-27	Forres Mechanics	1965-66	Nairn County		

Paisley Charity Cup

32-83	Paisley Athletic		1913-14	St. Mirren		1940-44	*No Competition*
33-84	Abercorn		1914-15	Abercorn		1944-45	St. Mirren
34-85	St. Mirren		1915-16	St. Mirren		1945-46	Airdrieonians
35-86	Abercorn		1916-17	St. Mirren		1946-47	St. Mirren
36-87	St. Mirren		1917-18	St. Mirren		1947-48	St. Mirren
37-88	*No Competition*		1918-19	St. Mirren		1948-49	St. Mirren
38-89	Abercorn		1919-20	St. Mirren		1949-50	Barnsley
39-90	St. Mirren		1920-21	St. Mirren		1950-51	St. Mirren
90-91	St. Mirren		1921-22	St. Mirren		1951-52	St. Mirren
91-92	Abercorn		1922-23	St. Mirren		1952-53	*No Competition*
92-93	St. Mirren		1923-24	St. Mirren		1953-54	St. Mirren
93-94	St. Mirren		1924-25	St. Mirren		1954-55	St. Mirren/Kilmarnock
94-95	Abercorn		1925-26	St. Mirren		1955-56	Leicester City
95-96	St. Mirren		1926-27	St. Mirren		1956-57	St. Mirren
96-00	*No Competition*		1927-28	St. Mirren		1957-58	St. Mirren
00-01	Westmarch		1928-29	St. Mirren		1958-59	*No Competition*
01-04	*No Competition*		1929-30	Morton		1959-60	St. Mirren
04-05	Abercorn		1930-31	St. Mirren		1960-61	Manchester City
05-06	*No Competition*		1931-32	St. Mirren		1961-62	St. Mirren
06-07	St. Mirren		1932-33	*No Competition*		1962-63	St. Mirren/Norwich City
07-08	*No Competition*		1933-34	Albion Rovers		1963-64	Chelsea
08-09	2nd Abercorn		1934-35	St. Mirren		1964-65	St. Mirren/ Norwich City
09-10	1st St. Mirren		1935-37	*No Competition*		1965-66	Northampton Town
10-11	1st St. Mirren		1937-38	St. Mirren/Partick Thistle		1966-67	St. Mirren/Ipswich Town
11-12	St. Mirren		1938-39	Clyde		1967-68	St. Mirren/Preston N. End
12-13	Abercorn		1939-40	Clyde			

mmary (Scottish clubs only): 45 - St. Mirren+; 9 - Abercorn; 2 - Clyde; 1 - Airdrieonians, bion Rovers, Kilmarnock*, Morton, Paisley Athletic, Partick Thistle*, Westmarch.
= including 6 shared, * = including 1 shared.

Penman Cup

(Originally for Fife and Lothians senior clubs, later extended to those in central and north-east Scotland. Like the Dewar Shield, was not played for every season,was ccasionally unfinished and often carried over more than one season. This is believed to be the complete list of winners.)

05-06	Raith Rovers		1916-17	East Fife		1936-37	Raith Rovers
06-07	Bathgate		1917-18	Dundee		1938-39	East Fife
07-08	St. Bernards		1919-20	Cowdenbeath		1945-46	Stenhousemuir
08-09	Raith Rovers		1920-21	Alloa		1949-50	Stenhousemuir
09-10	East Fife		1921-22	Dundee		1953-54	Stenhousemuir
10-11	Cowdenbeath		1923-24	Raith Rovers		1957-58	Stirling Albion
11-12	Raith Rovers		1924-25	St. Johnstone		1958-59	Raith Rovers
12-13	Armadale		1925-26	Alloa		1959-60	Dunfermline Athletic
13-14	Broxburn United		1928-29	Dundee		1961-62	East Fife
15-16	Cowdenbeath		1929-30	Dundee United			

mmary: 6 - Raith Rovers; 4 - East Fife; 3 - Cowdenbeath, Dundee; 2 - Alloa, Stenhousemuir, 'rling Albion; 1 - Armadale, Bathgate, Broxburn United, Dundee United, Dunfermline Athletic, Bernards, St. Johnstone.

Perthshire Cup

(For member clubs of the Perthshire (Senior) F.A.)

34-85	Dunblane		1887-88	Dunblane		1890-91	Dunblane
35-86	Dunblane		1888-89	Dunblane		1891-92	Dunblane
36-87	Coupar Angus		1889-90	St. Johnstone		1892-93	St. Johnstone

CONTINUED OVERLEAF

1893-94 Fair City Athletic	1922-23 Vale of Atholl	1952-53 Breadalbane
1894-95 St. Johnstone	1923-24 Blairgowrie	1953-54 Ballinluig
1895-96 St. Johnstone	1924-25 Dunkeld & Birnam	1954-55 Grandtully Vale
1896-97 Vale of Atholl	1925-26 St. Johnstone	1955-56 Vale of Atholl
1897-98 Fair City Athletic	1926-27 St. Johnstone	1956-57 Breadalbane
1898-99 Fair City Athletic	1927-28 St. Johnstone	1957-58 Breadalbane
1899-00 Dunblane	1928-29 St. Johnstone	1958-59 Breadalbane
1900-01 Dunblane	1929-30 St. Johnstone	1959-60 Breadalbane
1901-02 St. Johnstone	1930-31 St. Johnstone	1960-61 Breadalbane
1902-03 St. Johnstone	1931-32 St. Johnstone	1961-62 Breadalbane
1903-04 Dunblane	1932-33 Vale of Atholl	1962-63 Murthly
1904-05 St. Johnstone	1933-34 Blairgowrie	1963-64 St. Johnstone
1905-06 Dunblane	1934-35 Blairgowrie	1964-65 Grandtully Vale
1906-07 St. Johnstone	1935-36 Blairgowrie	1965-66 Breadalbane
1907-08 St. Johnstone	1936-37 Breadalbane	1966-67 Breadalbane
1908-09 St. Johnstone	1937-38 Blairgowrie	1967-68 Vale of Atholl
1909-10 Dunblane	1938-39 Blairgowrie	1968-69 Ballinluig
1910-11 St. Johnstone	1939-40 Black Watch	1969-70 Errol Amateurs
1911-12 St. Johnstone	*1940-46 No Competition*	1970-71 Vale of Atholl
1912-13 Dunblane	1946-47 Breadalbane	1971-72 Vale of Atholl
1913-14 St. Johnstone	1947-48 Grandtully Vale	1972-73 Vale of Atholl
1914-19 No Competition	1948-49 Vale of Atholl	1973-74 Grandtully Vale
1919-20 Blairgowrie Amateurs	1949-50 Grandtully Vale	1974-75 Grandtully Vale
1920-21 St. Johnstone	1950-51 Grandtully Vale	
1921-22 Vale of Atholl	1951-52 Breadalbane	

Summary: *22 - St. Johnstone; 12 - Breadalbane, Dunblane; 10 - Vale of Atholl; 7 - Grandtully Vale; 6 - Blairgowrie; 3 - Fair City Athletic; 2 - Ballinluig; 1 - Black Watch, Blairgowrie Amateurs, Coupar Angus, Dunkeld & Birnam, Errol Amateurs, Murthly.*

Potts Cup
(For South of Scotland F.A. Clubs)

1901-02 Maxwelltown Volunteers	1934-35 Creetown	1970-71 Stranraer 'A'
1902-03 Nithsdale Wanderers	1935-36 St. Cuthbert Wanderers	1971-72 St. Cuthbert Wanderers
1903-04 Maxwelltown Volunteers	1936-37 St. Cuthbert Wanderers	1972-73 Stranraer 'A'
1904-05 Dumfries	*1937-38 Not Completed*	1973-74 Stranraer 'A'
1905-06 Nithsdale Wanderers	1938-39 Wigtown & Bladnoch	1974-75 St. Cuthbert Wanderers
1906-07 Dumfries	*1939-46 No Competition*	1975-76 Stranraer 'A'
1907-08 Dumfries	1946-47 Stranraer	1976-77 Stranraer 'A'
1908-09 Nithsdale Wanderers	1947-48 Wigtown & Bladnoch	1977-78 Stranraer 'A'
1909-10 Nithsdale Wanderers	1948-49 Stranraer	*1978-79 Not Completed*
1910-11 St. Cuthbert Wanderers	1949-50 Tarff Rovers	*1979-80 No Competition*
1911-12 Dumfries	1950-51 Wigtown & Bladnoch	1980-81 Threave Rovers
1912-13 Solway Star	1951-52 Newton Stewart	1981-82 Creetown
1913-14 Nithsdale Wanderers	1952-53 Newton Stewart	1982-83 Dalbeattie Star
1914-15 St. Cuthbert Wanderers	1953-54 Tarff Rovers	1983-84 Stranraer 'A'
1915-19 No Competition	1954-55 St. Cuthbert Wanderers	1984-85 St. Cuthbert Wanderers
1919-20 Nithsdale Wanderers	1955-56 St. Cuthbert Wanderers	1985-86 Dalbeattie Star
1920-21 Queen of the South	1956-57 St. Cuthbert Wanderers	1986-87 St. Cuthbert Wanderers
1921-22 Douglas Wanderers	1957-58 Greystone Rovers	1987-88 Newton Stewart
1922-23 Nithsdale Wanderers	1958-59 Stranraer 'A'	1988-89 St. Cuthbert Wanderer
1923-24 Douglas Wanderers	1959-60 Queen of the South 'A'	1989-90 Wigtown & Bladnoch
1924-25 Dalbeattie Star	1960-61 Queen of the South 'A'	1990-91 Threave Rovers
1925-26 Stranraer	1961-62 Newton Stewart	1991-92 Dalbeattie Star
1926-27 Stranraer	1962-63 Threave Rovers	1992-93 Dalbeattie Star
1927-28 Stranraer	1963-64 Stranraer 'A'	1993-94 Threave Rovers
1928-29 Not Completed	1964-65 Tarff Rovers	1994-95 Threave Rovers
1929-30 St. Cuthbert Wanderers	1965-66 Threave Rovers	1995-96 Stranraer Athletic
1930-31 Stranraer	1966-67 Tarff Rovers	1996-97 St. Cuthbert Wanderer
1931-32 Wigtown	1967-68 Threave Rovers	1997-98 Tarff Rovers
1932-33 Dalbeattie Star	*1968-69 No Competition*	1998-99 Dalbeattie Star
1933-34 Creetown	1969-70 St. Cuthbert Wanderers	1999-00 Dalbeattie Star

mmary: *15 - St. Cuthbert Wanderers; 9 - Stranraer 'A', 8 - Dalbeattie Star; 7 - Nithsdale nderers, Threave Rovers; 6 - Stranraer; 5 - Tarff Rovers; 4 - Dumfries, Newton Stewart, Wigtown 3ladnoch; 3 - Creetown; 2 - Douglas Wanderers, Maxwelltown Volunteers, Queen of the South 'A', Greystone Rovers, Queen of the South, Solway Star, Stranraer Athletic, Wigtown.*

Premier Reserve League
(For under 21 teams from 1998-99)

'5-76	Rangers	1984-85	Celtic	1993-94	Celtic
'6-77	Rangers	1985-86	Rangers	1994-95	Celtic
'7-78	Rangers	1986-87	Aberdeen	1995-96	Rangers
'8-79	Rangers	1987-88	Dundee United	1996-97	Hearts
'9-80	Celtic	1988-89	Dundee United	1997-98	Rangers
30-81	Celtic	1989-90	Dundee United	1998-99	St. Johnstone
31-82	Aberdeen	1990-91	Celtic	1999-00	Hearts
32-83	Rangers	1991-92	Rangers		
33-84	Rangers	1992-93	Hearts		

mmary: *10 - Rangers; 6 - Celtic; 3 - Dundee United, Hearts; 2 - Aberdeen. 1 - St. Johnstone.*

Reid Charity Cup
(For Perth Senior Clubs)

39-90	St. Johnstone	1891-92	St. Johnstone
30-91	St. Johnstone	1892-93	Fair City Athletic

Renfrewshire Cup

'8-79	Thornliebank	1913-14	Morton	1949-50	St. Mirren
'9-80	Thornliebank	1914-15	Morton	1950-51	Morton
30-81	Arthurlie	*1915-17*	*No Competition*	1951-52	Morton
31-82	Arthurlie	1917-18	Morton	1952-53	Morton
32-83	St. Mirren	*1918-19*	*No Competition*	1953-54	Babcock & Wilcox
33-84	St. Mirren	1919-20	Morton	*1954-55*	*No Competition*
34-85	Port Glasgow Athletic	*1920-21*	*No Competition*	1955-56	Morton
35-86	Abercorn	1921-22	Morton	1956-57	Morton
36-87	Abercorn	1922-23	Morton	1957-58	Morton
37-88	St. Mirren	1923-24	St. Mirren	1958-59	St. Mirren
38-89	Abercorn	1924-25	St. Mirren	1959-60	St. Mirren
39-90	Abercorn	1925-26	St. Mirren	1960-61	St. Mirren
30-91	St. Mirren	1926-27	St. Mirren	1961-62	Morton
31-92	Abercorn	*1927-28*	*No Competition*	1962-63	St. Mirren
32-93	Morton	1928-29	St. Mirren	1963-64	Morton
33-94	St. Mirren	1929-30	St. Mirren	1964-65	Morton
34-95	Port Glasgow Athletic	1930-31	Morton	1965-66	Morton
35-96	Port Glasgow Athletic	1931-32	St. Miren	1966-67	St. Mirren
36-97	St. Mirren	1932-33	St. Mirren	1967-68	Morton
37-98	St. Mirren	1933-34	St. Mirren	*1968-71*	*Not Completed*
38-99	Morton	1934-35	Morton	1971-72	Morton
39-00	Port Glasgow Athletic	1935-36	St. Mirren	1972-73	Morton
30-01	Morton	1936-37	Morton	1973-74	St. Mirren
31-02	Morton	1937-38	St. Mirren	*1974-75*	*Not Completed*
32-03	Morton	1938-39	Morton	*1975-76*	*No Competition*
33-04	St. Mirren	*1939-40*	*Not Completed*	1976-77	St. Mirren
34-05	Morton	1940-41	St. Mirren	1977-78	Morton
35-06	Morton	1941-42	Morton	1978-79	St. Mirren
36-07	Morton	1942-43	Morton	1979-80	St. Mirren
37-08	Morton	1943-44	St. Mirren	1980-81	Morton
38-09	Port Glasgow Athletic	1944-45	Morton	*1981-82*	*No Competition*
39-10	St. Mirren	1945-46	St. Mirren	1982-83	St. Mirren
30-11	St. Mirren	1946-47	St. Mirren	1983-84	St. Mirren
31-12	Morton	1947-48	St. Mirren	1984-85	St. Mirren
32-13	Morton	1948-49	Morton	1985-86	St. Mirren

CONTINUED OVERLEAF

the winners 25

1986-87	Morton	1990-91	Morton	1997-98	St. Mirren
1987-88	St. Mirren	*1991-95*	*No Competition*	1998-99	St. Mirren
1988-89	Morton	1995-96	Morton		
1989-90	St. Mirren	1996-97	Morton		

Summary: *45 - Morton; 44 - St. Mirren; 5 - Abercorn, Port Glasgow Athletic; 2 - Arthurlie, Thornliebank; 1 - Babcock & Wilcox.*

Reserve League

(For competition between 1919 and 1938 see under Scottish Alliance League)

1909-10	Falkirk	1945-46	Hibernian	1964-65	Celtic
1910-11	Hearts	1946-47	Hibernian	1965-66	Celtic
1911-12	Partick Thistle	1947-48	Hibernian	1966-67	Rangers
1912-13	Motherwell	1948-49	Hibernian	1967-68	Rangers
1913-14	Hearts	*1949-55*	*No Competition*	1968-69	Rangers
1914-15	Kilmarnock	1955-56	Aberdee	1969-70	Celtic
1938-39	Rangers	1957-58	Hearts	1970-71	Celtic
1939-42	*No Competition*	1958-59	Celtic	1971-72	Ayr United
1942-43	(1) Motherwell *	1959-60	Celtic	1972-73	Aberdeen
	(2) Motherwell *	1960-61	Celtic	1973-74	Rangers
1943-44	(1) Motherwell *	1961-62	Rangers	1974-75	Rangers
	(2) Morton *	1962-63	Celtic		
1944-45	Motherwell	1963-64	Rangers		

* Played in two series

Summary: *8 - Celtic, Rangers; 5 - Motherwell; 4 - Hibernian; 3 - Hearts; 2 - Aberdeen; 1 - Ayr United, Falkirk, Kilmarnock, Morton, Partick Thistle.*

Reserve League Cup

1942-43	Motherwell	1966-67	Celtic	1984-85	Aberdeen
1943-45	*No Competition*	1967-68	Rangers	1985-86	Celtic
1945-46	Rangers	1968-69	Celtic	1986-87	Dundee
1946-47	Hibernian	1969-70	Celtic	1987-88	Motherwell
1947-48	Hibernian	1970-71	Celtic	1988-89	Hearts
1948-49	Hibernian	1971-72	Hearts	1989-90	Celtic
1949-55	*No Competition*	1972-73	Aberdeen	1990-91	Dundee United
1955-56	Falkirk	1973-74	Partick Thistle	1991-92	Celtic
1956-57	Aberdeen	1974-75	Rangers	1992-93	Rangers
1957-58	Aberdeen	1975-76	Rangers	1993-94	Celtic
1958-59	Falkirk	1976-77	Rangers	1994-95	Celtic
1959-60	Celtic	1977-78	St. Mirren	1995-96	Celtic
1960-61	Rangers	1978-79	Aberdeen	1996-97	Aberdeen
1961-62	Rangers	1979-80	Aberdeen	1997-98	Rangers
1962-63	Rangers	1980-81	Celtic	1998-99	Livingston
1963-64	Dundee United	1981-82	Ayr United	1999-00	Dunfermline Athletic
1964-65	Kilmarnock	1982-83	Airdrieonians		
1965-66	Hibernian	1983-84	Hamilton Academical		

Summary: *12 - Celtic; 10 - Rangers; 7 - Aberdeen; 4 - Hibernian; 2 - Dundee United, Falkirk, Hear. Motherwell; 1 - Airdrieonians, Ayr United, Dundee, Dunfermline Athletic, Hamilton Academical, Kilmarnock, Livingston, Partick Thistle, St. Mirren.*

Reserve League (East)

1978-79	Stirling Albion	1986-87	Dunfermline Athletic	1994-95	Raith Rovers
1979-80	Falkirk	1987-88	Raith Rovers	1995-96	St. Johnstone
1980-81	Dundee United	1988-89	Forfar Athletic	1996-97	St. Johnstone
1981-82 See Scottish Combined R. L.		1989-90	St. Johnstone	1997-98	Forfar Athletic
1982-83	Dundee United	1990-91	Dundee	1998-99	Raith Rovers
1983-84	Aberdeen	1991-92	Dundee United	1999-00	Dunfermline Athletic
1984-85 See Scottish Combined R.L.		1992-93	Dunfermline Athletic		
1985-86	Stenhousemuir	1993-94	Falkirk		

Summary: *3 - Dundee United, Dunfermline Athletic, Raith Rovers, St. Johnstone; 2 - Falkirk, Forfa Athletic; 1 - Aberdeen, Dundee, Stenhousemuir, Stirling Albion.*

Reserve League (West)

78-79	Hamilton Academical	1986-87	Airdrieonians	1994-95	Rangers
79-80	Hamilton Academical	1987-88	Clyde	1995-96	St. Mirren
80-81	Celtic	1988-89	Celtic	1996-97	Airdrieonians
81-82	*See Scottish Combined R.L.*	1989-90	Ayr United	1997-98	Hamilton Academical
82-83	Celtic	1990-91	Rangers	1998-99	Morton
83-84	Motherwell	1991-92	Clydebank	1999-00	Ayr United
84-85	*See Scottish Combined R.L.*	1992-93	Rangers		
85-86	Airdrieonians	1993-94	Rangers		

Summary: *4 - Rangers; 3 - Airdrieonians, Celtic, Hamilton Academical; 2 - Ayr United; 1 - Clyde, Clydebank, Morton, Motherwell, St. Mirren.*

Roseberry Charity Cup
(For competition between Edinburgh Clubs)

82-83	Hearts	1903-04	Hearts	1924-25	Hibernian
83-84	Hibernian	1904-05	Hearts	1925-26	Hearts
84-85	Hibernian	1905-06	Hibernian	1926-27	Hearts
85-86	Hearts	1906-07	Hearts	1927-28	Hearts
86-87	Hibernian	1907-08	St. Bernards	1928-29	Hearts
87-88	Hibernian	1908-09	Hibernian	1929-30	Hearts
88-89	Mossend Swifts	1909-10	Hibernian	1930-31	St. Bernards
89-90	Hearts	1910-11	Hibernian	1931-32	Leith Athletic
90-91	Leith Athletic	1911-12	Hibernian	1932-33	Hearts
91-92	Hearts	1912-13	Hibernian	1933-34	Hearts
92-93	Hearts	1913-14	Hearts	1934-35	Hearts
93-94	Hibernian	1914-15	St. Bernards	1935-36	Hearts
94-95	Hearts	1915-16	Hearts	1936-37	Hearts
95-96	Hearts	1916-17	Hearts	1937-38	St. Bernards
96-97	Hibernian	1917-18	Hibernian	1938-39	Leith Athletic
97-98	Hearts	1918-19	Hearts	1939-40	Hibernian
98-99	Hearts	1919-20	Hearts	1940-41	Hearts
99-00	Hearts	1920-21	Hearts	1941-42	Hearts
00-01	Hibernian	1921-22	Hibernian	1942-43	Hearts
01-02	Hibernian	1922-23	Hearts	1943-44	Hibernian
02-03	Hibernian	1923-24	Hibernian	1944-45	Hibernian

Summary: *33 - Hearts; 22 - Hibernian; 4 - St. Bernards; 3 - Leith Athletic; 1 - Mossend Swifts.*

St. Cuthbert's Cup
(For member clubs of the South of Scotland F.A.)

92-93	6th G.R.V.	1893-94	St. Cuthbert Wanderers

Scottish Alliance

91-92	Linthouse	1893-94	Royal Albert	1895-96	Wishaw Thistle
92-93	Cowlairs	1894-95	Wishaw Thistle	1896-97	Third Lanark 'A'

Scottish Alliance League
(Scottish League Reserve sides plus some former Third Division clubs. See also Reserve League)

19-20	Kilmarnock	1926-27	Hearts	1933-34	Celtic
20-21	St. Mirren	1927-28	Rangers	1934-35	Rangers
21-22	Celtic	1928-29	Rangers	1935-36	Aberdeen
22-23	Airdrieonians	1929-30	Rangers	1936-37	Celtic
23-24	Rangers	1930-31	Rangers	1937-38	Celtic
24-25	Hearts	1931-32	Rangers		
25-26	Airdrieonians	1932-33	Aberdeen		

Summary: *8 - Rangers; 4 - Celtic; 2 - Aberdeen, Airdrieonians, Hearts; 1 - Kilmarnock, St. Mirren.*

Scottish Central Combination

1897-98	East Stirlingshire	1899-00	Falkirk	1901-02	Stenhousemuir
1898-99	Stenhousemuir	1900-01	Arthurlie	1902-03	Alloa

Scottish Combined Reserve League

(Competition for reserve teams of Second Division and some third teams of First Divisio
Clubs. In some seasons played for in two separate series.)

1958-59	Morton		(2) Raith Rovers	*1971-72*	*Not Completed*
1959-60	(1) Queen of the South	1965-66	(1) East Fife	*1972-73*	*No Competition*
	(2)(E) Dundee United		(2) Celtic	*1973-74*	*Not Completed*
	(W) Queen of the South	1966-67	(1) Celtic	*1974-75*	*No Competition*
1960-61	Celtic		(2) Queen's Park	1975-76	Partick Thistle
1961-62	(1) Clyde	1967-68	(1) Hearts	*1976-77*	*No Competition*
	(2) Celtic		*(2) Not Completed*	1977-78	Morton
1962-63	(1) Celtic	1968-69	Motherwell	*1978-81 See Reserve Leagues E.& |*
	(2) Celtic	1969-70	(1) Rangers	1981-82	Aberdeen
1963-64	(1) Celtic		*(2) Not Completed*	*1982-84 See Reserve Leagues E.& V*
	(2) Celtic	1970-71	(1) Partick Thistle	1984-85	Motherwell
1964-65	(1) Arbroath		(2) Partick Thistle		

Summary: 7 - Celtic; 3 - Partick Thistle; 2 - Morton, Motherwell, Queen of the South; 1 - Aberdeen,
Arbroath, Clyde, Dundee United, East Fife, Hearts, Queens Park, Raith Rovers, Rangers.

Scottish Consolation Cup

1907-08	Alloa	1910-11	St. Johnstone	1913-14	St. Johnstone
1908-09	Wishaw Thistle	1911-12	Johnstone		
1909-10	Arthurlie	1912-13	Galston		

Scottish Cup

1873-74	Queen's Park	1903-04	Celtic	1937-38	East Fife
1874-75	Queen's Park	1904-05	Third Lanark	1938-39	Clyde
1875-76	Queen's Park	1905-06	Hearts	1939-46	No Competition
1876-77	Vale of Leven	1906-07	Celtic	1946-47	Aberdeen
1877-78	Vale of Leven	1907-08	Celtic	1947-48	Rangers
1878-79	Vale of Leven	1908-09	Cup Withheld	1948-49	Rangers
1879-80	Queen's Park	1909-10	Dundee	1949-50	Rangers
1880-81	Queen's Park	1910-11	Celtic	1950-51	Celtic
1881-82	Queen's Park	1911-12	Celtic	1951-52	Motherwell
1882-83	Dumbarton	1912-13	Falkirk	1952-53	Rangers
1883-84	Queen's Park	1913-14	Celtic	1953-54	Celtic
1884-85	Renton	1914-19	No Competition	1954-55	Clyde
1885-86	Queen's Park	1919-20	Kilmarnock	1955-56	Hearts
1886-87	Hibernian	1920-21	Partick Thistle	1956-57	Falkirk
1887-88	Renton	1921-22	Morton	1957-58	Clyde
1888-89	Third Lanark	1922-23	Celtic	1958-59	St. Mirren
1889-90	Queen's Park	1923-24	Airdrieonians	1959-60	Rangers
1890-91	Hearts	1924-25	Celtic	1960-61	Dunfermline Athletic
1891-92	Celtic	1925-26	St. Mirren	1961-62	Rangers
1892-93	Queen's Park	1926-27	Celtic	1962-63	Rangers
1893-94	Rangers	1927-28	Rangers	1963-64	Rangers
1894-95	St. Bernards	1928-29	Kilmarnock	1964-65	Celtic
1895-96	Hearts	1929-30	Rangers	1965-66	Rangers
1896-97	Rangers	1930-31	Celtic	1966-67	Celtic
1897-98	Rangers	1931-32	Rangers	1967-68	Dunfermline Athletic
1898-99	Celtic	1932-33	Celtic	1968-69	Celtic
1899-00	Celtic	1933-34	Rangers	1969-70	Aberdeen
1900-01	Hearts	1934-35	Rangers	1970-71	Celtic
1901-02	Hibernian	1935-36	Rangers	1971-72	Celtic
1902-03	Rangers	1936-37	Celtic	1972-73	Rangers

73-74	Celtic	1982-82	Aberdeen	1991-92	Rangers
74-75	Celtic	1983-84	Aberdeen	1992-93	Rangers
75-76	Rangers	1984-85	Celtic	1993-94	Dundee United
76-77	Celtic	1985-86	Aberdeen	1994-95	Celtic
77-78	Rangers	1986-87	St. Mirren	1995-96	Rangers
78-79	Rangers	1987-88	Celtic	1996-97	Kilmarnock
79-80	Celtic	1988-89	Celtic	1997-98	Hearts
80-81	Rangers	1989-90	Aberdeen	1998-99	Rangers
81-82	Aberdeen	1990-91	Motherwell	1999-00	Rangers

Summary: 30 - Celtic; 29 - Rangers; 10 - Queen's Park; 7 - Aberdeen; 6 - Hearts; 3 - Clyde, Kilmarnock, St. Mirren, Vale of Leven; 2 - Dunfermline Athletic, Falkirk, Hibernian, Motherwell, Renton, Third Lanark; 1 - Airdrieonians, Dumbarton, Dundee, Dundee United, East Fife, Morton, Partick Thistle, St. Bernards.

Scottish Federation

1891-92	Arthurlie	1892-93	Royal Albert

Scottish Football Combination

1896-97	Hearts 'A'	1902-03	Albion Rovers	1908-09	Galston
1897-98	Rangers 'A'	1903-04	Royal Albert	1909-10	Nithsdale Wand./Girvan
1898-99	Rangers 'A'	1904-05	Beith	*1910-11*	*Not Completed*
1899-00	Queen's Park Strollers	1905-06	Dumbarton	*1911-35*	*No Competition*
1900-01	Arthurlie	1906-07	Galston/Johnstone	1935-36	Dalbeattie Star
1901-02	Albion Rovers	1907-08	Galston	1936-37	Ayr United 'A

Scottish League - Division 1
(Prior to Reorganisation)

1890-91	Dumbarton/Rangers	1917-18	Rangers	1950-51	Hibernian
1891-92	Dumbarton	1918-19	Celtic	1951-52	Hibernian
1892-93	Celtic	1919-20	Rangers	1952-53	Rangers
1893-94	Celtic	1920-21	Rangers	1953-54	Celtic
1894-95	Hearts	1921-22	Celtic	1954-55	Aberdeen
1895-96	Celtic	1922-23	Rangers	1955-56	Rangers
1896-97	Hearts	1923-24	Rangers	1956-57	Rangers
1897-98	Celtic	1924-25	Rangers	1957-58	Hearts
1898-99	Rangers	1925-26	Celtic	1958-59	Rangers
1899-00	Rangers	1926-27	Rangers	1959-60	Hearts
1900-01	Rangers	1927-28	Rangers	1960-61	Rangers
1901-02	Rangers	1928-29	Rangers	1961-62	Dundee
1902-03	Hibernian	1929-30	Rangers	1962-63	Rangers
1903-04	Third Lanark	1930-31	Rangers	1963-64	Rangers
1904-05	Celtic	1931-32	Motherwell	1964-65	Kilmarnock
1905-06	Celtic	1932-33	Rangers	1965-66	Celtic
1906-07	Celtic	1933-34	Rangers	1966-67	Celtic
1907-08	Celtic	1934-35	Rangers	1967-68	Celtic
1908-09	Celtic	1935-36	Celtic	1968-69	Celtic
1909-10	Celtic	1936-37	Rangers	1969-70	Celtic
1910-11	Rangers	1937-38	Celtic	1970-71	Celtic
1911-12	Rangers	1938-39	Rangers	1971-72	Celtic
1912-13	Rangers	*1939-46*	*No Competition*	1972-73	Celtic
1913-14	Celtic	1946-47	Rangers	1973-74	Celtic
1914-15	Celtic	1947-48	Hibernian	1974-75	Rangers
1915-16	Celtic	1948-49	Rangers		
1916-17	Celtic	1949-50	Rangers		

Summary: 35 - Rangers*; 29 - Celtic; 4 - Hearts, Hibernian; 2 - Dumbarton*; 1 - Aberdeen, Dundee, Kilmarnock, Motherwell, Third Lanark.   * includes one shared.

Scottish League - Division 2

(Prior to reorganisation)

1893-94	Hibernian	1922-23	Queen's Park	1952-53	Stirling Albion
1894-95	Hibernian	1923-24	St. Johnstone	1953-54	Motherwell
1895-96	Abercorn	1924-25	Dundee United	1954-55	Airdrieonians
1896-97	Partick Thistle	1925-26	Dunfermline Athletic	1955-56	Queen's Park
1897-98	Kilmarnock	1926-27	Bo'ness	1956-57	Clyde
1898-99	Kilmarnock	1927-28	Ayr United	1957-58	Stirling Albion
1899-00	Partick Thistle	1928-29	Dundee United	1958-59	Ayr United
1900-01	St. Bernards	1929-30	Leith Athletic	1959-60	St. Johnstone
1901-02	Port Glasgow Athletic	1930-31	Third Lanark	1960-61	Stirling Albion
1902-03	Airdrieonians	1931-32	East Stirlingshire	1961-62	Clyde
1903-04	Hamilton Academical	1932-33	Hibernian	1962-63	St. Johnstone
1904-05	Clyde	1933-34	Albion Rovers	1963-64	Morton
1905-06	Leith Athletic	1934-35	Third Lanark	1964-65	Stirling Albion
1906-07	St. Bernards	1935-36	Falkirk	1965-66	Ayr United
1907-08	Raith Rovers	1936-37	Ayr United	1966-67	Morton
1908-09	Abercorn	1937-38	Raith Rovers	1967-68	St. Mirren
1909-10	Leith Athletic	1938-39	Cowdenbeath	1968-69	Motherwell
1910-11	Dumbarton	*1939-46*	*No Competition*	1969-70	Falkirk
1911-12	Ayr United	1946-47	Dundee	1970-71	Partick Thistle
1912-13	Ayr United	1947-48	East Fife	1971-72	Dumbarton
1913-14	Cowdenbeath	1948-49	Raith Rovers	1972-73	Clyde
1914-15	Cowdenbeath	1949-50	Morton	1973-74	Airdrieonians
1915-21	*No Competition*	1950-51	Queen of the South	1974-75	Falkirk
1921-22	Alloa	1951-52	Clyde		

Summary: *6 - Ayr United; 5 - Clyde; 4 - Stirling Albion; 3 - Airdrieonians, Cowdenbeath, Falkirk, Hibernian, Leith Athletic, Morton, Partick Thistle, Raith Rovers, St. Johnstone; 2 - Abercorn, Dumbarton, Dundee United, Kilmarnock, Motherwell, Queen's Park, St. Bernards, Third Lanark, 1 - Albion Rovers, Alloa, Bo'ness, Dundee, Dunfermline Athletic, East Fife, East Stirlingshire, Hamilton Academical, Port Glasgow Athletic, Queen of the South, St. Mirren.*

Scottish League - Division 3

(Prior to Reorganisation)

1923-24	Arthurlie	1924-25	Nithsdale Wanderers	1925-26	Helensburgh

Scottish League - Division 'C'

1946-47	Stirling Albion	1950-51	NE - Hearts Res.		SW - Rangers Res
1947-48	East Stirlingshire		SW - Clyde Res.	1953-54	NE - Brechin City
1948-49	Forfar Athletic	1951-52	NE - Dundee Res.		SW - Rangers Res.
1949-50	NE - Hibernian Res.		SW - Rangers Res.	1954-55	NE - Aberdeen Res.
	SW - Clyde Res.	1952-53	NE - Aberdeen Res.		SW - Partick Th. Res.

Scottish League - Premier Division

1975-76	Rangers	1984-85	Aberdeen	1993-94	Rangers
1976-77	Celtic	1985-86	Celtic	1994-95	Rangers
1977-78	Rangers	1986-87	Rangers	1995-96	Rangers
1978-79	Celtic	1987-88	Celtic	1996-97	Rangers
1979-80	Aberdeen	1988-89	Rangers	1997-98	Celtic
1980-81	Celtic	1989-90	Rangers	1998-99	Rangers
1981-82	Celtic	1990-91	Rangers	1999-00	Rangers
1982-83	Dundee United	1991-92	Rangers		
1983-84	Aberdeen	1992-93	Rangers		

Summary: *14 - Rangers; 7 - Celtic; 3 - Aberdeen; 1 - Dundee United.*

Scottish League - First Division
(After Reorganisation)

75-76	Partick Thistle	1983-84	Morton	1992-93	Raith Rovers
76-77	St. Mirren	1984-85	Motherwell	1993-94	Falkirk
77-78	Morton	1985-86	Hamilton Academical	1994-95	Raith Rovers
78-79	Dundee	1986-87	Morton	1995-96	Dunfermline Athletic
79-80	Hearts	1987-88	Hamilton Academical	1996-97	St. Johnstone
80-81	Hibernian	1988-89	St. Johnstone	1997-98	Dundee
81-82	Motherwell	1990-91	Falkirk	1998-99	Hibernian
82-83	St. Johnstone	1991-92	Dundee	1999-00	St. Mirren

Summary: *3 - Dundee, Morton, St. Johnstone; 2 - Falkirk, Hamilton Academical, Hibernian, Motherwell, Raith Rovers, St. Mirren;; 1 - Dunfermline Athletic, Hearts, Partick Thistle.*

Scottish League - Second Division
(After reorganisation)

75-76	Clydebank	1984-85	Montrose	1993-94	Stranraer
76-77	Stirling Albion	1985-86	Dunfermline Athletic	1994-95	Morton
77-78	Clyde	1986-87	Meadowbank Thistle	1995-96	Stirling Albion
78-79	Berwick Rangers	1987-88	Ayr United	1996-97	Ayr United
79-80	Falkirk	1988-89	Albion Rovers	1997-98	Stranraer
80-81	Queen's Park	1989-90	Brechin City	1998-99	Livingston
81-82	Clyde	1990-91	Stirling Albion	1999-00	Clyde
82-83	Brechin City	1991-92	Dumbarton		
83-84	Forfar Athletic	1992-93	Clyde		

Summary: *4 - Clyde; 3 - Stirling Albion; 2 - Ayr United, Brechin City, Livingston/Meadowbank Thistle, Stranraer; 1 - Albion Rovers, Berwick Rangers, Clydebank, Dumbarton, Dunfermline Athletic, Falkirk, Forfar Athletic, Montrose, Morton, Queen's Park.*

Scottish League - Division Three
(After Reorganisation)

94-95	Forfar Athletic	1996-97	Inverness Caledonian Th.	1998-99	Ross County
95-96	Livingston	1997-98	Alloa	1999-00	Queen's Park

Scottish League Challenge Cup

90-91	Dundee	1994-95	Airdrieonians	*1998-99*	*No Competition*
91-92	Hamilton Academical	1995-96	Stenhousemuir	1999-00	Alloa
92-93	Hamilton Academical	1996-97	Stranraer		
93-94	Falkirk	1997-98	Falkirk		

Scottish League Cup

45-46	Aberdeen	1961-62	Rangers	1977-78	Rangers
46-47	Rangers	1962-63	Hearts	1978-79	Rangers
47-48	East Fife	1963-64	Rangers	1979-80	Dundee United
48-49	Rangers	1964-65	Rangers	1980-81	Dundee United
49-50	East Fife	1965-66	Celtic	1981-82	Rangers
50-51	Motherwell	1966-67	Celtic	1982-83	Celtic
51-52	Dundee	1967-68	Celtic	1983-84	Rangers
52-53	Dundee	1968-69	Celtic	1984-85	Rangers
53-54	East Fife	1969-70	Celtic	1985-86	Aberdeen
54-55	Hearts	1970-71	Rangers	1986-87	Rangers
55-56	Aberdeen	1971-72	Partick Thistle	1987-88	Rangers
56-57	Celtic	1972-73	Hibernian	1988-89	Rangers
57-58	Celtic	1973-74	Dundee	1989-90	Aberdeen
58-59	Hearts	1974-75	Celtic	1990-91	Rangers
59-60	Hearts	1975-76	Rangers	1991-92	Hibernian
60-61	Rangers	1976-77	Aberdeen	1992-93	Rangers

CONTINUED OVERLEAF

1993-94	Rangers	1996-97	Rangers	1999-00	Celtic
1994-95	Raith Rovers	1997-98	Celtic		
1995-96	Aberdeen	1998-99	Rangers		

Summary: *21 - Rangers; 11 - Celtic; 6 - Aberdeen; 4 - Hearts; 3 - Dundee, East Fife; 2 - Dundee United, Hibernian; 1 - Motherwell, Partick Thistle, Raith Rovers.*

Scottish Qualifying Cup

1895-96	Annbank	1906-07	Raith Rovers	1920-21	East Fife
1896-97	Kilmarnock	1907-08	St. Bernards	1921-22	Montrose
1897-98	Port Glasgow Athletic	1908-09	Vale of Leven	1922-23	Royal Albert
1898-99	East Stirlingshire	1909-10	Leith Athletic	1923-24	Queen of the South
1899-00	Galston	1910-11	East Stirlingshire	1924-25	Royal Albert
1900-01	Stenhousemuir	1911-12	Dunfermline Athletic	1925-26	Leith Athletic
1901-02	Stenhousemuir	1912-13	Abercorn	1926-27	Mid-Annandale
1902-03	Motherwell	1913-14	Albion Rovers	1927-28	Beith
1903-04	Arbroath	1914-15	St. Bernards	1928-29	Murrayfield Amateurs
1904-05	Aberdeen	*1915-19*	*No Competition*	1929-30	Bathgate
1905-06	Leith Athletic	1919-20	Bathgate	1930-31	Bathgate

Summary: *3 - Bathgate, Leith Athletic; 2 - East Stirlingshire, Royal Albert, St. Bernards, Stenhousemuir; 1 - Abercorn, Aberdeen, Albion Rovers, Annbank, Arbroath, Beith, Dunfermline Athletic, East Fife, Galston, Kilmarnock, Mid-Annandale, Montrose, Motherwell, Murrayfield Amateur Port Glasgow Athletic, Queen of the South, Raith Rovers, Vale of Leven.*

Scottish Qualifying Cup (Midland)

1947-48	Forfar Athletic	1948-49	Montrose

Scottish Qualifying Cup (North)

1931-32	Inverness Citadel	1959-60	Elgin City	1981-82	Inverness Caledonain
1932-33	Inverness Thistle	1960-61	Keith	1982-83	Inverness Caledonian
1933-34	Rosyth Recreation	1961-62	Inverness Caledonian	1983-84	Inverness Caledonian
1934-35	Clachnacuddin	1962-63	Keith	1984-85	Keith
1935-36	Elgin City	1963-64	Forres Mechanics	1985-86	Peterhead
1936-37	Vale Ocoba	1964-65	Elgin City	1986-87	Inverness Caledonian
1937-38	Elgin City	1965-66	Inverness Caledonian	1987-88	Inverness Caledonian
1938-39	Clachnacuddin	1966-67	Inverness Caledonian	1988-89	Inverness Thistle
1939-46	*No Competition*	1967-68	Elgin City	1989-90	Elgin City
1946-47	Peterhead	1968-69	Nairn County	1990-91	Cove Rangers
1947-48	Clachnacuddin	1969-70	Inverness Caledonian	1991-92	Inverness Caledonian
1948-49	Inverness Caledonain	1970-71	Elgin City	1992-93	Huntly
1949-50	Inverness Caledonian	1971-72	Inverness Caledonian	1993-94	Ross County
1950-51	Inverness Caledonian	1972-73	Inverness Thistle	1994-95	Huntly
1951-52	Deveronvale	1973-74	Ross County	1995-96	Fraserburgh
1952-53	Buckie Thistle	1974-75	Clachnacuddin	1996-97	Huntly
1953-54	Buckie Thistle	1975-76	Peterhead	1997-98	Peterhead
1954-55	Forres Mechanics	1976-77	Inverness Thistle	1998-99	Clachnacuddin
1955-56	Inverness Thistle	1977-78	Peterhead	1999-00	Huntly
1956-57	Lossiemouth	1978-79	Peterhead		
1957-58	Fraserburgh	1979-80	Brora Rangers		
1958-59	Buckie Thistle	1980-81	Inverness Thistle		

Summary: *14 - Inverness Caledonian; 7 - Elgin City; 6 - Inverness Thistle, Peterhead; 5 - Clachnacuddin; 4 - Huntly: 3 - Buckie Thistle, Keith; 2 - Forres Mechanics, Fraserburgh, Ross County; 1 - Brora Rangers, Cove Rangers, Deveronvale, Inverness Citadel, Lossiemouth, Nairn Count Rosyth Recreation, Vale Ocoba.*

Scottish Qualifying Cup (South)

31-32	Beith	1959-60	Eyemouth United	1981-82	Hawick Royal Albert
32-33	Beith	1960-61	Duns	1982-83	Gala Fairydean
33-34	Penicuik Athletic	1961-62	Gala Fairydean	1983-84	Gala Fairydean
34-35	Beith	1962-63	Duns	1984-85	Gala Fairydean
35-36	Galston	1963-64	Duns	1985-86	Gala Fairydean
36-37	Duns	1964-65	Edinburgh University	1986-87	Whitehill Welfare
37-38	Stranraer	1965-66	Gala Fairydean	1987-88	Gala Fairydean
38-39	Penicuik Athletic	1966-67	Gala Fairydean	1988-89	Spartans
39-46	*No Competition*	1967-68	Hawick Royal Albert	1989-90	Gala Fairydean
46-47	Edinburgh City	1968-69	Glasgow University	1990-91	Vale of Leithen
47-48	Berwick Rangers	1969-70	Tarff Rovers	1991-92	Gala Fairydean
48-49	Leith Athletic	1970-71	Glasgow University	1992-93	Vale of Leithen
49-50	Leith Athletic	1971-72	St. Cuthbert Wanderers	1993-94	Whitehill Welfare
50-51	Brechin City	1972-73	Vale of Leithen	1994-95	Whitehill Welfare
51-52	Wigtown & Bladnoch	1973-74	Ferranti Thistle	1995-96	Whitehill Welfare
52-53	Eyemouth United	1974-75	Selkirk	1996-97	Spartans
53-54	Peebles Rovers	1975-76	Selkirk	1997-98	Whitehill Welfare
54-55	Eyemouth United	1976-77	Vale of Leithen	1998-99	Whitehill Welfare
55-56	Newton Stewart	1977-78	Selkirk	1999-00	Whitehill Welfare
56-57	Duns	1978-79	Gala Fairydean		
57-58	Vale of Leithen	1979-80	Spartans		
58-59	Eyemouth United	1980-81	Whitehill Welfare		

Summary: 11 - Gala Fairydean; 8 - Whitehill Welfare; 5 - Duns, Vale of Leithen; 4 - Eyemouth United; 3 - Beith, Selkirk, Spartans; 2 - Glasgow University, Hawick Royal Albert, Leith Athletic, Penicuik Athletic; 1 - Berwick Rangers, Brechin City, Edinburgh City, Edinburgh University, Ferranti Thistle, Galston, Newton Stewart, Peebles Rovers, St. Cuthbert Wanderers, Stranraer, Tarff Rovers, Wigtown & Bladnoch.

Scottish Second XI Cup

81-82	Dumbarton	1911-12	Rangers	1944-45	Hearts
82-83	Kilmarnock Athletic	1912-13	Rangers	1945-46	Hibernian
83-84	Kilmarnock Athletic	1913-14	Clyde	1946-47	Hibernian
84-85	Hibernian	1914-15	Clyde	1947-48	Airdrieonians
85-86	Abercorn	1915-19	*No Competition*	1948-49	Motherwell
86-87	Abercorn	1919-20	Queen's Park	1949-50	Falkirk
87-88	Ayr United	1920-21	Hearts	1950-51	Hearts
88-89	Cambuslang	1921-22	Airdrieonians	1951-52	Rangers
89-90	Rangers	1922-23	Airdrieonians	1952-53	Dundee
90-91	Celtic	1923-24	Rangers	1953-54	Hearts
91-92	Leith Athletic	1924-25	Rangers	1954-55	Aberdeen
92-93	Leith Athletic	1925-26	Rangers	1955-56	Aberdeen
93-94	Hearts	1926-27	St. Mirren	1956-57	Motherwell
94-95	Hearts	1927-28	Rangers	1957-58	Celtic
95-96	Queen's Park	1928-29	Rangers	1958-59	St. Mirren
96-97	Hearts	1929-30	Rangers	1959-60	*Cup Withheld*
97-98	Rangers	1930-31	Rangers	1960-61	St. Johnstone
98-99	Rangers	1931-32	Hearts	1961-62	Rangers
99-00	Third Lanark	1932-33	Rangers	1962-63	Dundee United
00-01	Hearts	1933-34	Hamilton Academical	1963-64	Rangers
01-02	Queen's Park	1934-35	St. Johnstone	1964-65	Rangers
02-03	Queen's Park	1935-36	Celtic	1965-66	Celtic
03-04	Queen's Park	1936-37	Rangers	1966-67	Dundee
04-05	Third Lanark	1937-38	Rangers	1967-68	Rangers
05-06	Hearts	1938-39	Hibernian	1968-69	Aberdeen
06-07	Rangers	1939-40	Ayr United	1969-70	Rangers
07-08	Dundee	1940-41	Rangers	1970-71	Celtic
08-09	Falkirk	1941-42	Clyde	1971-72	Partick Thistle
09-10	Falkirk	1942-43	Motherwell	1972-73	Hearts
10-11	Hearts	1943-44	Hearts	1973-74	Celtic

CONTINUED OVERLEAF

1974-75	Partick Thistle	1979-80	Kilmarnock	1984-85	Celtic
1975-76	Aberdeen	1980-81	Dundee United	*1985-87*	*No Competition*
1976-77	Rangers	1981-82	Aberdeen	1987-88	Dundee United
1977-78	Aberdeen	1982-83	Dundee		
1978-79	Rangers	1983-84	Airdrieonians		

Summary: *25 - Rangers; 13 - Hearts; 7 - Celtic; 6 - Aberdeen; 5 - Queen's Park; 4 - Airdrieonians, Dundee, Hibernian; 3 - Clyde, Dundee United, Falkirk, Motherwell; 2 - Abercorn, Ayr United, Kilmarnock Athletic, Leith Athletic, Partick Thistle, St. Johnstone, St. Mirren, Third Lanark; 1 - Cambuslang, Dumbarton, Hamilton Academical, Kilmarnock.*

Scottish Supplementary Cup
(Additional tournament for 'B'Division clubs)

1946-47	East Fife	1948-49	St. Johnstone	*1950-51*	*No Competition*
1947-48	East Fife	*1949-50*	*Not Completed*	1951-52	Clyde

Scottish Union

1906-07	Rangers 'A'	1909-10	Dumbarton Harp	1912-13	Dykehead
1907-08	Bathgate	1910-11	Peebles Rovers	1913-14	Queen's Park Victoria X
1908-09	Falkirk 'A'	1911-12	Galston		

Southern Counties Charity Cup

1883-84	5th K.R.V.	1901-02	Maxwelltown Volunteers	1922-23	Queen of the South
1884-85	Q.O.S. Wanderers	1902-03	Maxwelltown Volunteers	1923-24	Queen of the South
1885-86	Q.O.S. Wanderers	1903-04	Maxwelltown Volunteers	1924-25	Solway Star
1886-87	Q.O.S. Wanderers	1904-05	Maxwelltown Volunteers	1925-26	Queen of the South
1887-88	Moffat	1905-06	Maxwelltown Volunteers	1926-27	Mid-Annandale
1888-89	Q.O.S. Wanderers	1906-07	Dumfries	1927-28	Solway Star
1889-90	5th K.R.V.	1907-08	Dumfries	1928-29	Solway Star
1890-91	5th K.R.V.	1908-09	Dumfries	1929-30	Queen of the South
1891-92	Q.O.S. Wanderers	1909-10	Dumfries	1930-31	Queen of the South
1892-93	Q.O.S. Wanderers	1910-11	Nithsdale Wanderers	1931-32	Queen of the South
1893-94	5th K.R.V.	1911-12	5th K.O.S.B.	1932-33	Mid-Annandale
1894-97	*No Competition*	1912-13	Nithsdale Wanderers	1933-34	Queen of the South
1897-98	Dumfries Hibs	*1913-19*	*No Competition*	1934-35	Mid-Annandale
1898-99	Dumfries	1919-20	Queen of the South	1935-36	Mid-Annandale
1899-00	Dumfries	1920-21	Queen of the South	1936-37	Queen of the South
1900-01	Dumfries	1921-22	Queen of the South		

Summary: *11 - Queen of the South; 7 - Dumfries; 6 - Queen of the South Wanderers; 5 - Maxwelltown Volunteers; 4 - 5th K.R.V., Mid-Annandale, Solway Star; 2 - Nithsdale Wanderers; 1 - Dumfries Hibs, 5th K.O.S.B., Moffat.*

Southern Counties Cup

1891-92	5th KRV	1907-08	Maxwelltown Volunteers	1927-28	Nithsdale Wanderers
1892-93	Q.O.S. Wanderers	1908-09	Dalbeattie Star	1928-29	Mid-Annandale
1893-94	5th KRV	1909-10	Dumfries	1929-30	St. Cuthbert Wanderers
1894-95	Maxwelltown Thistle	1910-11	Nithsdale Wanderers	1930-31	Dalbeattie Star
1895-96	St. Cuthbert Wanderers	1911-12	Nithsdale Wanderers	1931-32	Stranraer
1896-97	6th GRV	1912-13	Solway Star	1932-33	Stranraer
1897-98	Dumfries	1913-14	Nithsdale Wanderers	1933-34	Dalbeattie Star
1898-99	Dumfries	*1914-19*	*No Competition*	1934-35	Queen of the South 'A'
1899-00	Dumfries	1919-20	Nithsdale Wanderers	1935-36	Queen of the South 'A'
1900-01	Dumfries	1920-21	Queen of the South	1936-37	Stranraer
1901-02	Dumfries	1921-22	Nithsdale Wanderers	*1937-38*	*Not Completed*
1902-03	Dumfries	1922-23	Nithsdale Wanderers	1938-39	Stranraer
1903-04	Nithsdale Wanderers	1923-24	Queen of the South 'A'	*1939-45*	*No Competition*
1904-05	Maxwelltown Volunteers	1924-25	Dalbeattie Star	1945-46	Nithsdale Wanderers
1905-06	Dumfries	1925-26	Stranraer	1946-47	Dalbeattie Star
1906-07	Nithsdale Wanderers	1926-27	Stranraer	1947-48	Stranraer

48-49	Newton Stewart	1966-67	Stranraer 'A'	1984-85	Creetown
49-50	Tarff Rovers	1967-68	Tarff Rovers	1985-86	Threave Rovers
50-51	Newton Stewart	1968-69	Stranraer 'A'	1986-87	Queen of the South 'A'
51-52	Tarff Rovers	1969-70	St. Cuthbert Wanderers	1987-88	Queen of the South 'A'
52-53	St. Cuthbert Wanderers	1970-71	Stranraer 'A'	1988-89	Stranraer 'A'
53-54	St. Cuthbert Wanderers	1971-72	Queen of the South 'A'	1989-90	Annan Athletic
54-55	Whithorn	1972-73	Tarff Rovers	1990-91	Queen of the South 'A'
55-56	Newton Stewart	1973-74	Stranraer 'A'	1991-92	Stranraer 'A'
56-57	Stranraer 'A'	1974-75	Tarff Rovers	1992-93	Dalbeattie Star
57-58	Greystone Rovers	1975-76	Queen of the South 'A'	1993-94	Stranraer 'A'
58-59	Newton Stewart	1976-77	Stranraer 'A'	1994-95	Stranraer 'A'
59-60	Stranraer 'A'	1977-78	Lincluden Swifts	1995-96	Annan Athletic
60-61	Stranraer 'A'	1978-79	Lincluden Swifts	1996-97	Queen of the South 'A'
61-62	Queen of the South 'A'	1979-80	Threave Rovers	1997-98	Threave Rovers
62-63	Newton Stewart	1980-81	Threave Rovers	1998-99	Annan Athletic
63-64	Stranraer 'A'	1981-82	Queen of the South 'A'	1999-00	Queen of the South 'A'
64-65	Threave Rovers	1982-83	Queen of the South 'A'		
65-66	Queen of the South 'A'	1983-84	Newton Stewart		

Summary: 14 - Queen of the South 'A'; 13 - Stranraer 'A'; 10 - Nithsdale Wanderers; 8 - Dumfries; - Stranraer; 6 - Dalbeattie Star, Newton Stewart; 5 - St. Cuthbert Wanderers, Tarff Rovers, Threave Rovers; 3 - Annan Athletic; 2 - 5th K.R.V., Lincluden Swifts, Maxwelltown Volunteers; 1 - Creetown, Greystone Rovers, Maxwelltown Thistle, Mid-Annandale, Queen of the South, Queen of the South Wanderers, 6th G.R.V., Solway Star, Whithorn.

Southern League
(Wartime competition for Scottish League clubs)
(Western League 1939-40; 'A' Division 1945-46)

39-40	Rangers	1942-43	Rangers	1945-46	Rangers
40-41	Rangers	1943-44	Rangers		
41-42	Rangers	1944-45	Rangers		

Southern League Cup
(Wartime competition for Scottish League clubs)

40-41	Rangers	1942-43	Rangers	1944-45	Rangers
41-42	Rangers	1943-44	Hibernian	1945-46	Aberdeen

South of Scotland Cup
(Formerly the Southern Counties Consolation Cup)

98-99	6th G.R.V.	1908-09	Douglas Wanderers	1922-23	Mid-Annandale
99-00	Dumfries Hibernians	1909-10	Mid-Annandale Amateurs	1923-24	Newton Stewart
00-01	Douglas Wanderers	1910-11	Douglas Wanderers	1924-25	Newton Stewart
01-02	Vale of Dryfe	1911-12	Dumfries	1925-26	St. Cuthbert Wanderers
02-03	Vale of Dryfe	1912-13	Nithsdale Wanderers	1926-27	St. Cuthbert Wanderers
03-04	Maxwelltown Volunteers	1913-14	Solway Star	*1927-28*	*Not Completed*
04-05	Dumfries	*1914-19*	*No Competition*	1928-29	Mid-Annandale
05-06	Maxwelltown Volunteers	1919-20	Mid-Annandale	1929-30	Dalbeattie Star
06-07	Maxwelltown Volunteers	*1920-21*	*Not Completed*	1930-31	Dalbeattie Star
07-08	Dumfries	1921-22	Queen of the South		

Summary: 3 - Douglas Wanderers, Dumfries, Maxwelltown Volunteers, Mid-Annandale; 2 - Dalbeattie Star, Newton Stewart, St. Cuthbert Wanderers, Vale of Dryfe; 1 - Dumfries Hibernian, Mid-Annandale Amateurs, Nithsdale Wanderers, Queen of the South, 6th G.R.V., Solway Star.

South of Scotland League
(Formerly the Southern Counties League)

27-28	St. Cuthbert Wanderers	1932-33	Dalbeattie Star	*1937-46*	*No Competition*
28-29	St. Cuthbert Wanderers	1933-34	Dalbeattie Star	1946-47	Ayr United 'A'
29-30	Dalbeattie Star	1934-35	St. Cuthbert Wanderers	1947-48	Ayr United 'A'
30-31	Dalbeattie Star	1935-36	St. Cuthbert Wanderers	1948-49	Stranraer
31-32	Dalbeattie Star	1936-37	St. Cuthbert Wanderers	1949-50	Tarff Rovers

CONTINUED OVERLEAF

1950-51	Newton Stewart	1967-68	Threave Rovers	1984-85	Annan Athletic
1951-52	Wigtown & Bladnoch	1968-69	Stranraer 'A'	1985-86	Newton Stewart
1952-53	Wigtown & Bladnoch	1969-70	St. Cuthbert Wanderers	1986-87	Wigtown & Bladnoch
1953-54	St. Cuthbert Wanderers	1970-71	St. Cuthbert Wanderers	1987-88	Threave Rovers
1954-55	Tarff Rovers	1971-72	Threave Rovers	1988-89	Dalbeattie Star
1955-56	Tarff Rovers	1972-73	St. Cuthbert Wanderers	1989-90	Threave Rovers
1956-57	Stranraer 'A'	1973-74	Stranraer 'A'	1990-91	Threave Rovers
1957-58	Stranraer 'A'	1974-75	St. Cuthbert Wanderers	1991-92	Girvan Amateurs
1958-59	Newton Stewart	1975-76	Girvan Amateurs	1992-93	Dalbeattie Star
1959-60	Tarff Rovers	1976-77	Stranraer 'A'	1993-94	Threave Rovers
1960-61	Tarff Rovers	1977-78	Girvan Amateurs	1994-95	Wigtown & Bladnoch
1961-62	Stranraer 'A'	1978-79	Lincluden Swifts	1995-96	St. Cuthbert Wanderers
1962-63	Threave Rovers	1979-80	Lincluden Swifts	1996-97	Queen of the South 'A'
1963-64	Stranraer 'A'	1980-81	Threave Rovers	1997-98	Tarff Rovers
1964-65	Tarff Rovers	1981-82	St. Cuthbert Wanderers	1998-99	Tarff Rovers
1965-66	Tarff Rovers	1982-83	Annan Athletic	1999-00	Tarff Rovers
1966-67	Threave Rovers	1983-84	Wigtown & Bladnoch		

Summary: *12 - St. Cuthbert Wanderers; 10 - Tarff Rovers; 9 - Threave Rovers; 7 - Dalbeattie Star, Stranraer 'A'; 5 - Wigtown & Bladnoch; 3 - Girvan Amateurs, Newton Stewart; 2 - Annan Athletic, Ayr United 'A', Lincluden Swifts; 1 - Queen of the South 'A', Stranraer.*

South of Scotland League Cup

1950-51	Newton Stewart	1967-68	Threave Rovers	1984-85	Annan Athletic
1951-52	Wigtown & Bladnoch	1968-69	Stranraer 'A'	1985-86	Newton Stewart
1952-53	Wigtown & Bladnoch	1969-70	St. Cuthbert Wanderers	1986-87	Wigtown & Bladnoch
1953-54	St. Cuthbert Wanderers	1970-71	St. Cuthbert Wanderers	1987-88	Threave Rovers
1954-55	Tarff Rovers	1971-72	Threave Rovers	1988-89	Dalbeattie Star
1955-56	Tarff Rovers	1972-73	St. Cuthbert Wanderers	1989-90	Threave Rovers
1956-57	Stranraer 'A'	1973-74	Stranraer 'A'	1990-91	Threave Rovers
1957-58	Stranraer 'A'	1974-75	St. Cuthbert Wanderers	1991-92	Girvan Amateurs
1958-59	Newton Stewart	1975-76	Girvan Amateurs	1992-93	Dalbeattie Star
1959-60	Tarff Rovers	1976-77	Stranraer 'A'	1993-94	Threave Rovers
1960-61	Tarff Rovers	1977-78	Girvan Amateurs	1994-95	Wigtown & Bladnoch
1961-62	Stranraer 'A'	1978-79	Lincluden Swifts	1995-96	St. Cuthbert Wanderers
1962-63	Threave Rovers	1979-80	Lincluden Swifts	1996-97	Queen of the South 'A'
1963-64	Stranraer 'A'	1980-81	Threave Rovers	1997-98	Tarff Rovers
1964-65	Tarff Rovers	1981-82	St. Cuthbert Wanderers	1998-99	Tarff Rovers
1965-66	Tarff Rovers	1982-83	Annan Athletic	1999-00	Tarff Rovers
1966-67	Threave Rovers	1983-84	Wigtown & Bladnoch		

Summary: *9 - Tarff Rovers,Threave Rovers; 7 - St. Cuthbert Wanderers, Stranraer 'A'; 5 - Wigtown & Bladnoch; 3 - Girvan Amateurs, Newton Stewart; 2 - Annan Athletic, Dalbeattie Star, Lincluden Swifts; 1 - Queen of the South 'A'.*

Stirling Charity Cup

(According to sources close to Stirling Albion, there never was an actual trophy for this competition. Any available cup was used for the presentation and then immediately reclaimed. Not played for every year, this is believed to be a complete list of winners.)

1885-86	King's Park	1894-95	Callander Rob Roy	1933-34	King's Park
1886-87	Dunblane	1895-96	Callander Rob Roy	1934-35	Hearts
1887-88	King's Park	1896-97	King's Park	1936-37	Hearts
1888-89	King's Park	1924-25	King's Park	*1939-45*	*No Competition*
1889-90	King's Park	1927-28	King's Park	1945-46	Stirling Albion
1890-91	King's Park	1928-29	St. Mirren	1948-49	Stirling Albion
1891-92	Bridge of Allan	1929-30	St. Mirren	1952-53	Stirling Albion
1892-93	King's Park	1931-32	Hearts		
1893-94	King's Park	1932-33	Hearts		

Summary: *11 - King's Park; 4 - Hearts; 3 - Stirling Albion; 2 - Callander Rob Roy, St. Mirren; 1 - Bridge of Allan, Dunblane.*

Stirlingshire Cup

83-84	Falkirk	1923-24	East Stirlingshire	1965-66	Alloa
84-85	Camelon	1924-25	East Stirlingshire	1966-67	Falkirk
85-86	East Stirlingshire	1925-26	Falkirk	1967-68	Falkirk
86-87	East Stirlingshire	1926-27	Falkirk	1968-69	East Stirlingshire
87-88	East Stirlingshire	1927-28	East Stirlingshire	1969-70	Falkirk
88-89	East Stirlingshire	1928-29	East Stirlingshire	1970-71	Stenhousemuir
89-90	Falkirk	1929-30	Falkirk	1971-72	Stirling Albion
90-91	East Stirlingshire	1930-31	Falkirk	1972-73	Dumbarton
91-92	Campsie	1931-32	East Stirlingshire	1973-74	Stirling Albion
92-93	East Stirlingshire	1932-33	Stenhousemuir	1974-75	Dumbarton
93-94	East Stirlingshire	1933-34	Alloa	1975-76	Stenhousemuir
94-95	Falkirk	1934-35	Falkirk	1976-77	Stirling Albon
95-96	Falkirk	1935-36	East Stirlingshire	1977-78	Stirling Albion
96-97	East Stirlingshire	1936-37	Stenhousemuir	1978-79	Clydebank
97-98	Camelon	1937-38	Falkirk	1979-80	Clydebank
98-99	King's Park	*1938-39*	*Not Completed*	1980-81	Dumbarton
99-00	Stenhousemuir	*1939-45*	*No Competition*	1981-82	Alloa
00-01	East Stirlingshire	*1945-46*	*Not Completed*	1982-83	Dumbarton
01-02	Stenhousemuir	1946-47	Alloa	1983-84	Stirling Albion
02-03	East Stirlingshire	*1947-48*	*Not Completed*	1984-85	East Stirlingshire
03-04	Falkirk	*1948-49*	*Not Completed*	1985-86	Dumbarton
04-05	Alloa	1949-50	Falkirk	1986-87	Stenhousemuir
05-06	Falkirk	1950-51	Falkirk	1987-88	Dumbarton
06-07	East Stirlingshire	1951-52	Falkirk	1988-89	Stirling Albion
07-08	Alloa	1952-53	Dumbarton	1989-90	Dumbarton
08-09	Alloa	1953-54	Stirling Albion	1990-91	Dumbarton
09-10	Falkirk	1954-55	Stirling Albion	1991-92	Stirling Albion
10-11	King's Park	1955-56	Alloa	1992-93	Falkirk
11-12	King's Park	1956-57	Dumbarton	1993-94	Dumbarton
12-13	Alloa	1957-58	Alloa	1994-95	Falkirk
13-14	East Stirlingshire	1958-59	Stirling Albion	1995-96	Dumbarton
14-15	King's Park	1959-60	Alloa	1996-97	Alloa
15-19	*No Competition*	1960-61	Falkirk	1997-98	Falkirk
19-20	Falkirk	1961-62	East Stirlingshire	1998-99	Stirling Albion
20-21	Alloa	1962-63	Stenhousemuir	1999-00	Falkirk
21-22	Stenhousemuir	1963-64	Falkirk		
22-23	Falkirk	1964-65	Dumbarton		

Summary: 27 - Falkirk; 21 - East Stirlingshire; 13 - Alloa, Dumbarton; 11 - Stirling Albion; - Stenhousemuir; 4 - King's Park; 2 - Camelon; Clydebank; 1 - Campsie.

Summer Cup

(Wartime competition for Scottish League clubs. Revived briefly in the mid 60's.)

40-41	Hibernian	1943-44	Motherwell	1964-65	Motherwell
41-42	Rangers	1944-45	Partick Thistle		
42-43	St. Mirren	1963-64	Hibernian		

Tweedie Cup

(For member clubs of the South of Scotland F.A.)

98-99	Newton Stewart Athletic	1909-10	Stranraer	1935-36	St. Cuthbert Wanderers
99-00	Stranraer	1910-11	Stranraer	1936-37	St. Cuthbert Wanderers
00-01	Newton Stewart Athletic	1911-12	Home Office Rovers	*1937-47*	*No Competition*
01-02	Barholm Rovers	1912-13	Dunragit	1947-48	Stranraer
02-03	Stranraer	*1913-26*	*No Competition*	1948-49	St. Cuthbert Wanderers
03-04	Stranraer	1926-27	Newton Stewart	1949-50	Stranraer
04-05	Stranraer	1927-28	Stranraer	*1950-52*	*Not Completed*
05-06	Newton Stewart	1928-29	Stranraer	1952-53	Stranraer 'A'
06-07	Newton Stewart	1929-30	Stranraer	*1953-54*	*Not Completed*
07-08	Garliestown	*1930-34*	*No Competition*	1954-55	St. Cuthbert Wanderers
08-09	Whithorn	1934-35	Creetown	*1955-56*	*Not Completed*

CONTINUED OVERLEAF

1956-57	Tarff Rovers	1970-71	Stranraer 'A'	*1988-89*	*No Competition*
1957-58	*Not Completed*	*1971-73*	*Not Completed*	1989-90	St. Cuthbert Wanderers
1958-59	Wigtown & Bladnoch	1973-74	St. Cuthbert Wanderers	*1990-91*	*No Competition*
1959-60	Stranraer'A'	*1974-79*	*No Competition*	1991-92	Newton Stewart
1960-61	*Not Completed*	1979-80	Lincluden Swifts	*1992-93*	*No Competition*
1961-62	Stranraer 'A'	*1980-81*	*Not Completed*	1993-94	Maxwelltown HSFP
1962-63	*Not Completed*	1981-82	Threave Rovers	*1994-95*	*No Competition*
1963-64	Threave R./St. Cuth. W.	*1982-83*	*Not Completed*	1995-96	Annan Athletic
1964-66	*Not Completed*	1983-84	Annan Athletic	1996-97	Threave Rovers
1966-67	Stranraer 'A'	*1984-85*	*No Competition*	1997-98	Tarff Rovers
1967-68	*Not Completed*	1985-86	Threave Rovers	1998-99	Tarff Rovers
1968-69	Threave Rovers	*1986-87*	*No Competition*	1999-00	Dalbeattie Star
1969-70	*Not Completed*	1987-88	Threave Rovers		

Summary: 11 - Stranraer; 7 - St. Cuthbert Wanderers*; 6 - Threave Rovers*; 5 - Stranraer 'A';
4 - Newton Stewart; 3 - Tarff Rovers; 2 - Annan Athletic, Newton Stewart Athletic; 1 - Barholm
Rovers, Creetown, Dalbeattie Star, Dunragit, Garlieston, Home Office Rovers, Lincluden Swifts,
Maxwelltown HSFP, Whithorn, Wigtown & Bladnoch. * includes one shared.

Upper Nithsdale Charity Cup

1904-05	Lanemark	1905-06	Maxwelltown V./Nithsdale	1906-07	Lanemark

Wemyss Cup
(For Fife senior clubs)

1897-98	Raith Rovers	1911-12	East Fife	1925-26	Cowdenbeath
1898-99	Cowdenbeath	1912-13	East Fife	1926-27	Cowdenbeath
1899-00	Dunf. A./Cowdenbeath	1913-14	Cowdenbeath	1927-28	Dunfermline Athletic
1900-01	Raith Rovers	1914-15	Raith Rovers	1928-29	Cowdenbeath
1901-02	Lochgelly United	1915-16	Cowdenbeath	1929-30	Dunfermline Athletic
1902-03	Lochgelly United	1916-17	Cowdenbeath	1930-31	Cowdenbeath
1903-04	Raith Rovers	1917-18	East Fife	1931-32	Cowdenbeath
1904-05	Raith Rovers	*1918-19*	*No Competition*	1932-33	Dunfermline Athletic
1905-06	Raith Rovers	1919-20	Cowdenbeath	1933-34	Dunfermline Athletic
1906-07	Hearts of Beath	1920-21	Raith Rovers	1934-35	East Fife
1907-08	Lochgelly United	1921-22	Lochgelly United	1935-36	East Fife
1908-09	Dunfermline Athletic	1922-23	Cowdenbeath	1936-37	East Fife
1909-10	Dunfermline Athletic	1923-24	Lochgelly United	1937-38	Cowdenbeath/Raith Rov
1910-11	Cowdenbeath	1924-25	Cowdenbeath	1938-39	Raith Rovers

Summary: 15 - Cowdenbeath **; 9 - Raith Rovers *; 7 - Dunfermline Athletic *; 6 - East Fife;
5 - Lochgelly United; 1 - Hearts of Beath. * includes 1 shared ** includes 2 shared

Western League

1898-99	St. Mirren	1904-05	Clyde	1918-19	Dumbarton Harp
1899-00	Morton / Kilmarnock	1905-06	Kilmarnock	1919-20	Stevenston United
1900-01	Morton	*1906-15*	*No Competition*	1920-21	Johnstone
1901-02	Port Glasgow Athletic	1915-16	Vale of Leven	1921-22	Arthurlie
1902-03	Motherwell	1916-17	Clydebank	1922-23	Arthurlie
1903-04	Clyde	1917-18	Albion Rovers		

West Fife Charity Cup

1913-14	Cowdenbeath	1916-17	Cowdenbeath	1921-22	Dunfermline Athletic
1914-15	Cowdenbeath	1917-18	Cowdenbeath	1922-23	Cowdenbeath
1915-16	Cowdenbeath	1919-20	Cowdenbeath		

Wigtownshire & District Cup

1890-91	Newton Stewart Athletic	1893-94	Newton Stewart Athletic	1896-97	Newton Stewart Athletic
1891-92	Garlieston	1894-95	Newton Stewart Athletic	1897-98	Newton Stewart Athletic
1892-93	Newton Stewart Athletic	1895-96	Newton Stewart Athletic	1898-99	Stranraer

99-00 Newton Stewart Athletic	1922-23 Whithorn	1947-48 St. Cuthbert Wanderers
00-01 Barholm Rovers	1923-24 Stranraer	1948-49 *No Competition*
01-02 Barholm Rovers	1924-25 Newton Stewart	1949-50 St. Cuthbert Wanderers
02-03 Maxwelltown Volunteers	1925-26 Newton Stewart	1950-56 *No Competition*
03-04 Douglas Wanderers	1926-27 St. Cuthbert Wanderers	1956-57 Stranraer 'A'
04-05 Stranraer	1927-28 Stranraer	1957-58 *No Competition*
05-06 Newton Stewart	1928-29 St. Cuthbert Wanderers	1958-59 St. Cuthbert Wanderers
06-07 Creetown Volunteers	1929-30 Newton Stewart	1959-60 Tarff Rovers
07-08 *No Competition*	1930-32 *No Competition*	1960-61 *No Competition*
08-09 Whithorn	1932-33 Stranraer	1961-62 Newton Stewart
09-10 Stranraer	1933-34 Wigtown & Bladnoch	1962-63 *No Competition*
10-11 Stranraer	1934-35 St. Cuthbert Wanderers	1963-64 Tarff Rovers
11-12 St. Cuthbert Wanderers	1935-36 Creetown	1964-67 *No Competition*
12-13 Stranraer	1936-37 *No Competition*	1967-68 Stranraer 'A'
13-14 Stranraer	1937-38 St. Cuthbert Wanderers	1968-69 *No Competition*
14-19 *No Competition*	1938-39 Stranraer	1969-70 St. Cuthbert Wanderers
19-20 Newton Stewart	1939-45 *No Competition*	1970-72 *No Competition*
20-21 Stranraer	1945-46 Tarff Rovers	1972-73 Stranraer 'A'
21-22 Stranraer	1946-47 R.A.F. Wig Bay	

Summary: 12 - Stranraer; 9 - St. Cuthbert Wanderers; 8 - Newton Stewart Athletic; 6 - Newton Stewart; 3 - Stranraer 'A', Tarff Rovers; 2 - Barholm Rovers, Whithorn; 1 - Creetown, Creetown Volunteers, Douglas Wanderers, Garlieston, Maxwelltown Volunteers, R.A.F. Wig Bay, Wigtown & Bladnoch.

Wigtownshire & Kirkcudbrightshire Cup
(Also known as the Cafolla Cup)

20-21 Whithorn	1933-34 Creetown	1950-51 Newton Stewart
21-22 Stranraer	1934-35 Creetown	1951-53 *No Competition*
22-23 Whithorn	1935-36 Wigtown & Bladnoch	1953-54 St. Cuthbert Wanderers
23-24 *No Competition*	1936-37 *No Competition*	1954-56 *No Competition*
24-25 Wigtown & Bladnoch	1937-38 Creetown	1956-57 Tarff Rovers
25-26 St. Cuthbert Wanderers	1938-39 St. Cuthbert Wanderers	1957-58 *No Competition*
26-27 St. Cuthbert Wanderers	1939-46 *No Competition*	1958-59 Wigtown & Bladnoch
27-28 Stranraer	1946-47 Stranraer	1959-60 *No Competition*
28-29 St. Cuthbert Wanderers	1947-48 *No Competition*	1960-61 Stranraer 'A'
29-32 *No Competition*	1948-49 Newton Stewart	1961-64 *No Competition*
32-33 Wigtown & Bladnoch	1949-50 *No Competition*	1964-65 Tarff Rovers

Summary: 5 - St. Cuthbert Wanderers; 4 - Wigtown & Bladnoch; 3 - Creetown, Stranraer; 2 - Newton Stewart, Tarff Rovers, Whithorn; 1 - Stranraer 'A'.

Wigtownshire Cup

89-90 Newton Stewart Athletic	1908-09 Newton Stewart	1931-32 *No Competition*
90-91 Tarff Rovers	1909-10 Stranraer	1932-33 Wigtown & Bladnoch
91-92 Newton Stewart Athletic	1910-11 Stranraer	1933-34 Wigtown & Bladnoch
92-93 Garlieston	1911-12 Newton Stewart	1934-35 Creetown
93-94 Garlieston	1912-13 Whithorn	1935-36 Creetown
94-95 Garlieston	1913-14 Newton Stewart	1936-37 St. Cuthbert Wanderers
95-96 Newton Stewart Athletic	1914-19 *No Competition*	1937-38 R.A.F. West Freugh
96-97 Newton Stewart Athletic	1919-20 Stranraer	1938-39 R.A.F. West Freugh
97-98 Newton Stewart Athletic	1920-21 Stranraer	1939-45 *No Competition*
98-99 Stranraer	1921-22 Newton Stewart	1945-46 St. Cuthbert Wanderers
99-00 Newton Stewart Athletic	1922-23 Tarff Rovers	1946-47 *No Competition*
00-01 Stranraer	1923-24 Stranraer	1947-48 Stranraer
01-02 Tarff Rovers	1924-25 Wigtown & Bladnoch	1948-49 Wigtown & Bladnoch
02-03 Newton Stewart	1925-26 Newton Stewart	1949-50 *No Competition*
03-04 Newton Stewart	1926-27 Stranraer	1950-51 Newton Stewart
04-05 Stranraer	1927-28 Stranraer	1951-52 *Not Completed*
05-06 Stranraer	1928-29 *No Competition*	1952-54 *No Competition*
06-07 Whithorn	1929-30 Garlieston	1954-55 Whithorn
07-08 Whithorn	1930-31 Wigtown & Bladnoch	1955-59 *No Competition*

CONTINUED OVERLEAF

1959-60	Threave Rovers	1962-63	Threave Rovers	1967-68	Newton Stewart
1960-61	Stranraer 'A'	*1963-64*	*No Competition*		
1961-62	*No Competition*	1964-65	Threave Rovers		

Summary: *12 - Stranraer; 9 - Newton Stewart; 6 - Newton Stewart Athletic; 5 - Wigtown & Bladnoch 4 - Garlieston, Tariff Rovers, Whithorn; 2 - Creetown, R.A.F. West Freugh, St. Cuthbert Wanderers, Threave Rovers; 1 - Stranraer 'A'*

Wilson Cup

(Competed for between Hearts and Hibernian, originally on New Year's Day. Cup presented in 1905 by Mr. Robert Wilson, then a director of Hearts)

1905-06	Hibernian	1919-20	Hearts	1933-34	Hearts
1906-07	Hearts	1920-21	Hibernian	1934-35	Hearts
1907-08	Hibernian	1921-22	Hibernian	1935-36	Hearts
1908-09	Hibernian	1922-23	Hearts	1936-37	Hearts
1909-10	Hearts	1923-24	Hearts	1937-38	Hearts
1910-11	Hibernian	1924-25	Hibernian	1938-39	Hearts
1911-12	Hearts	1925-26	Hearts	1939-40	Hearts
1912-13	Hibernian	1926-27	Hibernian	1940-41	Hearts
1913-14	Hearts	1927-28	Hibernian	1941-42	Hearts
1914-15	Hearts	1928-29	Hearts	*1942-43*	*No Competition*
1915-16	Hibernian	1929-30	Hibernian	1943-44	Hearts
1916-17	Hibernian	1930-31	Hibernian	1944-45	Hibernian
1917-18	Hibernian	1931-32	Hearts	1945-46	Hearts
1918-19	Hearts	1932-33	Hibernian		

Summary: *24 - Hearts; 16 - Hibernian.*

Special 'One-Off' Competitions

Coronation Cup	1952-53	Celtic	
Exhibition Cup	1937-38	Celtic	
St. Mungo Cup	1951-52	Celtic	'A' Division Clubs
St. Mungo Quaich	1951-52	Dumbarton	'B' Division Clubs
Victory Cup	1918-19	St. Mirren	
Victory Cup	1945-46	Rangers	

Aberdeen & District Junior League

1902-03	Abergeldie	1926-27	East End	1947-48	Banks o' Dee
1903-04	Abergeldie	1927-28	Mugiemoss	1948-49	St. Clement's
1904-05	Abergeldie	1928-29	Inverurie Loco Works	1949-50	Banks o' Dee
1905-06	Mugiemoss	1929-30	Inverurie Loco Works	1950-51	Parkvale
1906-07	Mugiemoss	1930-31	Inverurie Loco Works	1951-52	Sunnybank
1907-08	Mugiemoss	1931-32	Inverurie Loco Works	1952-53	Banks o' Dee
1908-09	Parkvale	1932-33	Inverurie Loco Works	1953-54	Sunnybank
1909-10	Mugiemoss	1933-34	East End	1954-55	Inverurie Loco Works
1910-11	Mugiemoss	1934-35	Inverurie Loco Works	1955-56	Sunnybank
1911-12	Mugiemoss	1935-36	Inverurie Loco Works	1956-57	Banks o' Dee
1912-13	Mugiemoss	1936-37	Inverurie Loco Works	1957-58	Banks o' Dee
1913-14	Richmond	1937-38	Hall Russell's	1958-59	Lads' Club
1914-18	*No Competition*	1938-39	Hall Russell's	1959-60	Inverurie Loco Works
1918-19	Hall Russell's	1939-40	Hall Russell's	1960-61	Inverurie Loco Works
1919-20	Richmond	1940-41	Hall Russell's	1961-62	Inverurie Loco Works
1920-21	Banks o' Dee	1941-42	A. Hall & Co.	1962-63	Rosemount
1921-22	Mugiemoss	1942-43	Inverurie Loco Works	1963-64	Lewis United
1922-23	Mugiemoss	1943-44	K.O.S.B. 'B'	1964-65	Rosemount
1923-24	Argyle	1944-45	Mugiemoss	1965-66	Sunnybank
1924-25	Inverurie Loco Works	1945-46	Inverurie Loco Works	1966-67	Sunnybank
1925-26	Inverurie Loco Works	1946-47	A. Hall & Co.	1967-68	Banks o' Dee

Summary of Wins: 16 - Inverurie Loco Works; 11 - Mugiemoss; 7 - Banks o' Dee; 5 - Hall Russell's, Sunnybank; 3 - Abergeldie; 2 - A. Hall & Co., East End, Parkvale, Richmond, Rosemount; 1 - Argyle, K.O.S.B. 'B', Lads' Club, Lewis United, St. Clement's.

Aberdeen & District Junior League Cup

1923-24	Banks o' Dee	1938-39	Mugiemoss	1953-54	Sunnybank
1924-25	Banks o' Dee	1939-40	Hall Russell's	1954-55	Sunnybank
1925-26	East End	1940-41	Hall Russell's	1955-56	Banks o' Dee
1926-27	Hawthorn	1941-42	A. Hall & Co.	1956-57	Banks o' Dee
1927-28	Inverurie Loco Works	1942-43	I.T.C.	1957-58	Lads' Club
1928-29	Inverurie Loco Works	1943-44	Mugiemoss	1958-59	Lads' Club
1929-30	Inverurie Loco Works	1944-45	A. Hall & Co.	1959-60	Banks o' Dee
1930-31	Woodside	1945-46	Inverurie Loco Works	1960-61	Banks o' Dee
1931-32	Inverurie Loco Works	1946-47	Mugiemoss	1961-62	Sunnybank
1932-33	Banks o' Dee	1947-48	St. Clement's	1962-63	Stonehaven
1933-34	Parkvale	1948-49	Sunnybank	1963-64	Stonehaven
1934-35	Hall Russell's	1949-50	Sunnybank	1964-65	Banks o' Dee
1935-36	Hall Russell's	1950-51	Woodside	1965-66	Sunnybank
1936-37	Banks o' Dee	1951-52	Lewis United	1966-67	Sunnybank
1937-38	Hall Russell's	1952-53	Banks o' Dee	1967-68	Banks o' Dee

Summary: 11 - Banks o' Dee; 7 - Sunnybank; 5 - Hall Russell's, Inverurie Loco Works; 3 - Mugiemoss; 2 - A. Hall & Co., Lads' Club, Stonehaven, Woodside; 1 - East End, Hawthorn, I.T.C., Lewis United, Parkvale, St. Clement's.

Aberdeen Cable TV Cup

1987-88	Bon Accord	1992-93	Sunnybank	1997-98	FC Stoneywood
1988-89	Turriff United	1993-94	FC Stoneywood	1998-99	Formartine United
1989-90	Culter	1994-95	Longside	*1999-00*	*No Competition*
1990-91	FC Stoneywood	1995-96	FC Stoneywood		
1991-92	Sunnybank	1996-97	Bon Accord		

Aberdeen County Trophy
(Also known as the Lovie Shield)

1904-05	East End	1928-29	Inverurie Rovers	1949-50	Banks o' Dee
1905-06	Abergeldie	1929-30	Hall Russell's	1950-51	Mugiemoss
1906-07	East End	1930-31	Hawthorn	1951-52	Lewis United
1907-08		1931-32	Richmond	1952-53	Sunnybank
1908-09	Morison Thistle	1932-33	Banks o' Dee	1953-54	Sunnybank
1909-10	Mugiemoss	1933-34	Banks o' Dee	1954-55	Inverurie Loco Works
1910-11	Parkvale	1934-35	Inverurie Loco Works	1955-56	Banks o' Dee
1911-12	Parkvale	1935-36	Inverurie Loco Works	1956-57	Banks o' Dee
1912-13	Inverurie Loco Works	1936-37	Banks o' Dee	1957-58	Mugiemoss
1913-14	Inverurie Loco Works	1937-38	Hall Russell's	1958-59	Sunnybank
1914-15	Banks o' Dee	1938-39	South United	1959-60	Woodside
1915-19	*No Competition*	1939-40	Inverurie Loco Works	1960-61	Inverurie Loco Works
1919-20	Richmond	1940-41	Incognitos	1961-62	Inverurie Loco Works
1920-21	Banks o' Dee	1941-42	I.T.C.	1962-63	East End
1921-22	Mugiemoss	1942-43	Inverurie Loco Works	1963-64	Rosemount
1922-23	Argyle	1943-44	K.O.S.B. 'B'	1964-65	Rosemount
1923-24	Argyle	1944-45	Inverurie Loco Works	1965-66	Banks o' Dee
1924-25	Hall Russell's	1945-46	Hall Russell's	1966-67	Banks o' Dee
1925-26	East End	1946-47	Hall Russell's	1967-68	Banks o' Dee
1926-27	Richmond	1947-48	Sunnybank		
1927-28	Banks o' Dee	1948-49	St. Clement's		

Summary: *12 - Banks o' Dee; 10 - Inverurie Loco Works; 5 - Hall Russell's; 4 - East End, Mugiemoss, Sunnybank; 3 - Richmond; 2 - Argyle, Parkvale, Rosemount; 1 - Abergeldie, Hawthorn, Incognitos, Inverurie Rovers, I.T.C., K.O.S.B. 'B', Lewis United, Morison Thistle, St. Clement's, South United, Woodside.*

Acorn Heating Cup
(See under DUTHIE CUP)

Angus Junior League
(Formerly the Forfar & District League)

1901-02	Forfar Hearts	1925-26	Brechin Victoria	1951-52	Alyth United
1902-03	Forfar West End	1926-27	Brechin Victoria	1952-53	Montrose Roselea
1903-04		1927-28	Brechin Victoria	1953-54	Arbroath Victoria
1904-05	Forfar Celtic	1928-29	Arbroath Victoria	1954-55	Arbroath Victoria
1905-06	Forfar Celtic	1929-30	Brechin Victoria	1955-56	Coupar Angus
1906-07	Forfar Celtic	1930-31	Forfar East End	1956-57	Arbroath Victoria
1907-08	Forfar West End	1931-32	Forfar East End	1957-58	Alyth United
1908-09	Forfar West End	1932-33	Forfar West End	1958-59	Alyth United
1909-10	Arbroath Ardenlea	1933-34	Arbroath Ardenlea	1959-60	Coupar Angus
1910-11		1934-35	Brechin Victoria	1960-61	Kirriemuir Thistle
1911-12	Forfar Celtic	1935-36	Alyth United	1961-62	Brechin Matrix
1912-13	Forfar East End	1936-37	Arbroath Victoria	1962-63	Brechin Matrix
1913-14	Arbroath Ardenlea	1937-38	Forfar East End	1963-64	Brechin Matrix
1914-19	*No Competition*	1938-39	Coupar Angus	1964-65	Alyth United
1919-20	Forfar North End	1938-39	Forfar East End	1965-66	Alyth United
1920-21	Forfar East End	*1939-47*	*No Competition*	1966-67	Alyth United
1921-22	Forfar East End	1947-48	Montrose Roselea	1967-68	Forfar East End
1922-23	Forfar East End	1948-49	Forfar Celtic	1968-69	Forfar East End
1923-24	Kirriemuir Celtic	1949-50	Montrose Roselea		
1924-25	Brechin Victoria	1950-51	Brechin Victoria		

Summary: *10 - Forfar East End; 7 - Alyth United, Brechin Victoria; 5 - Arbroath Victoria, Forfar Celtic; 4 - Forfar West End; 3 - Arbroath Ardenlea, Brechin Matrix, Coupar Angus, Montrose Roselea; 1 - Forfar Hearts, Forfar North End, Kirriemuir Celtic, Kirriemuir Thistle.*

Arbroath & District Cup
(For member clubs of the Angus Junior F.A.)

Year	Winner	Year	Winner	Year	Winner
1891-92	Forfar East End	1916-19	*No Competition*	1950-51	Kirriemuir Thistle
1892-93		1919-20	Forfar East End	1951-52	Alyth United
1893-94		1920-21	Arbroath Ardenlea	1952-53	Forfar West End
1894-95		1921-22	Arbroath Ardenlea	1953-54	Arbroath Victoria
1895-96		1922-23	Forfar Celtic	1954-55	Alyth United
1896-97		1923-24	Arbroath Victoria	1955-56	Forfar Celtic
1897-98		1924-25	Arbroath Ardenlea	1956-57	Kirriemuir Thistle
1898-99		1925-26	Forfar North End	1957-58	Kirriemuir Thistle
1899-00	Arbroath Rovers	1926-27	Arbroath Ardenlea	1958-59	Kirriemuir Thistle
1900-01	Arbroath Rovers	1927-28	Arbroath Victoria	1959-60	Kirriemuir Thistle
1901-02	Brechin Hearts	1928-29	Arbroath Victoria	1960-61	Coupar Angus
1902-03	Arbroath Ardenlea	1929-30	Arbroath Victoria	1961-62	Brechin Victoria
1903-04	Brechin Rovers	1930-31	Arbroath Victoria	1962-63	Montrose Roselea
1904-05	Brechin Hearts	1931-32	Forfar East End	1963-64	Alyth United
1905-06	Brechin Hearts	1932-33	Arbroath Ardenlea	1964-65	Alyth United
1906-07	Brechin Hearts	1933-34	Arbroath Ardenlea	1965-66	Forfar Celtic
1907-08	Forthill Athletic	1934-35	Kirriemuir Thistle	1966-67	Brechin Matrix
1908-09	St. Thomas	1935-36	Kirriemuir Thistle	1967-68	Arbroath Victoria
1909-10	Brechin Rovers	1936-37	Carnoustie Panmure	1968-69	Alyth United
1910-11	Arbroath Ardenlea	1937-38	Forfar West End	1969-70	
1911-12	Arbroath Fairfield	1938-39	Kirriemuir Thistle	1970-71	Arbroath Victoria
1912-13	Arbroath Ardenlea	1939-47	*No Competition*	1971-72	Kirriemuir Thistle
1913-14	Brechin Hearts	1947-48	Arbroath Victoria	1972-73	Kirriemuir Thistle
1914-15	Brechin Hearts	1948-49	Arbroath Westburn		
1915-16	Forfar East End	1949-50	Brechin Renton		

Summary: 10 - Kirriemuir Thistle; 9 - Arbroath Ardenlea, Arbroath Victoria; 6 - Brechin Hearts; - Alyth United; 4 - Forfar East End; 3 - Forfar Celtic; 2 - Arbroath Rovers, Brechin Rovers, Forfar West End; 1 - Arbroath Fairfield, Arbroath Westburn, Brechin Matrix, Brechin Renton, Brechin Victoria, Carnoustie Panmure, Coupar Angus, Forfar North End, Forthill, Montrose Roselea, St. Thomas.

Archibald Cup
(For Aberdeen & District clubs. Currently the Rollstud Archibald Cup)

Year	Winner	Year	Winner	Year	Winner
1921-22	Argyle	1953-54	Sunnybank	1977-78	East End
1922-23	Banks o' Dee	1954-55	Inverurie Loco Works	1978-79	East End
1923-26	*No Competition*	1955-56	Banks o' Dee	1979-80	Sunnybank
1926-27	Parkvale	1956-57	Banks o' Dee	1980-81	Inverurie Loco Works
1927-28	East End	1957-58	Lads' Club	1981-82	Banks o' Dee
1928-29	Inverurie Loco Works	1958-59	Banks o' Dee	1982-83	Mugiemoss
1929-30	East End	1959-60	Rosemount	1983-84	Sunnybank
1930-31	Mugiemoss	1960-61	Inverurie Loco Works	1984-85	Banks o' Dee
1931-32	Banks o' Dee	1961-62	Inverurie Loco Works	1985-86	Rosslyn Sports
1932-33	Inverurie Loco Works	1962-63	*No Competition*	1986-87	Banks o' Dee
1933-34	East End	1963-64	Sunnybank	1987-88	Culter
1934-35	Banks o' Dee	1964-65	Banks o' Dee	1988-89	Bon Accord
1935-36	Parkvale	1965-66	Banks o' Dee	1989-90	Culter
1936-37	Hall Russell's	1966-67	Lewis United	1990-91	FC Stoneywood
1937-38	Inverurie Loco Works	1967-68	Mugiemoss	1991-92	Buchanhaven Hearts
1938-39	Inverurie Loco Works	1968-69	Inverurie Loco Works	1992-93	FC Stoneywood
1939-40	Inverurie Loco Works	1969-70	Sunnybank	1993-94	East End
1940-47	*No Competition*	1970-71	Banks o' Dee	1994-95	Sunnybank
1947-48	Sunnybank	1971-72	Lewis United	1995-96	Sunnybank
1948-49	St. Clement's	1972-73	Mugiemoss	1996-97	FC Stoneywood
1949-50	Banks o' Dee	1973-74	Lewis United	1997-98	Sunnybank
1950-51	Woodside	1974-75	Sunnybank	1998-99	Formartine United
1951-52	Banks o' Dee	1975-76	Sunnybank	1999-00	Inverurie Loco Works
1952-53	Sunnybank	1976-77	East End		

Summary: *14 - Banks o' Dee; 12 - Sunnybank; 11 - Inverurie Loco Works; 7 - East End; 4 - Mugiemoss; 3 - FC Stoneywood, Lewis United; 2 - Culter, Parkvale, Rosemount/Rosslyn Sports; 1 - Argyle, Bon Accord, Buchanhaven Hearts, Formartine United, Hall Russell's, Lads' Club, St Clement's, Woodside*

Ayrshire League

1891-92	Annbank	1893-94	Saltcoats Victoria
1892-93	Annbank	1894-95	Dalry

Ayrshire Charity Cup

1901-02	Rugby XI	1906-07	Kilwinning Rangers	*1911-34*	*No competition*
1902-03	Ardeer Thistle	1907-08	Newmilns	1934-35	Irvine Meadow
1903-04	Vale of Garnock Strollers	1908-09	Newmilns	*1935-37*	*No competition*
1904-05	Vale of Garnock Strollers	1909-10	Glenbuck Cherrypickers	1937-38	Cumnock Juniors
1905-06	Glenbuck Cherrypickers	1910-11	Kilwinning Rangers	1938-39	Glengarnock Vale

Summary: *2 - Glenbuck Cherrypickers, Kilwinning Rangers, Newmilns, Vale of Garnock Strollers; 1 - Ardeer Thistle, Cumnock Juniors, Glengarnock Vale, Irvine Meadow, Rugby XI.*

Ayrshire Consolation Cup

1901-02	Cumnock Craigbank	1916-17	Hurlford Thistle	1931-32	Kilbirnie Ladeside
1902-03	Kilwinning Rangers	1917-18	Drongan	1932-33	Irvine Meadow
1903-04	Kilwinning Rangers	1918-19	Burnfoothill Primrose	1933-34	Kilwinning Rangers
1904-05	Troon Rangers	1919-20	Ardrossan Winton Rovers	1934-35	Glenafton Athletic
1905-06	Common Thistle	1920-21	Kilbirnie Ladeside	1935-36	Troon Athletic
1906-07	Irvine Victoria	1921-22	New Cumnock United	1936-37	Cumnock Juniors
1907-08	Kilbirnie Ladeside	1922-23	Ardrossan Winton Rovers	*1937-48*	*No competition*
1908-09	Newmilns	1923-24	Troon Athletic	1948-49	Ardrossan Winton Rovers
1909-10	Cronberry Eglinton	1924-25	Dalry Thistle	1949-50	Lugar Boswell Thistle
1910-11	Kilbirnie Ladeside	1925-26	Kilwinning Eglinton	1950-51	Craigmark Burntonians
1911-12	Kilwinning Eglinton	1926-27	Newmilns	1951-52	Annbank United
1912-13	Ardrossan Winton Rovers	1927-28	Saltcoats Victoria	1952-53	Glenafton Athletic
1913-14	Dreghorn Juniors	1928-29	Saltcoats Victoria	1953-54	Lugar Boswell Thistle
1914-15	Irvine Meadow	1929-30	Kello Rovers	1954-55	Glenafton Athletic
1915-16	Irvine Meadow	1930-31	Auchinleck Talbot	1955-56	Annbank United

Summary: *4 - Ardrossan Winton Rovers, Kilbirnie Ladeside; 3 - Glenafton Athletic, Irvine Meadow, Kilwinning Rangers; 2 - Annbank United, Kilwinning Eglinton, Lugar Boswell Thistle, Newmilns, Saltcoats Victoria, Troon Athletic; 1 - Auchinleck Talbot, Burnfoothill Primrose, Common Thistle, Craigmark Burntonians, Cronberry Eglinton, Cumnock Craigbank, Cumnock Juniors, Dalry Thistle, Dreghorn Juniors, Drongan, Hurlford Thistle, Irvine Victoria, Kello Rovers, New Cumnock United, Troon Rangers.*

Ayrshire Cup

1889-90	Glenbuck Cherrypickers	1905-06	Vale of Garnock Strollers	1921-22	Troon Athletic
1890-91	Glenbuck Cherrypickers	1906-07	Newmilns	1922-23	Largs Thistle
1891-92	Glenbuck Cherrypickers	1907-08	Vale of Garnock Strollers	1923-24	Kilbirnie Ladeside
1892-93	Irvine Rangers	1908-09	Kilwinning	1924-25	Stevenston Ardeer Ath.
1893-94	Darvel	1909-10	Newmilns	1925-26	Stevenston Ardeer Ath.
1894-95	Darvel	1910-11	Newmilns	1926-27	Ardrossan Winton Rovers
1895-96	Hurlford Thistle	1911-12	Saltcoats Victoria	1927-28	Lugar Boswell Thistle
1896-97	Shawbank	1912-13	Kilbirnie Ladeside	1928-29	Lugar Boswell Thistle
1897-98	Winton	1913-14	Irvine Meadow	1929-30	Cronberry Eglinton
1898-99	Irvine Meadow	1914-15	Muirkirk Athletic	1930-31	Glenbuck Cherrypickers
1899-00	Benquhat Heatherbell	1915-16	Cumnock Juniors	1931-32	Irvine Meadow
1900-01	Irvine Meadow	1916-17	Stevenston Thistle	1932-33	Ardeer Recreation
1901-02	Newmilns	1917-18	Cumnock Juniors	1933-34	Ardrossan Winton Rovers
1902-03	Stewarton	1918-19	Glenburn Rangers	1934-35	Kilwinning Rangers
1903-04	Irvine Meadow	1919-20	Auchinleck Talbot	1935-36	Glenafton Athletic
1904-05	Kilwinning	1920-21	Dreghorn Juniors	1936-37	Kello Rovers

the winners

937-38 Saltcoats Victoria	1958-59 Largs Thistle	1979-80 Auchinleck Talbot
938-39 Auchinleck Talbot	1959-60 Ardeer Thistle	1980-81 Cumnock Juniors
939-40 Saltcoats Victoria	1960-61 Dalry Thistle	1981-82 Auchinleck Talbot
940-41 Annbank United	1961-62 Glenafton Athletic	1982-83 Auchinleck Talbot
941-42 Ardeer Recreation	1962-63 Beith Juniors	1983-84 Irvine Meadow
942-43 Ardeer Recreation	1963-64 Beith Juniors	1984-85 Irvine Meadow
943-44 Annbank United	1964-65 Beith Juniors	1985-86 Kilwinning Rangers
944-45 Ardeer Recreation	1965-66 Ardeer Thistle	1986-87 Kilbirnie Ladeside
945-46 Annbank United	*1966-67 No competition*	1987-88 Auchinleck Talbot
946-47 Saltcoats Victoria	1967-68 Kello Rovers	1988-89 Glenafton Athletic
947-48 Kilbirnie Ladeside	1968-69 Hurlford United	1989-90 Cumnock Juniors
948-49 Cumnock Juniors	1969-70 Irvine Meadow	1990-91 Beith Juniors
949-50 Kilbirnie Ladeside	1970-71 Irvine Meadow	1991-92 Beith Juniors
950-51 Lugar Boswell Thistle	1971-72 Kilbirnie Ladeside	1992-93 Glenafton Athletic
951-52 Ardrossan Winton Rovers	1972-73 Hurlford United	1993-94 Auchinleck Talbot
952-53 Irvine Victoria	1973-74 Hurlford United	1994-95 Kilwinning Rangers
953-54 Irvine Meadow	1974-75 Kilbirnie Ladeside	1995-96 Auchinleck Talbot
954-55 Beith Juniors	1975-76 Kilbirnie Ladeside	1996-97 Auchinleck Talbot
955-56 Auchinleck Talbot	1976-77 Kilwinning Rangers	1997-98 Kilwinning Rangers
956-57 Largs Thistle	1977-78 Beith Juniors	1998-99 Kilwinning Rangers
957-58 Irvine Meadow	1978-79 Auchinleck Talbot	1999-00 Kilwinning Rangers

ummary: 11 - Auchinleck Talbot, Irvine Meadow; 8 - Kilbirnie Ladeside; 7 - Beith Juniors, ilwinning Rangers; 5 - Cumnock Juniors, Glenafton Athletic; 4 - Ardeer Recreation, Glenbuck herrypickers, Newmilns, Saltcoats Victoria; 3 - Annbank United, Ardrossan Winton Rovers, Hurlford Jnited, Largs Thistle, Lugar Boswell Thistle; 2 - Ardeer Thistle, Darvel, Kello Rovers, Kilwinning, tevenston Ardeer Athletic, Vale of Garnock Strollers; 1 - Benquhat Heatherbell, Cronberry Eglinton, Jalry Thistle, Dreghorn Juniors, Glenburn Rangers, Hurlford Thistle, Irvine Rangers, Irvine Victoria, Muirkirk Athletic, Shawbank, Stevenston Thistle, Stewarton, Troon Athletic, Winton.

Ayrshire District Cup
(Formerly the Irvine & District Cup)

891-92 Troon Athletic	1922-23 Darvel Juniors	1953-54 Gourock Juniors
892-93 Irvine Rangers	1923-24 Saltcoats Victoria	1954-55 Irvine Meadow
893-94 Dreghorn Juniors	1924-25 Saltcoats Victoria	1955-56 Irvine Meadow
894-95 Troon Athletic	1925-26 Ardeer Thistle	1956-57 Largs Thistle
895-96 Largs Thistle	1926-27 Ardrossan Winton Rovers	1957-58 Irvine Meadow
896-97 Troon	*1927-29 Competition in Dispute*	1958-59 Kilwinning Rangers
897-98 Dreghorn Juniors	1929-30 Lugar Boswell Thistle	1959-60 Glenafton Athletic
898-99 Newmilns	1930-31 Glenafton Athletic	1960-61 Beith Juniors
899-00 Irvine Meadow	1931-32 Kilwinning Rangers	1961-62 Ardeer Thistle
900-01 Stewarton Juniors	1932-33 Irvine Meadow	1962-63 Ardeer Thistle
901-02 Rugby XI	1933-34 Kilbirnie Ladeside	1963-64 Craigmark Burntonians
902-03 Springside	1934-35 Irvine Victoria	*1964-65 No Competition*
903-04 Irvine Meadow	1935-36 Ardrossan Winton Rovers	1965-66 Hurlford United
904-05 Kilbirnie Ladeside	1936-37 Kilbirnie Ladeside	1966-67 Kilbirnie Ladeside
905-06 Kilwinning Rangers	1937-38 Saltcoats Victoria	1967-68 Beith Juniors
906-07 Ardeer Thistle	1938-39 Irvine Meadow	1968-69 Hurlford United
907-08 Ardeer Thistle	1939-40 Dalry Thistle	1969-70 Kilbirnie Ladeside
908-09 Ardeer Thistle	1940-41 Ardeer Recreation	1970-71 Irvine Meadow
909-10 Irvine Meadow	1941-42 Ardeer Recreation	1971-72 Cumnock Juniors
910-11 Kilbirnie Ladeside	1942-43 Kello Rovers	1972-73 Kilbirnie Ladeside
911-12 Ardrossan Winton Rovers	1943-44 Annbank United	1973-74 Kilbirnie Ladeside
912-13 Kilbirnie Ladeside	1944-45 Hurlford United	1974-75 Kello Rovers
913-14 Irvine Meadow	1945-46 Ardeer Recreation	1975-76 Kello Rovers
914-15 Irvine Meadow	1946-47 Irvine Meadow	1976-77 Irvine Meadow
915-16 Ardeer Thistle	1947-48 Auchinleck Talbot	1977-78 Irvine Meadow
916-17 Stevenston Thistle	1948-49 Lugar Boswell Thistle	1978-79 Ardrossan Winton Rovers
917-19 No Competition	1949-50 Kilbirnie Ladeside	1979-80 Glenafton Athletic
919-20 Ardrossan Winton Rovers	1950-51 Irvine Meadow	1980-81 Auchinleck Talbot
920-21 Kilwinning Rangers	1951-52 Irvine Meadow	1981-82 Irvine Meadow
921-22 Darvel Juniors	1952-53 Saltcoats Victoria	1982-83 Auchinleck Talbot

CONTINUED OVERLEAF

1983-84	Cumnock Juniors	1989-90	Cumnock Juniors	1995-96	Kilwinning Rangers
1984-85	Auchinleck Talbot	1990-91	Beith Juniors	1996-97	Auchinleck Talbot
1985-86	Glenafton Athletic	1991-92	Auchinleck Talbot	1997-98	Glenafton Athletic
1986-87	Cumnock Juniors	1992-93	Kilbirnie Ladeside	1998-99	Kilwinning Rangers
1987-88	Irvine Meadow	1993-94	Glenafton Athletic	1999-00	Kilbirnie Ladeside
1988-89	Auchinleck Talbot	1994-95	Beith Juniors		

Summary: *18 - Irvine Meadow; 12 - Kilbirnie Ladeside; 7 - Ardeer Thistle, Auchinleck Talbot, Kilwinning Rangers; 6 - Glenafton Athletic; 5 - Ardrossan Winton Rovers; 4 - Beith Juniors, Cumnock Juniors, Saltcoats Victoria; 3 - Ardeer Recreation, Hurlford United, Kello Rovers; 2 - Darvel Juniors, Dreghorn Juniors, Largs Thistle, Lugar Boswell Thistle, Troon Athletic; 1 - Annbank United, Craigmark Burntonians, Dalry Thistle, Gourock Juniors, Irvine Rangers, Irvine Victoria, Newmilns, Rugby XI, Springside, Stevenston Thistle, Stewarton Juniors, Troon.*

Ayrshire Junior League

1928-29	Kello Rovers	1929-30	Cumnock Juniors	1930-31	Glenafton Athletic

Ayrshire League Cup

1968-69	Kello Rovers	1979-80	Glenafton Athletic	1990-91	Auchinleck Talbot
1969-70	Kello Rovers	1980-81	Craigmark Burntonians	1991-92	Beith Juniors
1970-71	Cumnock Juniors	1981-82	Beith Juniors	1992-93	Auchinleck Talbot
1971-72	Hurlford United	1982-83	Irvine Meadow	1993-94	Beith Juniors
1972-73	Kello Rovers	1983-84	Cumnock Juniors	1994-95	Kilbirnie Ladeside
1973-74	Irvine Victoria	1984-85	Cumnock Juniors	1995-96	Cumnock Juniors
1974-75	Kello Rovers	1985-86	Cumnock Juniors	1996-97	Cumnock Juniors
1975-76	Hurlford United	1986-87	Cumnock Juniors	1997-98	Auchinleck Talbot
1976-77	Cumnock Juniors	1987-88	Annbank United	1998-99	Kilwinning Rangers
1977-78	Auchinleck Talbot	1988-89	Kilbirnie Ladeside	1999-00	Glenafton Athletic
1978-79	Cumnock Juniors	1989-90	Auchinleck Talbot		

Summary: *9 - Cumnock Juniors; 5 - Auchinleck Talbot; 4 - Kello Rovers; 3 - Beith Juniors; 2 - Glenafton Athletic, Hurlford United, Kilbirnie Ladeside; 1 - Annbank United, Craigmark Burntonians, Irvine Meadow, Irvine Victoria, Kilwinning Rangers.*

Ayrshire Regional League
(Division 1 from 1977-78)

1968-69	Beith Juniors	1979-80	Auchinleck Talbot	1990-91	Auchinleck Talbot
1969-70	Irvine Meadow	1980-81	Cumnock Juniors	1991-92	Auchinleck Talbot
1970-71	Irvine Meadow	1981-82	Cumnock Juniors	1992-93	Glenafton Athletic
1971-72	Cumnock Juniors	1982-83	Glenafton Athletic	1993-94	Irvine Meadow
1972-73	Hurlford United	1983-84	Cumnock Juniors	1994-95	Auchinleck Talbot
1973-74	Cumnock Juniors	1984-85	Cumnock Juniors	1995-96	Cumnock Juniors
1974-75	Kello Rovers	1985-86	Auchinleck Talbot	1996-97	Auchinleck Talbot
1975-76	Kilbirnie Ladeside	1986-87	Auchinleck Talbot	1997-98	Cumnock Juniors
1976-77	Kilbirnie Ladeside	1987-88	Auchinleck Talbot	1998-99	Kilwinning Rangers
1977-78	Auchinleck Talbot	1988-89	Irvine Meadow	1999-00	Kilwinning Rangers
1978-79	Auchinleck Talbot	1989-90	Auchinleck Talbot		

Summary: *11 - Auchinleck Talbot; 8 - Cumnock Juniors; 4 - Irvine Meadow; 2 - Glenafton Athletic, Kilbirnie Ladeside, Kilwinning Rangers.; 1 - Beith Juniors, Hurlford United, Kello Rovers.*

Ayrshire Regional League - Division 2

1976-77	Kilwinning Rangers	1985-86	Whitletts Victoria	1994-95	Cumnock Juniors
1977-78	Kello Rovers	1986-87	Beith Juniors	1995-96	Lugar Boswell thistle
1978-79	Ardrossan Winton Rovers	1987-88	Ardrossan Winton Rovers	1996-97	Troon
1979-80	Whitletts Victoria	1988-89	Kilwinning Rangers	1997-98	Ardrossan Winton Rovers
1980-81	Kilwinning Rangers	1989-90	Annbank United	1998-99	Irvine Meadow
1981-82	Whitletts Victoria	1990-91	Kilwinning Rangers	1999-00	Lugar Boswell Thistle
1982-83	Craigmark Burntonians	1991-92	Ardeer Thistle		
1983-84	Largs Thistle	1992-93	Saltcoats Victoria		
1984-85	Muirkirk Juniors	1993-94	Largs Thistle		

Ayrshire Super Cup

986-87	Kilbirnie Ladeside	1991-92	Kello Rovers	1996-97	Cumnock Juniors
987-88	Annbank United	1992-93	Auchinleck Talbot	1997-98	Glenafton Athletic
988-89	Cumnock Juniors	1993-94	Auchinleck Talbot	1998-99	Auchinleck Talbot
989-90	Craigmark Burntonians	1994-95	Auchinleck Talbot	1999-00	Auchinleck Talbot
990-91	Ardrossan Winton Rovers	1995-96	Cumnock Juniors		

Bardon Aggregates Cup

(See under Cowdenbeath Cup)

Barrie Consolation Cup

(See under Forfarshire Junior Consolation Cup)

Brechin Rosebowl

(For member clubs of the Angus Junior F.A.)

928-29	Brechin Victoria	1947-48	Forfar East End	1959-60	Forfar West End
929-30	Brechin Victoria	1948-49	Arbroath Westburn	1960-61	Alyth United
930-31	Kirriemuir Thistle	1949-50	Brechin Renton	1961-62	Brechin Victoria
931-32	Forfar East End	1950-51	Brechin Victoria	1962-63	
932-33	Montrose Roselea	1951-52	Brechin Victoria	1963-64	Alyth United
933-34	Arbroath Ardenlea	1952-53	Coupar Angus	1964-65	Alyth United
934-35	Brechin Victoria	1953-54	Kirriemuir Thistle	1965-66	Brechin Victoria
935-36	Kirriemuir Thistle	1954-55	Arbroath Victoria	1966-67	Alyth United
936-37	Forfar East End	1955-56	Alyth United	1967-68	Arbroath Victoria
937-38	Montrose Roselea	1956-57	Kirriemuir Thistle	1968-69	Arbroath Victoria
938-39	Coupar Angus	1957-58	Forfar West End		
939-47	*No Competition*	1958-59	Forfar Celtic		

British Legion Cup

(For member clubs of the South of Scotland F.A.)

947-48	Annan Athletic	1949-50	Thornhill Juniors
948-49	Troqueer Juniors	1950-51	Troqueer Juniors

British Road Services Cup

(See under Scottish Road Services Cup)

Brown Cup

(Also Robertson Homes & National Steeplejacks Cups)

932-33	Tranent Juniors	*1940-41*	*No Competition*	1948-49	Arniston Rangers
933-34	Bonnyrigg Rose Athletic	1941-42	Bathgate Thistle	1949-50	Rosewell Rosedale
934-35	Kirkford Juniors	1942-43	Armadale Thistle	1950-51	Armadale Thistle
935-36	Bowhill Rovers	1943-44	Armadale Thistle	1951-52	Newtongrange Star
936-37	Lochgelly Albert	*1944-45*	*No Competition*	1952-53	Newtongrange Star
937-38	Arniston Rangers	1945-46	Fauldhouse United	1953-54	Armadale Thistle
938-39	Tranent Juniors	1946-47	Armadale Thistle	1954-55	Bo'ness United
939-40	Haddington Athletic	1947-48	Bo'ness United	1955-56	Dalkeith Thistle

CONTINUED OVERLEAF

the winners

1956-57	*No Competition*	1971-72	Whitburn	1986-87	Edinburgh United
1957-58	West Calder United	1972-73	Whitburn	1987-88	Bo'ness United
1958-59	*No Competition*	1973-74	Bonnyrigg Rose Athletic	1988-89	Edinburgh United
1959-60	Whitburn	1974-75	Linlithgow Rose	1989-90	Newtongrange Star
1960-61	Fauldhouse United	1975-76	Arniston Rangers	1990-91	Livingston United
1961-62	Newtongrange Star	1976-77	Camelon Juniors	1991-92	Newtongrange Star
1962-63	Dunbar United	1977-78	Bonnyrigg Rose Athletic	1992-93	Newtongrange Star
1963-64	Bonnyrigg Rose Athletic	1978-79	Haddington Athletic	1993-94	Newtongrange Star
1964-65	Linlithgow Rose	1979-80	Bo'ness United	1994-95	Linlithgow Roes
1965-66	New Blackburn Athletic	1980-81	Newtongrange Star	1995-96	Linlithgow Rose
1966-67	Linlithgow Rose	1981-82	Preston Athletic	1996-97	Bo'ness United
1967-68	Whitburn	1982-83	Bo'ness United	1997-98	Bo'ness United
1968-69	Arniston Rangers	1983-84	Bo'ness United	1998-99	Bo'ness United
1969-70	Dalkeith Thistle	1984-85	Linlithgow Rose	1999-00	Dunbar United
1970-71	Broxburn Athletic	1985-86	Bonnyrigg Rose Athletic		

Summary: 9 - Bo'ness United; 8 - Newtongrange Star; 6 - Linlithgow Rose; 5 - Armadale Thistle, Bonnyrigg Rose Athletic; 4 - Arniston Rangers, Whitburn; 2 - Dalkeith Thistle, Dunbar United, Edinburgh United, Fauldhouse United, Haddington Athletic, Tranent Juniors; 1 - Bathgate Thistle, Bowhill Rovers, Broxburn Athletic, Camelon Juniors, Kirkford Juniors, Livingston United, Lochgelly Albert, New Blackburn Athletic, Preston Athletic, Rosewell Rosedale, West Calder United.

Calder Cup
(See under East of Scotland Junior Cup)

Central League Cup
(Glasgow League Cup 21-27; Intermediate League Cup 27-31)

1921-22	Strathclyde	1948-49	Pollok	1975-76	Lanark United
1922-23	Strathclyde	1949-50	Bellshill Athletic	1976-77	Blantyre Victoria
1923-24	Kirkintilloch Rob Roy	1950-51	Petershill	1977-78	Pollok
1924-25	St. Roch's	1951-52	Petershill	1978-79	Maryhill
1925-26	Shawfield	1952-53	Ashfield	1979-80	Pollok
1926-27	Ashfield	1953-54	Kilsyth Rangers	1980-81	Maryhill
1927-28	Kirkintilloch Rob Roy	1954-55	Shettleston	1981-82	Renfrew
1928-29	Ashfield	1955-56	Maryhill	1982-83	Larkhall Thistle
1929-30	Clydebank Juniors	1956-57	Duntocher Hibs	1983-84	Pollok
1930-31	Pollok	1957-58	Port Glasgow Juniors	1984-85	Forth Wanderers
1931-32	Kirkintilloch Rob Roy	1958-59	Johnstone Burgh	1985-86	Larkhall Thistle
1932-33	Clydebank Juniors	1959-60	St. Roch's	1986-87	Arthurlie
1933-34	Vale of Clyde	1960-61	Greenock Juniors	1987-88	Pollok
1934-35	Clydebank Juniors	1961-62	St. Roch's	1988-89	Pollok
1935-36	Benburb	1962-63	Ashfield	1989-90	Vale of Clyde
1936-37	St. Roch's	1963-64	Renfrew	1990-91	Arthurlie
1937-38	Morton Juniors	1964-65	Petershill	1991-92	Petershill
1938-39	Arthurlie	1965-66	Greenock Juniors	1992-93	Lesmahagow
1939-40	Rutherglen Glencairn	1966-67	Greenock Juniors	1993-94	Shotts Bon Accord
1940-41	Strathclyde	1967-68	Kilsyth Rangers	*1994-95*	*Competition abandoned*
1941-42	Pollok	1968-69	Cambuslang Rangers	1995-96	Maryhill
1942-43	Benburb	1969-70	Cambuslang Rangers	1996-97	Arthurlie
1943-44	St. Roch's	1970-71	Maryhill	1997-98	Arthurlie
1944-45	Maryhill	1971-72	Renfrew	1998-99	Rutherglen Glencairn
1945-46	Renfrew	1972-73	Shettleston	1999-00	Benburb
1946-47	Ashfield	1973-74	Petershill		
1947-48	Yoker Athletic	1974-75	Petershill		

Summary: 8 - Pollok; 6 - Maryhill, Petershill; 5 - Arthurlie, Ashfield, St. Roch's; 4 - Renfrew; 3 - Benburb, Clydebank Juniors, Greenock Juniors, Kirkintilloch Rob Roy, Strathclyde; 2 -Cambuslang Rangers, Kilsyth Rangers, Larkhall Thistle, Rutherglen Glencairn, Shettleston, Vale of Clyde; 1 - Bellshill Athletic, Blantyre Victoria, Duntocher Hibs, Forth Wanderers, Johnstone Burgh, Lanark United, Lesmahagow, Morton Juniors, Port Glasgow Juniors, Shawfield, Yoker Athletic.

Central Regional League - Premier Division

68-69	Petershill	1979-80	East Kilbride Thistle	1990-91	Pollok
69-70	Renfrew	1980-81	Pollok	1991-92	Lesmahagow
70-71	Cumbernauld United	1981-82	East Kilbride Thistle	1992-93	Petershill
71-72	Cambuslang Rangers	1982-83	Petershill	1993-94	Arthurlie
72-73	Cambuslang Rangers	1983-84	Petershill	1994-95	Pollok
73-74	Cambuslang Rangers	1984-85	Pollok	1995-96	Pollok
74-75	East Kilbride Thistle	1985-86	Pollok	1996-97	Maryhill
75-76	East Kilbride Thistle	1986-87	Pollok	1997-98	Maryhill
76-77	Shettleston	1987-88	Arthurlie	1998-99	Shotts Bon Accord
77-78	Lesmahagow	1988-89	Arthurlie	1999-00	Benburb
78-79	Port Glasgow Juniors	1989-90	Petershill		

summary: *7 - Pollok; 5 - Petershill; 4 - East Kilbride Thistle; 3 - Arthurlie, Cambuslang Rangers; - Lesmahagow, Maryhill; 1 - Benburb, Cumbernauld United, Port Glasgow Juniors, Renfrew, Shettleston, Shotts Bon Acord.*

Central Regional League - Division 1

68-69	Pollok	1979-80	Forth Wanderers	1990-91	Cambuslang Rangers
69-70	Vale of Leven	1980-81	Blantyre Victoria	1991-92	Renfrew
70-71	Cambuslang Rangers	1981-82	Lesmahagow	1992-93	East Kilbride Thistle
71-72	Carluke Rovers	1982-83	Kilsyth Rangers	1993-94	Maryhill
72-73	St. Roch's	1983-84	St. Roch's	1994-95	Benburb
73-74	Bellshill Athletic	1984-85	Glasgow Perthshire	1995-96	Blantyre Victoria
74-75	Rutherglen Glencairn	1985-86	Shettleston	1996-97	Lanark United
75-76	Duntocher Hibs	1986-87	Pollok	1997-98	Shotts Bon Accord
76-77	Glasgow Perthshire	1987-88	Shotts Bon Accord	1998-99	Blantyre Victoria
77-78	Cumbernauld United	1988-89	Lesmahagow	1999-00	Larkhall Thistle
78-79	Pollok	1989-90	Benburb		

summary: *3 - Blantyre Victoria, Pollok; 2 - Benburb, Cambuslang Rangers, Glasgow Perthshire, Lesmahagow, St. Roch's, Shotts Bon Accord; 1 - Bellshill Athletic, Carluke Rovers, Cumbernauld United, Duntocher Hibs, East Kilbride Thistle, Forth Wanderers, Kilsyth Rangers, Lanark United, Larkhall Thistle, Maryhill, Renfrew, Rutherglen Glencairn, Shettleston, Vale of Leven.*

Central Regional League - Division 2

68-69	Ashfield	1979-80	Blantyre Victoria	1990-91	Ashfield
69-70	Lanark United	1980-81	Thorniewood United	1991-92	Johnstone Burgh
70-71	Neilston Juniors	1981-82	Dunipace Juniors	1992-93	Thorniewood United
71-72	St. Roch's	1982-83	Stonehouse Violet	1993-94	Cumbernauld United
72-73	Dunipace Juniors	1983-84	Cumbernauld United	1994-95	St. Roch's
73-74	Maryhill	1984-85	Lanark United	1995-96	Lanark United
74-75	Larkhall Thistle	1985-86	Cambuslang Rangers	1996-97	Shotts Bon Accord
75-76	Port Glasgow Juniors	1986-87	Bellshill Athletic	1997-98	Greenock Juniors
76-77	Shotts Bon Accord	1987-88	Maryhill	1998-99	Dunipace Juniors
77-78	Maryhill	1988-89	Yoker Athletic	1999-00	Port Glasgow Juniors
78-79	Vale of Leven	1989-90	Cambuslang Rangers		

summary: *3 - Dunipace Juniors, Lanark United, Maryhill; 2 - Ashfield, Cambuslang Rangers, Cumbernauld United, Port Glasgow Juniors, St. Roch's, Shotts Bon Accord, Thorniewood United; - Bellshill Athletic, Blantyre Victoria, Greenock Juniors, Johnstone Burgh, Larkhall Thistle, Neilston Juniors, Stonehouse Violet, Vale of Leven, Yoker Athletic.*

Central Regional League - Sectional League Cup

68-69	Benburb	1974-75	East Kilbride Thistle	1980-81	Larkhall Thistle
69-70	Shettleston	1975-76	Lanark United	1981-82	Petershill
70-71	Cambuslang Rangers	1976-77	Shettleston	1982-83	East Kilbride Thistle
71-72	Kirkintilloch Rob Roy	1977-78	Petershill	1983-84	Pollok
72-73	Benburb	1978-79	Arthurlie	1984-85	Shotts Bon Accord
73-74	Kirkintilloch Rob Roy	1979-80	Shettleston	1985-86	Yoker Athletic

CONTINUED OVERLEAF

1986-87	Arthurlie	1991-92	Rutherglen Glencairn	1996-97	Pollok
1987-88	Larkhall Thistle	1992-93	Pollok	1997-98	Shotts Bon Accord
1988-89	Shotts Bon Accord	1993-94	Lesmahagow	1998-99	Neilston Juniors
1989-90	Dunipace Juniors	1994-95	Petershill	1999-00	Pollok
1990-91	Pollok	1995-96	Blantyre Victoria		

Summary: *5 - Pollok; 3 - Petershill, Shettleston, Shotts Bon Accord; 2 - Arthurlie, Benburb, East Kilbride Thistle, Kirkintilloch Rob Roy, Larkhall Thistle; 1 - Blantyre Victoria, Cambuslang Rangers, Dunipace Juniors, Lanark United, Lesmahagow, Neilston Juniors, Rutherglen Glencairn, Yoker Athletic.*

Cherry Video Cup

1987-88	Downfield	1988-89	Forfar West End

City & District League
(See under Dundee Junior League Division 2)

Clark Beckett Cup

1992-93	Lochgelly Albert	1993-94	Kelty Hearts

Clackmannanshire Charity Cup

1890-91	Alva 2nd XI	1898-99	Alva Albion Rangers	1906-07	Alva Albion Rangers
1891-92	Alloa Hibernians	1899-00	Alloa Seafield Thistle	1907-08	Sauchie
1892-93	Alloa 2nd XI	1900-01	Alva Albion Rangers	1908-09	Sauchie
1893-94	Sauchie	1901-02	Alva Albion Rangers	1909-10	Sauchie
1894-95	Alloa 2nd XI	1902-03	Tillicoultry Rovers	1910-11	Sauchie
1895-96	Tillicoultry Victoria	1903-04	Clackmannan Juniors	1911-12	Alva Albion Rangers
1896-97	*No Competition*	1904-05	Clackmannan Juniors		
1897-98	Alva Albion Rangers	1905-06	Alva Albion Rangers		

Clackmannanshire Junior Challenge Cup

1901-02	Alva Albion Rangers	1905-06	Clackmannan Juniors	1909-10	Sauchie
1902-03	Clackmannan Juniors	1906-07	Alva Albion Rangers	1910-11	Alva Albion Rangers
1903-04	Alva Albion Rangers	1907-08	Alva Albion Rangers	1911-12	Sauchie
1904-05	Clackmannan Juniors	1908-09	Clackmannan Juniors	1912-13	Coalsnaughton United

Clackmannanshire Junior League

1896-97	Alva Albion Rangers	1900-01	Alva Albion Rangers	1904-05	Clackmannan Juniors
1897-98	Alva Albion Rangers	1901-02	Alva Albion Rangers	1905-06	Clackmannan Juniors
1898-99	Alloa Seafield Thistle	1902-03	Alva Albion Rangers	1906-07	Alva Albion Rangers
1899-00	Alloa Vale of Forth	1903-04	Alva Albion Rangers	1907-08	Denny Hibs

Clive Williamson Trophy
(For North Regional League North Clubs)

1998-99	Islavale	1999-00	Islavale

Concept Group Cup
(Formerly the Zamoyski Challenge Cup and the North End Centenary Cup.
For Tayside and North Regional Leagues' Clubs)

1988-89	Deveronside	1992-93	Forfar West End	1996-97	Dundee St. Joseph's
1989-90	Downfield	1993-94	Dundee St. Joseph's	1997-98	Dundee St. Joseph's
1990-91	Downfield	1994-95	Tayport	1998-99	Kirriemuir Thistle
1991-92	Tayport	1995-96	Dundee St. Joseph's	1999-00	Tayport

Connon Cup

For North Regional League North Section clubs. From 1998 presented to the runners-up in the North Regional League (North))

1931-32	Burghead Thistle	1959-60	Bishopmill United	1980-81	Lossiemouth United
1932-33	Rothes Victoria	1960-61	Burghead Thistle	1981-82	Buckie Rovers
1933-34	Hopeman	1961-62	Burghead Thistle	1982-83	RAF Kinloss
1934-35	Rothes Victoria	1962-63	Bishopmill United	1983-84	Bishopmill United
1935-36		1963-64	Fulmar	1984-85	Forres Thistle
1936-37		1964-65	Burghead Thistle	1985-86	Rothes Decimals
1937-38		1965-66	Lossiemouth United	1986-87	Nairn St. Ninian
1938-39		1966-67	Fulmar	1987-88	Nairn St. Ninian
1939-47	*No Competition*	1967-68	Islavale	1988-89	Lossiemouth United
1947-48	RAF Elgin	1968-69	Lossiemouth United	1989-90	Lossiemouth United
1948-49	New Elgin	1969-70	RAF Kinloss	1990-91	Bishopmill United
1949-50	Lossiemouth United	1970-71		1991-92	New Elgin
1950-51		1971-72		1992-93	Deveronside
1951-52	Bishopmill United	1972-73		1993-94	Fochabers
1952-53	Forres Thistle	1973-74	Nairn St. Ninian	1994-95	Bishopmill United
1953-54	Forres Thistle	1974-75		1995-96	Burghead Thistle
1954-55	Islavale	1975-76		1996-97	Burghead Thistle
1955-56	Burghead Thistle	1976-77		1997-98	Strathspey Thistle
1956-57	Islavale	1977-78	Bishopmill United	1998-99	Islavale
1957-58	Forres Thistle	1978-79		1999-00	Forres Thistle
1958-59	Burghead Thistle	1979-80	Forres Thistle		

Summary: *8 - Burghead Thistle; 7 - Bishopmill United; 6 - Forres Thistle, Lossiemouth United; - Islavale; 3 - Nairn St. Ninian; 2 - Fulmar, New Elgin, RAF Kinloss, Rothes Victoria; 1 - Buckie Rovers, Deveronside, Fochabers, Hopeman, RAF Elgin, Rothes Decimals, Strathspey Thistle.*

Constitutional Cup

(Also known as the Perthshire Junior Consolation Cup)

1920-21	Perth Caledonian	1937-38	Perth Craigie	1954-55	*No Competition*
1921-22	Perth Caledonian	1938-39	Coupar Angus	1955-56	Alyth United
1922-23	Perth Caledonian	1939-40	St. Johnstone YMCA	1956-57	Crieff Earngrove
1923-24	Stanley	1940-41	Luncarty	1957-58	Alyth United
1924-25	Vale of Earn	1941-42	Perth St. James	1958-59	Blairgowrie
1925-26	Stanley	1942-43	Jeanfield Swifts	1959-60	Crieff Earngrove
1926-27	Perth Violet	1943-44	Jeanfield Swifts	1960-61	Coupar Angus
1927-28	Perth Roselea	1944-45	Jeanfield Swifts	1961-62	Alyth United
1928-29	St. Johnstone YMCA	1945-46	Jeanfield Swifts	1962-63	Blairgowrie
1929-30	Vale of Earn	1946-47	Crieff Earngrove	1963-64	Jeanfield Swifts
1930-31	St. Johnstone YMCA	1947-48	Blairgowrie	1964-65	Luncarty
1931-32	St. Leonard's	1948-49	St. Johnstone YMCA	1965-66	Kinnoull
1932-33	Alyth United	1949-50	Jeanfield Swifts	1966-67	Jeanfield Swifts
1933-34	Alyth United	1950-51	Newburgh	1967-68	Jeanfield Swifts
1934-35	Alyth United	1951-52	Crieff Earngrove	1968-69	Jeanfield Swifts
1935-36	St. Johnstone YMCA	1952-53	Stanley		
1936-37	Crieff Earngrove	1953-54	Comrie Rovers		

Summary: *9 - Jeanfield Swifts; 6 - Alyth United; 5 - Crieff Earngrove, St. Johnstone YMCA; - Blairgowrie, Perth Caledonian, Stanley; 2 - Coupar Angus, Luncarty, Vale of Earn; 1 - Comrie Rovers, Kinnoull, Newburgh, Perth Craigie, Perth Roselea, Perth St. James, Perth Violet, St. Leonard's.*

Coronation Cup

(Played between Kilsyth Rangers and Kirkintilloch Rob Roy)

1952-53	Kilsyth Rangers	1955-56	Kilsyth Rangers	1958-59	*No Competition*
1953-54	Kilsyth Rangers	1956-57	*No Competition*	1959-60	Kilsyth Rangers
1954-55	Kirkintilloch Rob Roy	1957-58	Kirkintilloch Rob Roy	1960-61	Kirkintilloch Rob Roy

Courier Cup
(For member clubs of the Dundee Junior F.A.)

1891-92	Dundee Violet	1920-21	Forthill	1947-48	Osborne
1892-93		1921-22	Dundee Celtic	1948-49	Lochee Harp
1893-94	Dundee North End	1922-23	Dundee North End	1949-50	Carnoustie Panmure
1894-95	Dundee North End	1923-24	Dundee North End	1950-51	Lochee Harp
1895-96	Dundee North End	1924-25	Lochee United	1951-52	Carnoustie Panmure
1896-97	Dundee Violet	1925-26	Lochee Central	1952-53	Lochee Harp
1897-98	Stobswell	1926-27	Logie	1953-54	Carnoustie Panmure
1898-99	Dundee Violet	1927-28	Lochee Harp	1954-55	Lochee Harp
1899-00	Dundee Violet	1928-29	Lochee Harp	1955-56	Arnot
1900-01	East Craigie	1929-30	Osborne	1956-57	Dundee North End
1901-02	Edenbank	1930-31	Dundee North End	1957-58	Dundee North End
1902-03	East Craigie	1931-32	East Craigie	1958-59	Lochee Harp
1903-04	Stobswell	1932-33	Stobswell	1959-60	Broughty Athletic
1904-05	Stobswell	1933-34	Lochee Harp	1960-61	Dundee North End
1905-06	Dundee West End	1934-35	Dundee Violet	1961-62	Dundee St. Joseph's
1906-07	Arnot	1935-36	Dundee Violet	1962-63	Lochee Harp
1907-08	Dundee St. Joseph's	1936-37	Forthill Athletic	1963-64	Downfield
1908-09	Arnot	1937-38	Dundee Violet	1964-65	Lochee United
1909-10	Dundee North End	1938-39	Lochee Harp	1965-66	Lochee Harp
1910-11	Dundee Violet	1939-40	Dundee Violet	1966-67	Lochee Harp
1911-12	Fairfield	1940-41	Stobswell	1967-68	Dundee Violet
1912-13	Fairfield	1941-42	Dundee Violet	1968-69	Osborne
1913-14	Dundee North End	1942-43	Lochee Harp	1969-70	Dundee North End
1914-15	Dundee North End	1943-44	Lochee Harp	1970-71	Lochee United
1915-16	Osborne	1944-45	Stobswell	1971-72	Broughty Athletic
1916-19	*No Competition*	1945-46	Dundee Violet	1972-73	Elmwood
1919-20	Dundee North End	1946-47	Elmwood		

Summary: *14 - Dundee North End, Lochee Harp; 13 - Dundee Violet; 6 - Stobswell; 4 - Osborne; 3 - Arnot, Carnoustie Panmure, East Craigie, Lochee United; 2 - Broughty Athletic, Dundee St. Joseph's, Elmwood, Fairfield, Forthill Athletic; 1 - Downfield, Dundee Celtic, Dundee West End, Edenbank, Lochee Central, Logie.*

Cowdenbeath Cup
(Currently the Bardon Aggregates Cup)

1886-87	St. Leonards	1910-11	Glencraig Celtic	1935-36	Hearts of Beath
1887-88	St. Leonards	1911-12	Denbeath Star	1936-37	Blairhall Colliery
1888-89	Kirkcaldy Albion	1912-13	Inverkeithing United	1937-38	Blairhall Colliery
1889-90	Kirkcaldy Albion	1913-14	Glencraig Celtic	1938-39	Thornton Hibs
1890-91	Pathhead United	1914-15	Glencraig Celtic	*1939-40*	*Unfinished*
1891-92	Donibristle Heatherbell	1915-16	Glencraig Celtic	1940-41	Bowhill Rovers
1892-93	Cowdenbeath Juniors	1916-17	Denbeath Star	*1941-46*	*No Competition*
1893-94	Lochgelly Rangers	*1917-19*	*No Competition*	1946-47	Lochgelly Albert
1894-95	Raith Athletic	1919-20	Dunfermline DDSS	1947-48	Lochgelly Violet
1895-96	Hearts of Beath	1920-21	Hearts of Beath	1948-49	Markinch Victoria Rangers
1896-97	Leven Thistle	1921-22	Inverkeithing Juniors	1949-50	Rosyth Recreation
1897-98	Leven Thistle	1922-23	Inverkeithing Juniors	1950-51	Valleyfield
1898-99	Leven Thistle	1923-24	Wellesley	1951-52	Kelty Rangers
1899-00	Lochgelly Rangers	1924-25	Rosslyn Juniors	1952-53	Lochore Welfare
1900-01	Dunfermline Our Boys	1925-26	Denbeath Star	1953-54	Lochgelly Albert
1901-02	Lochgelly Rangers	1926-27	Inverkeithing Juniors	1954-55	Lochgelly Albert
1902-03	Kelty Rangers	1927-28	Dunnikier Juniors	1955-56	Lochore Welfare
1903-04	Kelty Rangers	1928-29	Crossgates Primrose	1956-57	Blairhall Colliery
1904-05	Clackmannan Juniors	1929-30	Rosslyn Juniors	1957-58	St. Andrew's United
1905-06	Clackmannan Juniors	1930-31	Dunnikier Juniors	1958-59	Lochgelly Albert
1906-07	Pathhead United	1931-32	Rosslyn Juniors	1959-60	Thornton Hibs
1907-08	Buckhaven	1932-33	Blairhall Juniors	1960-61	Newburgh
1908-09	Glencraig Celtic	1933-34	Rosslyn Juniors	1961-62	Lochore Welfare
1909-10	Kingseat Ath/Kelty R.	1934-35	Kirkford Juniors	1962-63	Thornton Hibs

963-64	Lochore Welfare	1976-77	Glenrothes	1989-90	Hill o' Beath Hawthorn
964-65	Dundonald Bluebell	1977-78	Glenrothes	1990-91	St. Andrew's United
965-66	St. Andrew's United	1978-79	Halbeath	1991-92	Hill o' Beath Hawthorn
966-67	Newburgh	1979-80	Leven Juniors	1992-93	Kelty Hearts
967-68	Lochore Welfare	1980-81	Jubilee Athletic	1993-94	Hill o' Beath Hawthorn
968-69	St. Andrew's United	1981-82	Kelty Hearts	1994-95	Hill o' Beath Hawthorn
969-70	Glenrothes	1982-83	Oakley United	1995-96	Oakley United
970-71	Oakley United	1983-84	Glenrothes	1996-97	Hill o' Beath Hawthorn
971-72	Glenrothes	1984-85	Kelty Hearts	1997-98	Hill o' Beath Hawthorn
972-73	Glenrothes	1985-86	Kelty Hearts	1998-99	Oakley United
973-74	Glenrothes	1986-87	Kelty Hearts	1999-00	Kelty Hearts
974-75	Lochore Welfare	1987-88	Jubilee Athletic		
975-76	Newburgh	1988-89	Hill o' Beath Hawthorn		

summary: 7 - Glenrothes, Hill o' Beath Hawthorn; 6 - Lochore Welfare, Kelty Hearts; 5 - Glencraig Celtic; 4 - Kelty Rangers*, Lochgelly Albert, Oakley United, Rosslyn Juniors, St. Andrews United; - Blairhall Colliery, Denbeath Star, Hearts of Beath, Inverkeithing Juniors, Leven Thistle, Lochgelly Rangers, Newburgh, Thornton Hibs; 2 - Clackmannan Juniors, Dunnikier Juniors, Jubilee Athletic, Kirkcaldy Albion, Pathhead United, St. Leonards; 1 - Blairhall Juniors, Bowhill Rovers, Buckhaven, Cowdenbeath Juniors, Crossgates Primrose, Donibristle Heatherbell, Dundonald Bluebell, Dunfermline DDSS, Dunfermline Our Boys, Halbeath, Inverkeithing United, Kingseat Athletic*, Kirkford Juniors, Leven Juniors, Lochgelly Violet, Markinch V.R., Raith Athletic, Rosyth Recreation, Valleyfield, Wellesley.
* = including 1 shared.

Craig Stephen Cup
(For member clubs of the Tayside Junior F.A.)

974-75	Crieff Earngrove	1978-79	Jeanfield Swifts	1982-83	Dundee North End
975-76	Jeanfield Swifts	1979-80	Arbroath S.C.	1983-84	Kinnoull
976-77	Jeanfield Swifts	1980-81	Broughty Athletic	1984-85	Downfield
977-78	Forfar Albion	1981-82	Jeanfield Swifts	1985-86	Dundee North End

Cream of the Barley Trophy
(For member clubs of the Tayside Junior F.A.)

975-76	Dundee North End	1982-83	Forfar West End	1989-90	Downfield
976-77	Dundee Violet	1983-84	Arbroath Victoria	1990-91	Arbroath SC
977-78	Carnoustie Panmure	1984-85	Lochee United	1991-92	Downfield
978-79	Lochee United	1985-86	Downfield	1992-93	Dundee St. Joseph's
979-80	Dundee Violet	1986-87	Lochee Harp	1993-94	Downfield
980-81	Dundee North End	1987-88	Dundee Violet	1994-95	Tayport
981-82	Lochee United	1988-89	Forfar West End		

Cumnock & Doon Valley Cup

986-87	Cumnock Juniors	1989-90	Craigmark Burntonians	1992-93	Auchinleck Talbot
987-88	Cumnock Juniors	1990-91	Auchinleck Talbot	1993-94	Auchinleck Talbot
988-89	Cumnock Juniors	1991-92	Kello Rovers	1994-95	Auchinleck Talbot

Cunningham District Cup

982-83	Irvine Meadow	1987-88	Irvine Meadow	1992-93	Ardrossan Winton Rovers
983-84	Irvine Meadow	1988-89	Irvine Victoria	1993-94	Beith Juniors
984-85	Irvine Victoria	1989-90	Ardrossan Winton Rovers	1994-95	Irvine Meadow
985-86	Irvine Meadow	1990-91	Ardrossan Winton Rovers		
986-87	Kilbirnie Ladeside	1991-92	Irvine Meadow		

Currie Cup

(Presented by Messrs. J. & T. Currie, Wine & Spirit Merchants, Perth, on 21 January 191
Competition for Perthshire Junior clubs until league reorganisation in 1969 - thereafter
opened to all Tayside Region clubs. Whyte & MacKay Cup from 1991-1999, Findlay & Co
Cup from 2000.)

1910-11	St. Leonards	1943-44	Jeanfield Swifts	1972-73	Arbroath Victoria
1911-12	Perth Violet	1944-45	Jeanfield Swifts	1973-74	Dundee Osborne
1912-13	Perth Craigie	1945-46	Jeanfield Swifts	1974-75	Blairgowrie
1913-14	Perth Craigie	1946-47	Crieff Earngrove	1975-76	Carnoustie Panmure
1914-19	*No Competition*	1947-48	Jeanfield Swifts	1976-77	Lochee United
1919-20	Perth Celtic	1948-49	Jeanfield Swifts	1977-78	Carnoustie Panmure
1920-21	*Not Completed*	1949-50	Blairgowrie	1978-79	Dundee Violet
1921-22	Perth Roselea	1950-51	Jeanfield Swifts	1979-80	Brechin Victoria
1922-23	Vale of Earn	1951-52	Blairgowrie	1980-81	Lochee Harp
1923-24	Stanley	1952-53	Blairgowrie	1981-82	Dundee Violet
1924-25	Scone Thistle	1953-54	Newburgh	1982-83	Forfar West End
1925-26	Vale of Earn	1954-55	Newburgh	1983-84	Forfar West End
1926-27	Perth YMCA	1955-56	Blairgowrie	1984-85	Kinnoull
1927-28	Scone Thistle	1956-57	Blairgowrie	1985-86	Lochee Harp
1928-29	Kinnoull	1957-58	Luncarty	1986-87	Lochee United
1929-30	Perth YMCA	1958-59	Alyth United	1987-88	Jeanfield Swifts
1930-31	Perth Violet	1959-60	Blairgowrie	1988-89	Forfar West End
1931-32	Perth YMCA	1960-61	Alyth United	1989-90	Dundee North End
1932-33	Scone Thistle	1961-62	Alyth United	1990-91	Tayport
1933-34	*Not Completed*	1962-63	Blairgowrie	1991-92	Tayport
1934-35	Alyth United	1963-64	Alyth United	1992-93	Tayport
1935-36	Alyth United	1964-65	Blairgowrie	1993-94	Tayport
1936-37	Crieff Earngrove	1965-66	Blairgowrie	1994-95	Downfield
1937-38	Perth Craigie	1966-67	Jeanfield Swifts	1995-96	Dundee St. Joseph's
1938-39	Coupar Angus	1967-68	Errol	1996-97	Dundee St. Joseph's
1939-40	Perth Y.M.C.A.	1968-69	Downfield	1997-98	Dundee St. Joseph's
1940-41	Jeanfield Swifts	1969-70	Kinnoull	1998-99	Tayport
1941-42	St. James	1970-71	East Craigie	1999-00	Lochee United
1942-43	Perth YMCA	1971-72	Carnoustie Panmure		

Summary: *10 - Blairgowrie; 9 - Jeanfield Swifts; 6 - Alyth United; 5 - Perth YMCA, Tayport;
3 - Carnoustie Panmure, Dundee St. Joseph's, Forfar West End, Kinnoull, Lochee United, Perth
Craigie, Scone Thistle; 2 - Crieff Earngrove, Downfield, Dundee Violet, Lochee Harp, Newburgh, Pert
Violet, Vale of Earn; 1 - Arbroath Victoria, Brechin Victoria, Coupar Angus, Dundee North End, East
Craigie, Errol, Luncarty, Osborne, Perth Celtic, Perth Roselea, St. James, St. Leonards, Stanley.*

Dalkeith Glazing Cup

(See under St. Michael Cup)

Dalmeny Cup

(Presented by Lord Dalmeny. For member clubs of the Edinburgh & District Junior F.A.)

1907-08	Arniston Rangers	1912-13	Penicuik Juniors	1920-21	Broxburn Athletic
1908-09	Musselburgh Athletic	1913-14	Pumpherston Rangers	1921-22	Edinburgh Emmet
1909-10	Arniston Rangers	1914-15	Tranent Juniors	1922-23	Bonnyrigg Rose Athleti
1910-11	Dalkeith Thistle	*1915-19*	*No Competition*	1923-24	Portobello Thistle
1911-12	Musselburgh Athletic	1919-20	Loanhead Mayflower		

D.J. Laing Homes Cup

(For member clubs of the Tayside Junior F.A.)

1995-96	Downfield	1997-98	Tayport Juniors	1999-00	Arbroath S.C.
1996-97	Dundee St. Joseph's	1998-99	Dundee North End		

Downfield S.C. Cup
(See under Tayside Regional League Cup)

Dumfries & District Junior Cup

92-93	5th KRV 2nd XI	1901-02	Balmoral	1912-13	Ashfield
93-94	5th KRV 2nd XI	1902-03	Primrose	1913-14	
94-95	Dumfries Thistle	1903-04		*1914-19*	*No Competition*
95-96	5th KRV 2nd XI	1904-05	Roslyn	1919-20	Kello Rovers
96-97	Nithsdale	1905-06	Roslyn	1920-21	Nithbank
97-98	Rob Roy	1906-07		1921-22	Maxwelltown Juniors
98-99	Rob Roy	1907-08		1922-23	Nithbank
99-00	Rosefield	*1908-11*	*No Competition*	1923-24	Dalbeattie Trades
00-01	Rosefield	1911-12	Ashfield	1924-25	Craigielands

Dumfries & District Junior League

45-46	Kirkconnel Athletic	1947-48	Annan Athletic	1949-50	Annan Athletic
46-47	Annan Athletic	1948-49	LMS Rovers	1950-51	Annan Athletic

Dumfries & District Junior Shield

00-01	Maxwelltown Volunteers	1906-07	Maxwelltown Juniors	*1914-19*	*No Competition*
01-02	Balmoral	1907-08		1919-20	St. Andrew's
02-03	Balmoral	*1908-11*	*No Competition*	1920-21	Tayleurians
03-04	Primrose	1911-12	Ashfield	1921-22	St. Andrew's / Railway
04-05		1912-13	Ashfield		Juniors
05-06	Balmoral	1913-14		1922-23	Maxwelltown Juniors

Dunbartonshire Junior Charity Cup

13-14	Kirkintilloch Harp	*1927-35*	*No Competition*	1948-49	Clydebank Juniors
14-15	Clydebank Juniors	1935-36	Duntocher Hibs	1949-50	Clydebank Juniors
15-16	Clydebank Juniors	1936-37	Duntocher Hibs	1950-51	Kirkintilloch Rob Roy
16-17	Clydebank Juniors	1937-38	Clydebank Juniors	1951-52	Kirkintilloch Rob Roy
17-18	Clydebank Juniors	1938-39	Duntocher Hibs	1952-53	Vale of Leven
18-19	Clydebank Juniors	1939-40	Clydebank Juniors	1953-54	Vale of Leven
19-20	Duntocher Hibs	*1940-41*	*No Competition*	1954-55	Kirkintilloch Rob Roy
20-21	Duntocher Hibs	1941-42	Clydebank Juniors	1955-56	Duntocher Hibs
21-22	Duntocher Hibs	1942-43	Vale of Leven	1956-57	Kirkintilloch Rob Roy
22-23	Duntocher Hibs	1943-44	Yoker Athletic	1957-58	Duntocher Hibs
23-24	Old Kilpatrick	1944-45	Yoker Athletic	1958-59	Yoker Athletic
24-25	Dumbarton Harp Athletic	1945-46	Vale of Leven	1959-60	Kirkintilloch Rob Roy
25-26	Kirkintilloch Rob Roy	1946-47	Vale of Leven	1960-61	Kirkintilloch Rob Roy
26-27	Clydebank Juniors	1947-48	Duntocher Hibs	1961-62	Kirkintilloch Rob Roy

Summary: 11 - Clydebank Juniors; 10 - Duntocher Hibs; 8 - Kirkintilloch Rob Roy; 5 - Vale of Leven; - Yoker Athletic; 1 - Dumbarton Harp Athletic, Kirkintilloch Harp, Old Kilpatrick.

Dunbartonshire Junior Cup

95-96	Yoker Athletic	1906-07	Clydebank Juniors	1917-18	Yoker Athletic
96-97	Duntocher Hibs	1907-08	Mossfield Amateurs	1918-19	Kirkintilloch Rob Roy
97-98	Yoker Athletic	1908-09	Kirkintilloch Rob Roy	1919-20	Clydebank Juniors
98-99	Duntocher Hibs	1909-10	Clydebank Juniors	1920-21	Vale of Leven
99-00	Clydebank Juniors	1910-11	Clydebank Juniors	1921-22	Duntocher Hibs
00-01	Smithston Albion	1911-12	Kirkintilloch Rob Roy	1922-23	Yoker Athletic
01-02	Old Kilpatrick	1912-13	Yoker Athletic	1923-24	Dumbarton Harp Juniors
02-03	Duntocher Hibs	1913-14	Yoker Athletic	1924-25	Duntocher Hibs
03-04	Duntocher Corinthians	1914-15	Clydebank Juniors	1925-26	Clydebank Juniors
04-05	Kirkintilloch Rob Roy	1915-16	Kirkintilloch Rob Roy	1926-27	Dumbarton Harp Juniors
05-06	Clydebank Juniors	1916-17	Clydebank Juniors	*1927-28*	*No Competition*

CONTINUED OVERLEAF

1928-29	Clydebank Juniors	1942-43	Clydebank Juniors	1956-57	Duntocher Hibs
1929-30	Croy Celtic	1943-44	Clydebank Juniors	1957-58	Duntocher Hibs
1930-31	Croy Celtic	1944-45	Clydebank Juniors	1958-59	Yoker Athletic
1931-32	Yoker Athletic	1945-46	Yoker Athletic	1959-60	Duntocher Hibs
1932-33	Clydebank Juniors	1946-47	Yoker Athletic	1960-61	Kirkintilloch Rob Roy
1933-34	Clydebank Juniors	1947-48	Duntocher Hibs	1961-62	Kirkintilloch Rob Roy
1934-35	Yoker Athletic	1948-49	Duntocher Hibs	1962-63	Kirkintilloch Rob Roy
1935-36	Kirkintilloch Rob Roy	1949-50	Yoker Athletic	1963-64	Duntocher Hibs
1936-37	Duntocher Hibs	1950-51	Clydebank Juniors	1964-65	Vale of Leven
1937-38	Yoker Athletic	1951-52	Kirkintilloch Rob Roy	1965-66	Kilsyth Rangers
1938-39	Clydebank Juniors	1952-53	Clydebank Juniors	1966-67	Yoker Athletic
1939-40	Vale of Leven	1953-54	Duntocher Hibs	1967-68	Kirkintilloch Rob Roy
1940-41	Clydebank Juniors	1954-55	Duntocher Hibs		
1941-42	Clydebank Juniors	1955-56	Duntocher Hibs		

Summary: *20 - Clydebank Juniors; 15 - Duntocher Hibs; 14 - Yoker Athletic; 11 - Kirkintilloch Rob Roy; 3 - Vale of Leven; 2 - Croy Celtic, Dumbarton Harp Juniors; 1 - Duntocher Corinthians, Kilsyth Rangers, Mossfield Amateurs, Old Kilpatrick, Smithston Albion.*

Dundee Junior Charity Cup
(See under Kiddie Cup)

Dundee Junior League

1895-96	Dundee North End	1919-20	Forthill	1948-49	Lochee Harp
1896-97	Dundee Violet	1920-21	Fairfield	1949-50	Lochee Harp
1897-98	Stobswell	1921-22	Osborne	1950-51	Carnoustie Panmure
1898-99	Dundee Violet	1922-23	Lochee Harp	1951-52	Carnoustie Panmure
1899-00	Dundee Violet	1923-24	Lochee Harp	1952-53	Carnoustie Panmure
1900-01	Stobswell	1924-25	Dundee Central	1953-54	Lochee Harp
1901-02	Ardenlea	1925-26	Logie	1954-55	Lochee Harp
1902-03	Stobswell	1926-27	Lochee Harp	1955-56	Carnoustie Panmure
1903-04	Fairfield	1927-28	Dundee Violet	1956-57	Dundee North End
1904-05	Lochee Harp	1928-29	Lochee Harp	1957-58	Carnoustie Panmure
1905-06	Dundee North End	1929-30	Lochee Harp	1958-59	Lochee Harp
1906-07	Lochee Harp	1930-31	Lochee Harp	1959-60	Dundee North End
1907-08	Dundee Violet	1931-32	Lochee Harp	1960-61	Lochee Harp
1908-09	Dundee North End	1932-33	Stobswell	1961-62	Dundee St. Joseph's
1909-10	Dundee Violet	1933-34	Dundee St. Joseph's	1962-63	Lochee Harp
1910-11	Lochee Harp	1934-35	Lochee Harp	1963-64	Downfield
1911-12	Fairfield	1935-36	Lochee Harp	1964-65	Carnoustie Panmure
1912-13	Fairfield	1936-37	Dundee Violet	1965-66	Carnoustie Panmure
1913-14	Dundee Violet	1937-38	Lochee Harp	1966-67	Downfield
1914-15	Dundee North End	1938-39	Arnot	1967-68	Dundee Violet
1915-16	Dundee Violet	*1939-47*	*No Competition*	1968-69	Lochee United
1916-19	*No Competition*	1947-48	Stobswell		

Summary: *20 - Lochee Harp; 10 - Dundee Violet; 7 - Carnoustie Panmure; 6 - Dundee North End; 5 - Stobswell; 4 - Fairfield; 2 - Downfield, Dundee St. Joseph's; 1 - Ardenlea, Arnot, Dundee Central, Forthill, Lochee United, Logie, Osborne.*

Dundee Junior League - Division 2
(Previously the City & District League)

1913-14	Osborne	1921-22	Arbroath Roselea	1925-26	Osborne
1914-19	*No Competition*	1922-23	Lochee Central	1926-27	Dundee St. Joseph's
1919-20	Lochee Central	1923-24	Logie		
1920-21	Lochee Central	1924-25	Downfield		

Dunfermline Cup
(See under West Fife Cup)

Dunfermline Shield
(See under Fife Shield)

Duthie Cup
(For Aberdeen & District Clubs. Currently the Acorn Heating Cup)

Year	Winner	Year	Winner	Year	Winner
13-04	Abergeldie	1938-39	Cattofield	1970-71	Banks o' Dee
04-05	East End	1939-40	Inverurie Loco Works	1971-72	Lewis United
05-06	Mugiemoss	1940-41	Incognitos	1972-73	Banks o' Dee
06-07	East End	1941-42	Aberdeen Juniors	1973-74	Banks o' Dee
07-08	Mugiemoss	1942-43	I.T.C.	1974-75	Banks o' Dee
08-09	Mugiemoss	1943-44	K.O.S.B. 'B'	1975-76	Banks o' Dee
09-10	Mugiemoss	1944-45	Belmont	1976-77	Lads' Club
10-11	Richmond	1945-46	Mugiemoss	1977-78	Fraserburgh United
11-12	Parkvale	1946-47	Banks o' Dee	1978-79	Parkvale
12-13	Mugiemoss	1947-48	Hall Russell's	1979-80	Banks o' Dee
13-14	Richmond	1948-49	Mugiemoss	1980-81	Banks o' Dee
14-15	Banks o' Dee	1949-50	Hall Russell's	1981-82	FC Stoneywood
15-19	No Competition	1950-51	Lewis United	1982-83	Banks o' Dee
19-20	Hall Russell's	1951-52	Woodside	1983-84	Banks o' Dee
20-21	Banks o' Dee	1952-53	Banks o' Dee	1984-85	Sunnybank
21-22	Mugiemoss	1953-54	Lewis United	1985-86	Banks o' Dee
22-23	East End	1954-55	25th Old Boys	1986-87	FC Stoneywood
23-24	Banks o' Dee	1955-56	Banks o' Dee	1987-88	Turriff United
24-25	Mugiemoss	1956-57	Banks o' Dee	1988-89	Buchanhaven Hearts
25-26	Hawthorn	1957-58	Banks o' Dee	1989-90	Sunnybank
26-27	Woodside	1958-59	Lads' Club	1990-91	Bon Accord
27-28	East End	1959-60	Rosemount	1991-92	Buchanhaven Hearts
28-29	Inverurie Loco Works	1960-61	Inverurie Loco Works	1992-93	Banks o' Dee
29-30	East End	1961-62	Lewis United	1993-94	Stonehaven
30-31	Woodside	1962-63	Lewis United	1994-95	Sunnybank
31-32	East End	1963-64	Stonehaven	1995-96	Banks o' Dee
32-33	Inverurie Loco Works	1964-65	Lewis United	1996-97	Bon Accord
33-34	Inverurie Loco Works	1965-66	Lewis United	1997-98	F.C. Stoneywood
34-35	Woodside	1966-67	East End	1998-99	Sunnybank
35-36	Inverurie Loco Works	1967-68	Formartine United	1999-00	Cruden Bay
36-37	Hall Russell's	1968-69	Stonehaven		
37-38	Hall Russell's	1969-70	Banks o' Dee		

Summary: *21 – Banks o' Dee; 9 – Mugiemoss; 7 – East End, Lewis United; 5 – Hall Russell's, Inverurie Loco Works, Woodside; 4 – Sunnybank; 3 – FC Stoneywood, Stonehaven; 2 – Bon Accord, Buchanhaven Hearts, Lads' Club, Parkvale, Richmond; 1 – Aberdeen Juniors, Abergeldie, Belmont, Cattofield, Cruden Bay, Formartine United, Fraserburgh United, Hawthorn, Incognitos, I.T.C., K.O.S.B. 'B', Rosemount, Turriff United, 25th Old Boys.*

East Ayrshire Cup

Year	Winner	Year	Winner	Year	Winner
95-96	Cumnock Juniors	1997-98	Glenafton Athletic	1999-00	Auchinleck Talbot
96-97	Auchinleck Talbot	1998-99	Auchinleck Talbot		

East Coast Windows Cup

Year	Winner	Year	Winner
87-88	St. Andrews United	1989-90	St. Andrews United
88-89	St. Andrews United	1990-91	Hill o' Beath Hawthorn

East Fife Cup
(Also known as the Montrave Cup - presented by the Earl of Montrave)

Year	Winner	Year	Winner	Year	Winner
94-95	Leven Thistle	1899-00	Buckhaven United	1904-05	Tayport
95-96	Leven Thistle	1900-01	Vale of Wemyss	1905-06	
96-97	Leven Thistle	1901-02	Buckhaven	1906-07	Pathhead United
97-98	Leven Thistle	1902-03	Vale of Wemyss	1907-08	Leslie Hearts
98-99	Leven Thistle	1903-04	Vale of Wemyss	1908-09	Buckhaven

1909-10	Buckhaven	1924-25	Anstruther Rangers	1936-37	Newburgh
1910-11	Denbeath Star	*1925-26*	*Not Completed*	1937-38	Thornton Hibs
1911-12	Denbeath Star	1926-27	St. Andrews United	1938-39	Wellesley
1912-13	Denbeath Star	1927-28	St. Andrews United	*1939-65*	*No Competition*
1913-14	Denbeath Star	1928-29	St. Andrews United	1965-66	Newburgh
1914-15	Windygates Rangers	1929-30	Denbeath Star	1966-67	Glenrothes
1915-19	*No Competition*	1930-31	Wellesley	1967-68	Thornton Hibs
1919-20	Denbeath Star	1931-32	Dunnikier Juniors	1968-69	Thornton Hibs
1920-21	Denbeath Star	1932-33	Rosslyn Juniors	1969-70	Dundonald
1921-22	Pittenweem Hearts	1933-34	Denbeath Star	1970-71	Glenrothes
1922-23	Dunnikier Juniors	1934-35	Denbeath Star	1971-72	Glenrothes
1923-24	Newburgh West End	1935-36	Denbeath Star	1972-73	Newburgh

Summary: *10 - Denbeath Star; 5 - Leven Thistle; 3 - Buckhaven, Glenrothes, Newburgh, St. Andrews United, Thornton Hibs, Vale of Wemyss; 2 - Dunnikier Juniors, Wellesley; 1 - Anstruther Rangers, Buckhaven United, Dundonald, Leslie Hearts, Newburgh West End, Pathhead United, Pittenweem Hearts, Rosslyn Juniors, Tayport, Windygates Rangers.*

East Lothian Cup

1891-92	Elphinstone Athletic	1902-03	Prestonpans Athletic	1923-24	Musselburgh Bruntonia
1892-93	Prestonpans Athletic	*1903-11*	*No Competition*	1924-25	Edinburgh Emmet
1893-94	Elphinstone Athletic	1911-12	Musselburgh Athletic	1925-26	Musselburgh Bruntonia
1894-95	Elphinstone Athletic	1912-13	Wemyss Athletic	1926-27	Newtongrange Star
1895-96	Ormiston Primrose	1913-14	Musselburgh Athletic	1927-28	Prestonpans Athletic
1896-97	Macmerry St. Clair	1914-15	Wemyss Athletic	1928-29	Dunbar United
1897-98	Prestonpans Athletic	*1915-19*	*No Competition*	1929-30	Elphinstone Athletic
1898-99	Dunbar Star	1919-20	Wemyss Athletic	*1930-32*	*No Competition*
1899-00	Tranent United	1920-21	Musselburgh Bruntonians	1932-33	Dunbar Star
1900-01	Tranent United	1921-22	Tranent Juniors		
1901-02	Tranent United	1922-23	Musselburgh Bruntonians		

Summary: *4 - Elphinstone Athletic, Musselburgh Bruntonians, Prestonpans Athletic; 3 - Tranent United, Wemyss Athletic; 2 - Dunbar Star, Musselburgh Athletic; 1 - Dunbar United, Edinburgh Emmet, Macmerry St. Clair, Newtongrange Star, Ormiston Primrose, Tranent Juniors.*

East of Scotland Junior Cup
(Currently the Calder Cup)

1896-97	Broxburn Athletic	1921-22	Arniston Rangers	1946-47	Stoneyburn Juniors
1897-98	Bonnyrigg Rose Athletic	1922-23	Arniston Rangers	1947-48	Arniston Rangers
1898-99	Leith Ivanhoe	1923-24	Musselburgh Bruntonians	1948-49	Armadale Thistle
1899-00	Niddrie Bluebell	1924-25	Edinburgh Emmet	1949-50	Stoneyburn Juniors
1900-01	Vale of Grange	1925-26	Newtongrange Star	1950-51	Broxburn Athletic
1901-02	Leith Ivanhoe	1926-27	Portobello Thistle	1951-52	Bo'ness United
1902-03	Vale of Grange	1927-28	Portobello Thistle	1952-53	Armadale Thistle
1903-04	Broxburn Athletic	1928-29	Edinburgh Emmet	1953-54	Linlithgow Rose
1904-05	Vale of Grange	1929-30	Newtongrange Star	1954-55	Bo'ness United
1905-06	Alva Albion Rangers	1930-31	Tranent Juniors	1955-56	Loanhead Mayflower
1906-07	Newtongrange Star	1931-32	Tranent Juniors	1956-57	Haddington Athletic
1907-08	Alva Albion Rangers	1932-33	Rosewell Rosedale	1957-58	Newtongrange Star
1908-09	Penicuik Juniors	1933-34	Tranent Juniors	1958-59	Newtongrange Star
1909-10	Arniston Rangers	1934-35	Thorntree United	1959-60	Tranent Juniors
1910-11	Penicuik Juniors	1935-36	Tranent Juniors	1960-61	Dunbar United
1911-12	Wemyss Athletic	1936-37	Musselburgh Athletic	1961-62	Armadale Thistle
1912-13	Arniston Rangers	1937-38	Tranent Juniors	1962-63	Bonnyrigg Rose Athlet
1913-14	Tranent Juniors	1938-39	Stoneyburn Juniors	1963-64	Dunbar United
1914-15	Denbeath Star	1939-40	Polkemmet Juniors	1964-65	Linlithgow Rose
1915-16	Loanhead Mayflower	1940-41	Haddington Athletic	1965-66	Whitburn Juniors
1916-17	Denbeath Star	1941-42	Bathgate Thistle	1966-67	Dalkeith Thistle
1917-18	Winchburgh Violet	1942-43	Burnbank Athletic	1967-68	Linlithgow Rose
1918-19	Winchburgh Violet	1943-44	Armadale Thistle	1968-69	Whitburn Juniors
1919-20	Tranent Juniors	1944-45	Fauldhouse United	1969-70	Whitburn Juniors
1920-21	Musselburgh Bruntonians	1945-46	Fauldhouse United	1970-71	Arniston Rangers

1-72	Dalkeith Thistle	1981-82	Newtongrange Star	1991-92	Newtongrange Star
2-73	Haddington Athletic	1982-83	Sauchie Juniors	1992-93	Linlithgow Rose
3-74	Whitburn Juniors	1983-84	Ormiston Primrose	1993-94	Camelon Juniors
4-75	Newtongrange Star	1984-85	Bo'ness United	1994-95	Ormiston Primrose
5-76	Linlithgow Rose	1985-86	Bonnyrigg Rose Athletic	1995-96	Linlithgow Rose
6-77	Newtongrange Star	1986-87	Bonnyrigg Rose Athletic	1996-97	Newtongrange Star
7-78	Linlithgow Rose	1987-88	Broxburn Athletic	1997-98	Whitburn Juniors
8-79	Tranent Juniors	1988-89	Linlithgow Rose	1998-99	Bo'ness United
9-80	Newtongrange Star	1989-90	Dunbar United	1999-00	Linlithgow Rose
0-81	Arniston Rangers	1990-91	Linlithgow Rose		

mmary: *11 - Newtongrange Star; 10 - Linlithgow Rose; 9 - Tranent Juniors; 7 - Arniston ngers; 5 - Whitburn Juniors; 4 - Armadale Thistle, Bo'ness United, Bonnyrigg Rose Athletic, oxburn Athletic; 3 - Dunbar United, Haddington Athletic, Stoneyburn Juniors, Vale of Grange; Alva Albion Rangers, Dalkeith Thistle, Denbeath Star, Edinburgh Emmet, Fauldhouse United, th Ivanhoe, Loanhead Mayflower, Musselburgh Bruntonians, Ormiston Primrose, Penicuik Juniors, tobello Thistle, Winchburgh Violet; 1 - Bathgate Thistle, Burnbank Athletic, Camelon Juniors, sselburgh Athletic, Niddrie Bluebell, Polkemmet Juniors, Rosewell Rosedale, Sauchie Juniors, orntree United, Wemyss Athletic.*

East Regional League - Division 1

8-69	Bo'ness United	1979-80	Camelon Juniors	1990-91	Newtongrange Star
9-70	Arniston Rangers	1980-81	Penicuik Athletic	1991-92	Newtongrange Star
0-71	Musselburgh Athletic	1981-82	Linlithgow Rose	1992-93	Fauldhouse United
1-72	Arniston Rangers	1982-83	Fauldhouse United	1993-94	Camelon Juniors
2-73	Broxburn Athletic	1983-84	Linlithgow Rose	1994-95	Camelon Juniors
3-74	Broxburn Athletic	1984-85	Bonnyrigg Rose Athletic	1995-96	Whitburn
4-75	Linlithgow Rose	1985-86	Whitburn	1996-97	Linlithgow Rose
5-76	Bonnyrigg Rose Athletic	1986-87	Whitburn	1997-98	Whitburn
6-77	Bonnyrigg Rose Athletic	1987-88	Linlithgow Rose	1998-99	Linlithgow Rose
7-78	Linlithgow Rose	1988-89	Whitburn	1999-00	Linlithgow Rose
8-79	Penicuik Athletic	1989-90	Whitburn		

mmary: *8 - Linlithgow Rose; 6 - Whitburn; 3 - Bonnyrigg Rose Athletic, Camelon Juniors; Arniston Rangers, Broxburn Athletic, Fauldhouse United, Newtongrange Star, Penicuik Athletic; Bo'ness United, Musselburgh Athletic.*

East Regional League - Division 2

3-74	Tranent Juniors	1982-83	Ormiston Primrose	1991-92	Livingston United
4-75	Newtongrange Star	1983-84	Bonnyrigg Rose Athletic	1992-93	Harthill Royal
5-76	Dunbar United	1984-85	Armadale Thistle	1993-94	Dunbar United
6-77	Newtongrange Star	1985-86	Edinburgh United	1994-95	Harthill Royal
7-78	Whitburn	1986-87	Bathgate Thistle	1995-96	Tranent Juniors
8-79	Broxburn Athletic	1987-88	Livingston United	1996-97	Fauldhouse United
9-80	Dalkeith Thistle	1988-89	Armadale Thistle	1997-98	Dunbar United
0-81	Livingston United	1989-90	Dalkeith Thistle	1998-99	Haddington Athletic
1-82	Fauldhouse United	1990-91	Bathgate Thistle	1999-00	Harthill Royal

mmary: *3 - Dunbar United, Harthill Royal, Livingston United; 2 - Armadale Thistle, Bathgate istle, Dalkeith Thistle, Fauldhouse United, Newtongrange Star, Tranent Juniors; 1 - Bonnyrigg Rose hletic, Broxburn Athletic, Edinburgh United, Haddington Athletic, Ormiston Primrose, Whitburn.*

East Regional League Cup

7-78	Linlithgow Rose	1985-86	Linlithgow Rose	1993-94	Camelon Juniors
8-79	Tranent Juniors	1986-87	Ormiston Primrose	1994-95	Linlithgow Rose
9-80	Tranent Juniors	1987-88	Bonnyrigg Rose Athletic	1995-96	Whitburn
0-81	Livingston United	1988-89	Whitburn	1996-97	Newtongrange Star
1-82	Fauldhouse United	1989-90	Newtongrange Star	1997-98	Whitburn
2-83	Fauldhouse United	1990-91	Linlithgow Rose	1998-99	Whitburn
3-84	Bonnyrigg Rose Athletic	1991-92	Newtongrange Star	1999-00	Harthill Royal
4-85	Bonnyrigg Rose Athletic	1992-93	Newtongrange Star		

SUMMARY OVERLEAF

Summary: *4 - Linlithgow Rose, Newtongrange Star, Whitburn; 3 - Bonnyrigg Rose Athletic; 2 - Fauldhouse United, Tranent Juniors; 1 - Camelon Juniors, Harthill Royal, Livingston United, Ormiston Primrose.*

Edinburgh & District Junior League

1922-23	Newtongrange Star	1937-38	Bonnyrigg Rose Athletic	1955-56	Dalkeith Thistle
1923-24	Newtongrange Star	1938-39	Stoneyburn Juniors	1956-57	Haddington Athletic
1924-25	Newtongrange Star	1939-40	Armadale Thistle	1957-58	Bo'ness United
1925-26	Newtongrange Star	1940-41	Armadale Thistle	1958-59	Newtongrange Star
1926-27	Newtongrange Star	*1941-45*	*No Competition*	1959-60	Loanhead Mayflower
1927-28	Dunbar United	1945-46	Fauldhouse United	1960-61	Dalkeith Thistle
1928-29	Tranent Juniors	1946-47	Bo'ness United	1961-62	Dunbar United
1929-30	Newtongrange Star	1947-48	Bo'ness United	1962-63	Sauchie Juniors
1930-31	Tranent Juniors	1948-49	Bo'ness United	1963-64	Bonnyrigg Rose Athlet
1931-32	Dalkeith Thistle	1949-50	Armadale Thistle	1964-65	Linlithgow Rose
1932-33	Newtongrange Star	1950-51	Newtongrange Star	1965-66	Linlithgow Rose
1933-34	Blackburn Athletic	1951-52	Newtongrange Star	1966-67	Linlithgow Rose
1934-35	Stoneyburn Juniors	1952-53	Armadale Thistle	1967-68	Linlithgow Rose
1935-36	Bo'ness Cadora	1953-54	Arniston Rangers		
1936-37	Tranent Juniors	1954-55	Newtongrange Star		

Summary: *11 - Newtongrange Star; 4 - Armadale Thistle, Bo'ness United, Linlithgow Rose; 3 - Dalkeith Thistle, Tranent Juniors; 2 - Bonnyrigg Rose Athletic, Dunbar United, Stoneyburn Junior; 1 - Arniston Rangers, Blackburn Athletic, Bo'ness Cadora, Fauldhouse United, Haddington Athletic, Loanhead Mayflower, Sauchie Juniors.*

Elder Cottage Hospital Cup

1922-23	Benburb	1930-31	Yoker Athletic	1938-39	Benburb
1923-24	St. Anthony's	1931-32	Clydebank Juniors	1939-40	Yoker Athletic
1924-25	Benburb	1932-33	Clydebank Juniors	*1940-44*	*No Competition*
1925-26	Shawfield	1933-34	Clydebank Juniors	1944-45	St. Anthony's
1926-27	Shawfield	1934-35	Benburb	1945-46	Renfrew
1927-28	Clydebank Juniors	1935-36	St. Anthony's	1946-47	Pollok
1928-29	Yoker Athletic	1936-37	Yoker Athletic		
1929-30	Yoker Athletic	1937-38	Yoker Athletic		

Erskine Charity Cup

1949-50	Shawfield	1964-65	Benburb	1979-80	Vale of Clyde
1950-51	St. Anthony's	1965-66	Johnstone Burgh	1980-81	Port Glasgow Juniors
1951-52	St. Anthony's	1966-67	Benburb	1981-82	St. Roch's
1952-53	Benburb	1967-68	Johnstone Burgh	1982-83	Arthurlie
1953-54	Pollok	1968-69	Rutherglen Glencairn	1983-84	Shettleston
1954-55	Arthurlie	1969-70	Vale of Leven	1984-85	Shettleston
1955-56	Renfrew	1970-71	Port Glasgow Juniors	1985-86	Shettleston
1956-57	Benburb	1971-72	Pollok	1986-87	Benburb
1957-58	Pollok	1972-73	Pollok	1987-88	Port Glasgow Juniors
1958-59	Yoker Ath/Johnstone B.	1973-74	Johnstone Burgh	1988-89	Arthurlie
1959-60	Greenock Juniors	1974-75	Renfrew	1989-90	Vale of Clyde
1960-61	Renfrew	1975-76	Arthurlie	1990-91	Neilston Juniors
1961-62	Benburb	1976-77	St. Anthony's	1991-92	Johnstone Burgh
1962-63	Renfrew	1977-78	Arthurlie	1992-93	Arthurlie
1963-64	Johnstone Burgh	1978-79	Benburb	1993-94	Neilston Juniors

Summary: *7 - Benburb; 6 - Arthurlie, Johnstone Burgh*; 4 - Pollok, Renfrew; 3 - Port Glasgow Juniors, St. Anthony's, Shettleston; 2 - Neilston Juniors, Vale of Clyde; 1 - Greenock Juniors, Rutherglen Glencairn, St. Roch's, Shawfield, Vale of Leven, Yoker Athletic.   * = one shared.*

Evening Times Cup Winners Cup
(Central League Championship until 1978-79)

31-32	Shawfield	1954-55	Ashfield	1977-78	Cumbernauld United
32-33	Petershill	1955-56	Petershill	1978-79	Pollok
33-34	Rutherglen Glencairn	1956-57	Kilsyth Rangers	1979-80	Blantyre Victoria
34-35	Clydebank Juniors	1957-58	Duntocher Hibs	1980-81	Pollok
35-36	Blantyre Victoria	1958-59	Johnstone Burgh	1981-82	Lesmahagow
36-37	Arthurlie	1959-60	Baillieston	1982-83	East Kilbride Thistle
37-38	Morton Juniors	1960-61	Greenock Juniors	1983-84	Pollok
38-39	Petershill	1961-62	Kirkintilloch Rob Roy	1984-85	Pollok
39-40	Petershill	1962-63	Kirkintilloch Rob Roy	1985-86	Pollok
40-41	Clydebank Juniors	1963-64	Petershill	1986-87	Arthurlie
41-42	Clydebank Juniors	1964-65	Johnstone Burgh	1987-88	Pollok
42-43	Rutherglen Glencairn	1965-66	Greenock Juniors	1988-89	Arthurlie
43-44	St. Roch's	1966-67	Rutherglen Glencairn	1989-90	Vale of Clyde
44-45	Clydebank Juniors	1967-68	Johnstone Burgh	1990-91	Cambuslang Rangers
45-46	Arthurlie	1968-69	Petershill	1991-92	Petershill
46-47	Vale of Leven	1969-70	Vale of Leven	1992-93	Lesmahagow
47-48	Kilsyth Rangers	1970-71	Cambuslang Rangers	1993-94	Arthurlie
48-49	Blantyre Celtic	1971-72	Cambuslang Rangers	1994-95	*No Competition*
49-50	Clydebank Juniors	1972-73	Cambuslang Rangers	1995-96	Maryhill
50-51	Duntocher Hibs	1973-74	Cambuslang Rangers	1996-97	Maryhill
51-52	Petershill	1974-75	East Kilbride Thistle	1997-98	Maryhill
52-53	Ashfield	1975-76	East Kilbride Thistle	1998-99	Dunipace Juniors
53-54	Kilsyth Rangers	1976-77	Glasgow Perthshire	1999-00	Port Glasgow Juniors

Summary: 8 - Petershill; 6 - Arthurlie, Pollok; 5 - Cambuslang Rangers, Clydebank Juniors; 3 - East Kilbride Thistle, Johnstone Burgh, Kilsyth Rangers, Maryhill, Rutherglen Glencairn; 2 - Ashfield, Blantyre Victoria, Duntocher Hibs, Greenock Juniors, Kirkintilloch Rob Roy, Lesmahagow, Vale of Leven; 1 - Baillieston, Blantyre Celtic, Cumbernauld United, Dunipace Juniors, Glasgow Perthshire, Morton Juniors, Port Glasgow Juniors, St. Roch's, Shawfield Juniors, Vale of Clyde.

Express Cup
(For member clubs of Fife Junior F.A.)

58-59	St. Andrews United	1961-62	Newburgh	1964-65	Nairn Thistle
59-60	Lochgelly Albert	1962-63	Tulliallan Thistle	1965-66	Dundonald Bluebell
60-61	Lochore Welfare	1963-64	Lochore Welfare	1966-67	Newburgh

Falkirk & District Junior Cup
(Stirlingshire Junior F.A. member clubs)

00-01	Grange Rovers	1913-14	Grange Rovers	1931-32	Camelon Juniors
01-02	Dunipace Juniors	1914-20	*No Competition*	1932-33	St. Ninians Thistle
02-03	Dunipace Juniors	1920-21	Dunipace Juniors	1933-34	Camelon Juniors
03-04	Dunipace Juniors	1921-22	Dunipace Juniors	1934-35	Camelon Juniors
04-05	Falkirk Juniors	1922-23	Dunipace Juniors	1935-36	St. Ninians Thistle
05-06	Dunipace Juniors	1923-24	Denny Hibs	1936-37	Banknock
06-07	Stenhousemuir Hearts	1924-25	Grange Rovers	1937-38	Forth Rangers
07-08	Forth Rangers	1925-26	Camelon Juniors	1938-39	Camelon Juniors
08-09	Dunipace Juniors	1926-27	*Not Completed*	1939-55	*No Competition*
09-10	Grange Rovers	1927-28	Dunipace Juniors	1955-56	Kilsyth Rangers
10-11	Denny Athletic	1928-29	Grange Rovers	1956-57	Kilsyth Rangers
11-12	Dunipace Juniors	1929-30	Dunipace Juniors	1957-58	Kilsyth Rangers
12-13	Dunipace Juniors	1930-31	Denny Hibs		

Summary: 12 - Dunipace Juniors; 5 - Camelon Juniors, Grange Rovers; 3 - Kilsyth Rangers; Denny Hibs, Forth Rangers, St. Ninians Thistle; 1 - Banknock, Denny Athletic, Falkirk Juniors, Stenhousemuir Hearts.

Fife & Lothians Cup
(Current trophy is the former Roseberry Junior Cup)

1968-69	Linlithgow Rose	1979-80	Linlithgow Rose	1990-91	Newtongrange Star
1969-70	Whitburn	1980-81	Penicuik Athletic	1991-92	Whitburn
1970-71	Camelon Juniors	1981-82	Bonnyrigg Rose Athletic	1992-93	Fauldhouse United
1971-72	Glenrothes	1982-83	Oakley United	1993-94	Bo'ness United
1972-73	Linlithgow Rose	1983-84	Linlithgow Rose	1994-95	St. Andrews United
1973-74	Linlithgow Rose	1984-85	Linlithgow Rose	1995-96	Hill o' Beath Hawthorn
1974-75	Linlithgow Rose	1985-86	Linlithgow Rose	1996-97	Bo'ness United
1975-76	Arniston Rangers	1986-87	Whitburn	1997-98	Arniston Rangers
1976-77	Penicuik Athletic	1987-88	Newtongrange Star	1998-99	Whitburn
1977-78	Newtongrange Star	1988-89	Edinburgh United	1999-00	Linlithgow Rose
1978-79	Linlithgow Rose	1989-90	Newtongrange Star		

Summary: *10 - Linlithgow Rose; 4 - Newtongrange Star, Whitburn; 2 - Arniston Rangers, Bo'ness United, Penicuik Athletic; 1 - Bonnyrigg Rose Athletic, Camelon Juniors, Edinburgh United, Fauldhouse, Glenrothes, Hill o' Beath Hawthorn, St. Andrews United.*

Fife County League
(Formerly the Fife Junior League)

1913-14	Windygates Rangers	1931-32	Rosslyn Juniors	1950-51	Steelend Victoria
1914-15	Glencraig Celtic	1932-33	Rosslyn Juniors	1951-52	Dundonald Bluebell
1915-16	Glencraig Celtic	1933-34	Inverkeithing Juniors	1952-53	Thornton Hibs
1916-17	Denbeath Star	1934-35	Bowhill Rovers	1953-54	Lochore Welfare
1917-18	Denbeath Star	1935-36	Hearts of Beath	1954-55	Lochgelly Albert
1918-19	*No Competition*	1936-37	Blairhall Colliery	1955-56	Lochore Welfare
1919-20	Inverkeithing Juniors	1937-38	East: Thornton Juniors	1956-57	Dundonald Bluebell
1920-21	Kingseat Juniors		West: Lochgelly Albert	1957-58	Dundonald Bluebell
1921-22	Kingseat Juniors	1938-39	East: Rosslyn Juniors	1958-59	Thornton Hibs
1922-23	Dunnikier Juniors		West: Lochore Welfare	1959-60	St. Andrews United
1923-24	East Fife Juniors	1939-40	East: Dunnikier Juniors	1960-61	St. Andrews United
1924-25	Newburgh West End		West: Hearts of Beath	1961-62	Lochore Welfare
1925-26	Anstruther Rangers	1940-41	Lochgelly Violet	1962-63	Lochore Welfare
1926-27	St. Andrews United	*1941-46*	*No Competition*	1963-64	Lochore Welfare
1927-28	St. Andrews United	1946-47	Lochgelly Albert	1964-65	St. Andrews United
1928-29	St. Andrews United	1947-48	Lochore Welfare	1965-66	Glenrothes
1929-30	Rosslyn Juniors	1948-49	Lochgelly Albert	1966-67	Glenrothes
1930-31	Bowhill Rovers	1949-50	Rosyth Recreation	1967-68	Glenrothes

Summary: *7 - Lochore Welfare; 6 - St. Andrews United; 4 - Lochgelly Albert, Rosslyn Juniors; 3 - Dundonald Bluebell, Glenrothes; 2 - Bowhill Rovers, Denbeath Star, Dunnikier Juniors, Glencraig Celtic, Hearts of Beath, Inverkeithing Juniors, Kingseat Juniors, Thornton Hibs; 1 - Anstruther Rangers, Blairhall Colliery, East Fife Juniors, Lochgelly Violet, Newburgh West End, Rosyth Recreation, Steelend Victoria, Thornton Juniors, Windygates Rangers.*

Fife Cup
(Currently the Peddie Smith Malocco Cup)

1885-86	Kirkcaldy Albion	1898-99	Leven Thistle	1911-12	Denbeath Star
1886-87	Raith Rovers	1899-00	Raith Athletic	1912-13	Denbeath Star
1887-88	Raith Rovers	1900-01	Buckhaven United	1913-14	Hearts of Beath
1888-89	Raith Rovers	*1901-02*	*Not Completed*	1914-15	Glencraig Celtic
1889-90	Kirkcaldy Albion	1902-03	Vale of Wemyss	1915-16	Hearts of Beath
1890-91	Kirkcaldy Albion	1903-04	Kelty Rangers	1916-17	Hearts of Beath
1891-92	Pathhead United	1904-05	Dunnikier Athletic	*1917-19*	*No Competition*
1892-93	Kinghorn	1905-06	Bowhill Thistle	1919-20	Denbeath Star
1893-94	Dunfermline Ath. Jnrs	1906-07	Pathhead United	1920-21	Hearts of Beath
1894-95	Dunfermline Juniors	1907-08	Leslie Hearts	1921-22	Rosslyn Juniors
1895-96	Methil Rovers	1908-09	Glencraig Celtic	1922-23	Dunnikier Juniors
1896-97	Methil Rovers	1909-10	Glencraig Celtic	1923-24	East Fife Juniors
1897-98	Raith Athletic	1910-11	Glencraig Celtic	1924-25	Dunnikier Juniors

25-26	Inverkeithing Juniors	1953-54	Lochgelly Albert	1977-78	Lochgelly Albert
26-27	St. Andrews United	1954-55	Dundonald Bluebell	1978-79	Glenrothes
27-28	St. Andrews United	1955-56	Crossgates Primrose	1979-80	Lochore Welfare
28-29	St. Andrews United	1956-57	Lochgelly Albert	1980-81	Jubilee Athletic
29-30	Rosslyn Juniors	1957-58	Lochgelly Albert	1981-82	Leven Juniors
30-31	Wellesley	1958-59	Thornton Hibs	1982-83	Kelty Hearts
31-32	Bowhill Rovers	1959-60	St. Andrews United	1983-84	Kelty Hearts
32-33	Newburgh West End	1960-61	Lochore Welfare	1984-85	Kelty Hearts
33-34	Bowhill Rovers	1961-62	Newburgh	1985-86	Glenrothes
34-35	Lochgelly Albert	1962-63	Blairhall Colliery	1986-87	Kelty Hearts
35-36	Thornton Hibs	1963-64	Lochore Welfare	1987-88	Oakley United
36-37	Bowhill Rovers	1964-65	Newburgh	1988-89	St. Andrews United
37-38	Lochore Welfare	1965-66	St. Andrews United	1989-90	St. Andrews United
38-39	Kelty Our Boys	1966-67	Newburgh	1990-91	Hill o' Beath Hawthorn
39-40	Hearts of Beath	1967-68	Glenrothes	1991-92	Dundonald Bluebell
40-41	Lochgelly Albert	1968-69	Frances Colliery	1992-93	Kelty Hearts
41-46	*No Competition*	1969-70	Newburgh	1993-94	Hill o' Beath Hawthorn
46-47	Steelend Victoria	1970-71	Glenrothes	1994-95	Hill o' Beath Hawthorn
47-48	Crossgates Primrose	1971-72	Glenrothes	1995-96	Hill o' Beath Hawthorn
48-49	Rosyth Recreation	1972-73	Glenrothes	1996-97	Thornton Hibs
49-50	Rosyth Recreation	1973-74	Newburgh	1997-98	Glenrothes
50-51	Lochore Welfare	1974-75	Thornton Hibs	1998-99	Thornton Hibs
51-52	Valleyfield	1975-76	Glenrothes	1999-00	Glenrothes
52-53	Newburgh	1976-77	Glenrothes		

Summary: 10 - Glenrothes; 7 - St. Andrews United; 6 - Lochgelly Albert, Newburgh; 5 - Hearts of Beath, Kelty Hearts, Lochore Welfare, Thornton Hibs; 4 - Glencraig Celtic, Hill o' Beath Hawthorn; 3 - Bowhill Rovers, Denbeath Star, Kirkcaldy Albion, Raith Rovers; 2 - Crossgates Primrose, Dundonald Bluebell, Dunnikier Juniors, Methil Rovers, Pathhead United, Raith Athletic, Rosslyn Juniors, Rosyth Recreation; 1 - Blairhall Colliery, Bowhill Thistle, Buckhaven United, Dunfermline Juniors, Dunfermline Athletic Juniors, Dunnikier Athletic, East Fife Juniors, Frances Colliery, Inverkeithing Juniors, Jubilee Athletic, Kelty Our Boys, Kelty Rangers, Kinghorn, Leslie Hearts, Leven Juniors, Leven Thistle, Newburgh West End, Oakley United, Steelend Victoria, Vale of Wemyss, Valleyfield, Wellesley.

Fife Drybrough Cup

73-74	Lochgelly Albert	1978-79	Glenrothes	1983-84	Glenrothes
74-75	Glenrothes	1979-80	Halbeath	1984-85	Glenrothes
75-76	Lochgelly Albert	1980-81	Oakley United	1985-86	Hill o' Beath Hawthorn
76-77	Oakley United	1981-82	Kelty Hearts		
77-78	Thornton Hibs	1982-83	Oakley United		

Fife Regional League

68-69	Thornton Hibs	1979-80	Oakley United	1990-91	Kelty Hearts
69-70	Glenrothes	1980-81	Halbeath	1991-92	Kelty Hearts
70-71	Glenrothes	1981-82	Leven Juniors	1992-93	Kelty Hearts
71-72	Oakley United	1982-83	Dundonald Bluebell	1993-94	Hill o' Beath Hawthorn
72-73	Newburgh	1983-84	Glenrothes	1994-95	Hill o' Beath Hawthorn
73-74	Lochgelly Albert	1984-85	Glenrothes	1995-96	Hill o' Beath Hawthorn
74-75	Glenrothes	1985-86	Oakley United	1996-97	Kelty Hearts
75-76	Glenrothes	1986-87	Hill o' Beath Hawthorn	1997-98	Hill o' Beath Hawthorn
76-77	Newburgh	1987-88	Oakley United	1998-99	Kelty Hearts
77-78	Glenrothes	1988-89	Hill o' Beath Hawthorn	1999-00	Hill o' Beath Hawthorn
78-79	Oakley United	1989-90	St. Andrews United		

Summary: 7 - Glenrothes, Hill o' Beath Hawthorn; 5 - Kelty Hearts, Oakley United; 2 - Newburgh; 1 - Dundonald Bluebell, Halbeath, Leven Juniors, Lochgelly Albert, St. Andrews United, Thornton Hibs.

Fife Regional League - Division 2

1978-79	Tulliallan Thistle	1979-80	Kirkcaldy YMCA

Fife Shield
(Also known as the Dunfermline Shield)

1893-94	Dunfermline Ath. Juniors	1906-07	Sauchie	1920-21	Hearts of Beath
1894-95	Dunfermline Ath. Juniors	1907-08	Alva Albion Rangers	1921-22	Rosslyn Juniors
1895-96	Dunfermline Ath. Juniors	1908-09	Glencraig Celtic	1922-23	Dunnikier Juniors
1896-97	Leven Thistle	1909-10	Glencraig Celtic	1923-24	Inverkeithing Juniors
1897-98	Dunfermline Ath. Juniors	1910-11	Kelty Rangers	1924-25	East Fife Juniors
1898-99	Dunfermline Ath. Juniors	1911-12	Glencraig Celtic	1925-26	Rosslyn Juniors
1899-00		1912-13	Denbeath Star	1926-27	St. Andrews United
1900-01	Buckhaven United	1913-14	Leslie Hearts	1927-28	St. Andrews United
1901-02	Buckhaven United	1914-15	Denbeath Star	1928-29	St. Andrews Athletic
1902-03	Lassodie	1915-16	Glencraig Celtic	1929-30	Denbeath Star
1903-04	Kelty Rangers	1916-17	Denbeath Star	1930-31	Wellesley
1904-05		*1917-19*	*No Competition*	1931-32	Dunnikier Juniors
1905-06	Lochgelly Rangers	1919-20	Inverkeithing Juniors	1932-33	Rosslyn Juniors

Summary: *5 - Dunfermline Athletic Juniors; 4 - Denbeath Star, Glencraig Celtic; 3 - Rosslyn Juniors; 2 - Buckhaven United, Dunnikier Juniors, Inverkeithing Juniors, Kelty Rangers, St. Andrews United; 1 - Alva Albion Rangers, East Fife Juniors, Hearts of Beath, Lassodie, Leslie Hearts, Leven Thistle, Lochgelly Rangers, St. Andrews Athletic, Sauchie, Wellesley.*

Findlay & Co. Cup
(See under Currie Cup)

Forfar & District Junior Charity Cup

1902-03	Forfar West End	1920-21	Forfar West End	1936-37	Forfar East End
1903-04		1921-22	Forfar Central	1937-38	Forfar East End
1904-05		1922-23	Forfar Celtic	1938-39	Kirriemuir Thistle
1905-06		1923-24	Forfar North End	1939-40	Forfar Celtic
1906-07	Forfar West End	1924-25	Forfar Celtic	*1940-48*	*No Competition*
1907-08		1925-26	Forfar North End	1948-49	Forfar Celtic
1908-09	Forfar West End	1926-27	Forfar North End	1949-50	Forfar Celtic
1909-10	Forfar West End	1927-28	Forfar Celtic	1950-51	Forfar Celtic
1910-11	Forfar West End	1928-29	Arbroath Victoria	1951-52	Forfar Celtic
1911-12	Forfar Celtic	1929-30	Forfar Celtic	1952-53	Forfar East End
1912-13		1930-31	Forfar East End	1953-54	Forfar East End
1913-14	Forfar East End	1931-32	Forfar East End	1954-55	
1914-15		1932-33	Kirriemuir Thistle	1955-56	Forfar Celtic
1915-16		1933-34	Forfar West End	1956-57	Forfar Celtic
1916-19	*No Competition*	1934-35	Forfar Celtic	1957-58	Forfar West End
1919-20	Forfar Celtic	1935-36	Forfar East End	1958-59	Forfar Celtic

Summary: *15 - Forfar Celtic; 8 - Forfar East End, Forfar West End; 3 - Forfar North End; 2 - Kirriemuir Thistle; 1 - Arbroath Victoria, Forfar Central.*

Forfar & District Cup
(For member clubs of the Angus Junior F.A.)

1892-93	Forfar East End	1898-99		1904-05	Brechin Harp
1893-94		1899-00		1905-06	Brechin Harp
1894-95		1900-01	Forfar East End	1906-07	Forfar Celtic
1895-96		1901-02	Forfar Corinthians	1907-08	Forfar West End
1896-97	Arbroath Dauntless	1902-03	Forfar West End	1908-09	Forfar West End
1897-98	Arbroath Dauntless	1903-04		1909-10	

10-11	1926-27 Forfar West End	1939-47 *No Competition*
11-12 Brechin Rovers	1927-28 Forfar East End	1947-48 Montrose Roselea
12-13 Forfar North End	1928-29 Arbroath Victoria	1948-49 Forfar Celtic
13-14 Arbroath Parkhead	1929-30 Forfar West End	1949-50 Brechin Renton
14-15 Forfar East End	1930-31 Forfar Celtic	1950-51 Kirriemuir Thistle
15-19 No Competition	1931-32 Arbroath Woodside	1951-52 Arbroath Victoria
19-20 Arbroath Comrades	1932-33 Arbroath Ardenlea	1952-53 Coupar Angus
20-21 Forfar East End	1933-34 Forfar Celtic	1953-54 Alyth United
21-22 Forfar Celtic	1934-35 Forfar West End	1954-55 Coupar Angus
22-23 Forfar Celtic	1935-36 Forfar West End	1955-56 Forfar West End
23-24 Forfar East End	1936-37 Brechin Victoria	1956-57 Coupar Angus
24-25 Brechin Victoria	1937-38 Alyth United	1957-58 Kirriemuir Thistle
25-26 Forfar West End	1938-39 Kirriemuir Thistle	

ummary: *9 - Forfar West End; 6 - Forfar Celtic, Forfar East End; 3 - Coupar Angus, Kirriemuir istle; 2 - Alyth United, Arbroath Dauntless, Arbroath Victoria, Brechin Harp, Brechin Victoria; - Arbroath Ardenlea, Arbroath Comrades, Arbroath Parkhead, Arbroath Woodside, Brechin Renton, echin Rovers, Forfar Corinthians, Forfar North End, Montrose Roselea.*

Forfar & Distrct League
(See under Angus Junior League)

Forfar Businessman's Trophy
(For member clubs of the Angus Junior F.A.)

61-62 Kirriemuir Thistle	1965-66 Arbroath Victoria	1969-70 Brechin Victoria
62-63 Kirriemuir Thistle	1966-67 Forfar Celtic	1970-71 Arbroath Victoria
63-64 Alyth United	1967-68 Alyth United	1971-72 Arbroath Victoria
64-65 Arbroath Victoria	1968-69 Forfar Celtic	1972-73 Kirriemuir Thistle

Fofarshire Junior Consolation Cup
(Also known as the Barrie Consolation Cup)

06-07 Lochee Harp	1929-30 Forfar West End	1950-51 Osborne
07-08 Arbroath Fairfield	1930-31 Osborne	1951-52 Carnoustie Panmure
08-09 Dundee West End	1931-32 East Craigie	1952-53 Stobswell
09-10 Dundee North End	1932-33 Broughty Athletic	1953-54 Dundee North End
10-11 Fairfield (Dundee)	1933-34 Dundee North End	1954-55 Carnoustie Panmure
11-12 Fairfield (Dundee)	1934-35 Stobswell	1955-56 Arnot
12-13 Fairfield (Dundee)	1935-36 Broughty Athletic	1956-57 Dundee St. Joseph's
13-14 Fairfield (Dundee)	1936-37 Dundee Violet	1957-58 Montrose Roselea
14-15 Stobswell	1937-38 Arnot	1958-59 Kirriemuir Thistle
15-16 Dundee St. Joseph's	1938-39 Anchorage	1959-60 Arbroath Victoria
16-19 No Competition	1939-40 Dundee North End	1960-61 Broughty Athletic
19-20 East Craigie	1940-41 Dundee North End	1961-62 Dundee St. Joseph's
20-21 Dundee North End	1941-42 Arnot	1962-63 Kirriemuir Thistle
21-22 Dundee Celtic	1942-43 Anchorage	1963-64 Carnoustie Panmure
22-23 Osborne	1943-44 Arnot	1964-65 Carnoustie Panmure
23-24 Stobswell	1944-45 Stobswell	1965-66 Downfield
24-25 Stobswell	1945-46 Stobswell	1966-67 Lochee Harp
25-26 Lochee United	1946-47 Dundee North End	1967-68 Broughty Athletic
26-27 Logie	1947-48 Elmwood	
27-28 East Craigie	1948-49 Downfield	
28-29 Dundee Violet	1949-50 Dundee North End	

ummary: *8 - Dundee North End; 7 - Stobswell; 4 - Arnot, Broughty Athletic, Carnoustie Panmure, irfield; 3 - Dundee St. Joseph's, East Craigie, Osborne; 2 - Anchorage, Downfield, Dundee Violet, rriemuir Thistle, Lochee Harp; 1 - Arbroath Fairfield, Arbroath Victoria, Dundee Celtic, Dundee West d, Elmwood, Forfar West End, Lochee United, Logie, Montrose Roselea.*

Forfarshire Junior Cup
(Also known as the Inglis Cup)

1898-99	Dundee Violet	1923-24	Lochee United	1946-47	Stobswell
1899-00	East Craigie	1924-25	Arbroath Woodside	1947-48	Dundee Violet
1900-01	Arbroath Rovers	1925-26	Stobswell	1948-49	Forfar Celtic
1901-02	Dundee Violet	1926-27	Lochee Harp	1949-50	Carnoustie Panmure
1902-03	Forfar West End	1927-28	Dundee Violet	1950-51	Carnoustie Panmure
1903-04	St. Leonard's	1928-29	Dundee St. Joseph's	1951-52	Lochee Harp
1904-05	Dundee St. Joseph's	1929-30	Lochee Central	1952-53	Carnoustie Panmure
1905-06	Dundee Violet	1930-31	Forfar East End	1953-54	Arbroath Victoria
1906-07	Forfar West End	1931-32	Dundee Celtic	1954-55	Dundee Violet
1907-08	Lochee Harp	1932-33	Dundee North End	1955-56	Carnoustie Panmure
1908-09	Dundee Violet	1933-34	Arbroath Victoria	1956-57	Lochee Harp
1909-10	Lochee Harp	1934-35	Dundee Violet	1957-58	Dundee North End
1910-11	Dundee St. Joseph's	1935-36	Lochee Harp	1958-59	Dundee North End
1911-12	Lochee Central	1936-37	Lochee Harp	1959-60	Dundee North End
1912-13	Arnot	1937-38	Forfar Celtic	1960-61	Lochee Harp
1913-14	Arbroath Ardenlea	1938-39	Dundee Violet	1961-62	Kirriemuir Thistle
1914-15	East Craigie	1939-40	Lochee Harp	1962-63	Carnoustie Panmure
1915-16	Dundee Violet	1940-41	Forfar Celtic	1963-64	Downfield
1916-19	*No Competition*	1941-42	Arbroath Victoria	1964-65	Lochee United
1919-20	Forfar North End	1942-43	Lochee Harp	1965-66	Dundee Violet
1920-21	Fairfield	1943-44	Carnoustie Panmure	1966-67	Dundee St. Joseph's
1921-22	Osborne	1944-45	Anchorage	1967-68	Osborne
1922-23	Lochee Central	1945-46	Dundee North End		

Summary: *11 - Dundee Violet, Lochee Harp; 6 - Carnoustie Panmure; 5 - Dundee North End; 4 - Dundee St. Joseph's; 3 - Arbroath Victoria, Forfar Celtic, Lochee Central; 2 - East Craigie, Forfar West End, Osborne, Stobswell; 1 - Anchorage, Arbroath Ardenlea, Arbroath Rovers, Arbroath Woodside, Arnot, Downfield, Dundee Celtic, Fairfield, Forfar East End, Forfar North End, Kirriemuir Thistle, Lochee United, St. Leonard's.*

Glasgow & District Intermediate Cup

1927-28	Ashfield	1929-30	St. Roch's
1928-29	Clydebank Juniors	1930-31	Strathclyde

Glasgow Intermediate Consolation Cup

1927-28	Clydebank Juniors	1929-30	Yoker Athletic
1928-29	Glasgow Perthshire	1930-31	Blantyre Celtic

Glasgow Intermediate North-Eastern Cup

1927-28	Glasgow Perthshire	1929-30	Pollok
1928-29	Bridgeton Waverley	1930-31	St. Roch's

Glasgow Charity Cup

1889-90	Benburb	1900-01	Glasgow Perthshire	1911-12	Parkhead
1890-91	Vale of Clyde	1901-02	Glasgow Perthshire	1912-13	Parkhead
1891-92	Minerva	1902-03	Petershill	1913-14	Maryhill
1892-93	Ashfield	1903-04	Maryhill	1914-15	Cambuslang Rangers
1893-94	Parkhead	1904-05	Maryhill	1915-16	Petershill
1894-95	Ashfield	1905-06	Ashfield	1916-17	Cambuslang Rangers
1895-96	Jordanhill	1906-07	Maryhill	1917-18	St. Anthony's
1896-97	Glasgow Perthshire	1907-08	Ashfield	1918-19	St. Anthony's
1897-98	Ashfield	1908-09	Ashfield	1919-20	Petershill
1898-99	Ashfield	1909-10	Cambuslang Rangers	1920-21	St. Anthony's
1899-00	Maryhill	1910-11	Ashfield	1921-22	Cambuslang Rangers

22-23	St. Anthony's	1934-35	Glasgow Perthshire
23-24	Rutherglen Glencairn	1935-36	Glasgow Perthshire
24-25	Strathclyde	1936-37	Petershill
25-26	St. Roch's	1937-38	Shettleston
26-27	Maryhill	1938-39	Strathclyde
27-28	Maryhill	1939-40	Petershill
28-29	Baillieston	1940-41	Strathclyde
29-30	Shettleston	1941-42	Rutherglen Glencairn
30-31	Yoker Athletic	1942-43	Rutherglen Glencairn
31-32	Benburb	1943-44	Rutherglen Glencairn
32-33	Rutherglen Glencairn	1944-45	Maryhill Harp
33-34	Shawfield	1945-46	Petershill

1946-47	Pollok
1947-48	Dennistoun Waverley
1948-49	St. Roch's
1949-50	St. Roch's
1950-51	Ashfield
1951-52	Parkhead
1952-53	Glasgow Perthshire
1953-54	St. Roch's
1954-55	Ashfield
1955-56	Ashfield
1956-57	Shettleston
1957-58	Pollok

Summary: *11 - Ashfield; 7 - Maryhill; 6 - Glasgow Perthshire, Petershill; 5 - Rutherglen Glencairn; - Cambuslang Rangers, Parkhead, St. Anthony's, St. Roch's; 3 - Shettleston, Strathclyde; - Benburb, Pollok; 1 - Baillieston, Dennistoun Waverley, Jordanhill, Maryhill Harp, Minerva, Shawfield, Vale of Clyde, Yoker Athletic.*

Glasgow Eastern Charity Cup

24-25	Strathclyde	1937-38	Strathclyde
25-26	Strathclyde	1938-39	Vale of Clyde
26-27	Shettleston	1939-40	Strathclyde
27-28	Baillieston	1940-41	*No Competition*
28-29	Baillieston	1941-42	Parkhead
29-30	Strathclyde	1942-43	Bridgeton Waverley
30-31	Bridgeton Waverley	1943-44	Strathclyde
31-32	Strathclyde	1944-45	Parkhead
32-33	Cambuslang Rangers	1945-46	Strathclyde
33-34	Shawfield	1946-47	Strathclyde
34-35	Vale of Clyde	1947-48	Bridgeton Waverley
35-36	Bridgeton Waverley	1948-49	Rutherglen Glencairn
36-37	Strathclyde	1949-50	Shettleston

1950-51	Shawfield
1951-52	Shettleston
1952-53	Cambuslang Rangers
1953-54	Parkhead
1954-55	Baillieston
1955-56	Baillieston
1956-57	Shawfield
1957-58	Baillieston
1958-59	Parkhead
1959-60	Shettleston
1960-61	Baillieston
1961-62	Strathclyde
1962-63	Vale of Clyde

Summary: *11 – Strathclyde; 6 – Baillieston; 4 – Bridgeton Waverley, Parkhead, Shettleston; – Shawfield, Vale of Clyde; 2 – Cambuslang Rangers; 1 – Rutherglen Glencairn.*

Glasgow Junior Cup

84-85	Wellpark	1908-09	Ashfield
85-86	Govanhill	1909-10	Ashfield
86-87	Fairfield	1910-11	Strathclyde
87-88	Westburn	1911-12	Cambuslang Rangers
88-89	Possilpark	1912-13	Petershill
89-90	Benburb	1913-14	Glasgow Perthshire
90-91	Minerva	1914-15	Ashfield
91-92	Vale of Clyde	1915-16	Parkhead
92-93	Vale of Clyde	1916-17	Benburb
93-94	Ashfield	1917-18	Vale of Clyde
94-95	Jordanhill	1918-19	St. Anthony's
95-96	Strathclyde	1919-20	Benburb
96-97	Cambuslang Hibs	1920-21	Cambuslang Rangers
97-98	Vale of Clyde	1921-22	St. Anthony's
98-99	Parkhead	1922-23	Bellshill Athletic
99-00	Rutherglen Glencairn	1923-24	Rutherglen Glencairn
00-01	Parkhead	1924-25	Parkhead
01-02	Parkhead	1925-26	Ashfield
02-03	Parkhead	1926-27	Cambuslang Rangers
03-04	Petershill	1927-28	Kilsyth Emmet
04-05	Maryhill	1928-29	Carluke Rovers
05-06	Ashfield	1929-30	Maryhill Hibs
06-07	Ashfield	1930-31	Kilsyth Rangers
07-08	Ashfield	1931-32	Shawfield Juniors

1932-33	Cambuslang Rangers
1933-34	Petershill
1934-35	Rutherglen Glencairn
1935-36	Strathclyde
1936-37	Strathclyde
1937-38	Rutherglen Glencairn
1938-39	Shawfield
1939-40	Benburb
1940-41	St. Anthony's
1941-42	Pollok
1942-43	Rutherglen Glencairn
1943-44	Petershill
1944-45	Maryhill
1945-46	St. Anthony's
1946-47	Cambuslang Rangers
1947-48	Strathclyde
1948-49	Benburb
1949-50	Petershill
1950-51	Parkhead
1951-52	Ashfield
1952-53	Ashfield
1953-54	Pollok
1954-55	Petershill
1955-56	Parkhead

CONTINUED OVERLEAF

the winners

1956-57	Parkhead	1961-62	Pollok	1966-67	Cambuslang Rangers
1957-58	Shettleston	1962-63	Ashfield	1967-68	Shettleston
1958-59	Shettleston	1963-64	Cambuslang Rangers		
1959-60	Shettleston	1964-65	Petershill		
1960-61	Petershill	1965-66	Cambuslang Rangers		

Summary: *11 - Ashfield; 9 - Parkhead; 8 - Cambuslang Rangers, Petershill; 5 - Benburb, Rutherglen Glencairn, Strathclyde; 4 - St. Anthony's, Shettleston, Vale of Clyde; 3 - Pollok; 2 - Maryhill, Shawfield; 1 - Bellshill Athletic, Cambuslang Hibs, Carluke Rovers, Fairfield, Glasgow perthshire, Govanhill, Jordanhill, Kilsyth Emmet, Kilsyth Rangers, Maryhill Hibs, Minerva, Possilpark, Wellpark, Westburn.*

Glasgow Junior Consolation Cup

1903-04	Rockbank	1915-16	Cambuslang Rangers	1927-28	Burnbank Athletic
1904-05	Co-operative United	1916-17	Cambuslang Rangers	1928-29	Royal Albert
1905-06	Postal Athletic	1917-18	Pollok	1929-31	No Competition
1906-07	Queen's Park Hampden XI	1918-19	Pollok	1931-32	Ashfield
1907-08	Petershill	1919-20	Glasgow Perthshire	1932-33	Strathclyde
1908-09	Cambuslang Rangers	1920-21	St. Roch's	1933-34	Cambuslang Rangers
1909-10	Petershill	1921-22	Parkhead	1934-35	Petershill
1910-11	Glasgow Perthshire	1922-23	Baillieston	1935-36	St. Roch's
1911-12	Rutherglen Glencairn	1923-24	Benburb	1936-37	Benburb
1912-13	Strathclyde	1924-25	Bridgeton Waverley	1937-38	Shettleston
1913-14	Parkhead	1925-26	Shettleston	1938-39	Vale of Clyde
1914-15	Maryhill	1926-27	Petershill		

Summary: *4 – Cambuslang Rangers, Petershill; 2 – Benburb, Glasgow Perthshire, Parkhead, Pollok, St. Roch's, Shettleston, Strathclyde; 1 – Ashfield, Baillieston, Bridgeton Waverley, Burnbank Ahletic, Co-operative United, Maryhill, Postal Athletic, Queen's Park Hampden XI, Rockbank, Royal Albert, Rutherglen Glencairn, Vale of Clyde.*

Glasgow Junior League

1895-96	Cambuslang Hibs	1906-07	Ashfield	1917-18	Vale of Clyde
1896-97	Strathclyde	1907-08	Ashfield	1918-19	Rutherglen Glencairn
1897-98	Parkhead	1908-09	Ashfield	1919-20	Vale of Clyde
1898-99	Rutherglen Glencairn	1909-10	Ashfield	1920-21	Ashfield
1899-00	Parkhead	1910-11	Cambuslang Rangers	1921-22	Rutherglen Glencairn
1900-01	Maryhill	1911-12	Cambuslang Rangers	1922-23	Strathclyde
1901-02	Rutherglen Glencairn	1912-13	Vale of Clyde	1923-24	Shettleston
1902-03	Parkhead	1913-14	Benburb	1924-25	St. Roch's
1903-04	Maryhill	1914-15	Cambuslang Rangers	1925-26	St. Roch's
1904-05	Maryhill	1915-16	Cambuslang Rangers	1926-27	Shettleston
1905-06	Ashfield	1916-17	Parkhead		

Summary: *6 - Ashfield; 4 - Cambuslang Rangers, Parkhead, Rutherglen Glencairn; 3 - Maryhill, Vale of Clyde; 2 - St. Roch's, Shettleston, Strathclyde; 1 - Benburb, Cambuslang Hibs.*

Glasgow Junior League Cup

1921-22	Strathclyde	1923-24	Kirkintilloch Rob Roy	1925-26	Shawfield
1922-23	Strathclyde	1924-25	St. Roch's	1926-27	Ashfield

Glasgow North-Eastern Cup

1890-91	Vale of Clyde	1897-98	Vale of Clyde	1904-05	Ashfield
1891-92	Vale of Clyde	1898-99	Glasgow Perthshire	1905-06	Maryhill
1892-93	Lambhill Harp	1899-00	Glasgow Perthshire	1906-07	Glasgow Perthshire
1893-94	Ashfield	1900-01	Cambuslang Hibs	1907-08	Strathclyde
1894-95	Parkhead	1901-02	Clyde Juniors	1908-09	R. Glencairn/Ashfield
1895-96	Parkhead	1902-03	Petershill	1909-10	Cambuslang Rangers
1896-97	Benburb	1903-04	Parkhead	1910-11	Strathclyde

11-12	Rutherglen Glencairn	1928-29	Saltcoats Victoria	1945-46	Pollok
12-13	Parkhead	1929-30	Croy Celtic	1946-47	Shawfield
13-14	Cambuslang Rangers	1930-31	Port Glasgow Juniors	1947-48	Petershill
14-15	Benburb	1931-32	St. Roch's	1948-49	Rutherglen Glencairn
15-16	Strathclyde	1932-33	St. Anthony's	1949-50	Strathclyde
16-17	Parkhead	1933-34	Rutherglen Glencairn	1950-51	Ashfield
17-18	Rutherglen Glencairn	1934-35	St. Francis	1951-52	St. Roch's
18-19	St. Anthony's	1935-36	Shawfield	1952-53	Ashfield
19-20	Vale of Clyde	1936-37	Shetleson	1953-54	Ashfield
20-21	Ashfield	1937-38	Strathclyde	1954-55	Maryhill Harp
21-22	Rutherglen Glencairn	1938-39	Vale of Clyde	1955-56	St. Anthony's
22-23	Ashfield	1939-40	Benburb	1956-57	Maryhill
23-24	Shawfield	1940-41	Maryhill Harp	1957-58	Cambuslang Rangers
24-25	Parkhead	1941-42	Glasgow Perthshire	1958-59	Maryhill Harp
25-26	Bridgeton Waverley	1942-43	Petershill	1959-60	Shettleston
26-27	Petershill	1943-44	Maryhill	1960-61	Shettleston
27-28	Maryhill Hibs	1944-45	Pollok		

ummary: *8 - Ashfield*; 6 - Parkhead, Rutherglen Glencairn*; 5 - Strathclyde, Vale of Clyde; - Glasgow Perthshire, Petershill; 3 - Benburb, Cambuslang Rangers, Maryhill, Maryhill Harp, . Anthony's, Shawfield, Shettleston; 2 - Croy Celtic, Pollok, St. Roch's; 1 - Bridgeton Waverley, ambuslang Hibs, Clyde Juniors, Lambhill Harp, Maryhill Hibs, St. Francis, Saltcoats Victoria. = one shared.*

GNT North Regional Cup

(For all North Regional Junior F.A. Clubs)

87-88	Bon Accord	1992-93	Hall Russell United	1997-98	Hermes
88-89	Bon Accord	1993-94	Sunnybank	1998-99	F.C. Stoneywood
89-90	Culter	1994-95	F.C. Stoneywood	1999-00	Culter
90-91	Stonehaven	1995-96	Inverurie Loco Works		
91-92	F.C. Stoneywood	1996-97	Sunnybank		

Gordon Campbell Construction Cup

(See under McLeman Cup)

Gordon Williamson Cup

(For North Regional League North Clubs)

55-56	Lossiemouth United	1970-71	Burghead Thistle	1985-86	Deveronside
56-57	New Elgin	1971-72	Burghead Thistle	1986-87	Deveronside
57-58	New Elgin	1972-73	Lossiemouth United	1987-88	Deveronside
58-59	Fochabers	1973-74	Burghead Thistle	1988-89	Bishopmill United
59-60	New Elgin	1974-75	Burghead Thistle	1989-90	Islavale
60-61	Lossiemouth United	1975-76	Buckie Rovers	1990-91	Islavale
61-62	Buckie Rovers	1976-77	Lossiemouth United	1991-92	Nairn St. Ninian
62-63	New Elgin	1977-78	Bishopmill United	1992-93	Islavale
63-64	Buckie Rovers	1978-79	Deveronside	1993-94	RAF Kinloss
64-65	Buckie Rovers	1979-80	New Elgin	1994-95	New Elgin
65-66	Islavale	1980-81	Buckie Rovers	1995-96	Deveronside
66-67	Forres Thistle	1981-82	New Elgin	1996-97	Deveronside
67-68	Forres Thistle	1982-83	Nairn St. Ninian	1997-98	Deveronside
68-69	Burghead Thistle	1983-84	Fochabers	1998-99	Islavale
69-70	Nairn St. Ninian	1984-85	Deveronside	1999-00	Nairn St. Ninian

ummary: *8 - Deveronside; 7 - New Elgin; 5 - Buckie Rovers, Burghead Thistle, Islavale; - Lossiemouth United, Nairn St. Ninian; 2 - Bishopmill United, Fochabers, Forres Thistle; - RAF Kinloss.*

Guide Cup

897-98	Arbroath Ardenlea	1900-01	Arbroath Ardenlea	1903-04	Arbroath Ardenlea
898-99	Forthill Athletic	1901-02	Arbroath Ardenlea		
899-00	Forthill Athletic	1902-03	Arbroath Ardenlea		

Heineken Cup
(See under Fife & Lothians Cup)

Hozier Cup
(For Lanarkshire League Clubs)

1888-89	Carluke (Milton) Rovers	1924-25	Lanark United	1947-48	Carluke Rovers
1889-90	Carluke (Milton) Rovers	1925-26	Lanark United	1948-49	Douglas Water Thistle
1890-91	Haywood Wanderers	1926-27	Carluke Rovers	1949-50	Douglasdale
1891-92	Haywood Wanderers	1927-28	Law Scotia	1950-51	Wishaw Juniors
1892-93	Haywood Wanderers	1928-29	Law Scotia	1951-52	Douglas Water Thistle
1893-94	Glespin Thistle	1929-30	Coalburn Juniors	1952-53	Coltness United
1894-95	Nethanvale Thistle	1930-31	Coalburn Juniors	1953-54	Douglas Water Thistle
1895-96	Lanark Athletic	1931-32	Coalburn Juniors	1954-55	Carluke Rovers
1896-97	Lanark Athletic	*1932-33*	*No Competition*	1955-56	Douglas Water Thistle
1897-98	Haywood Wanderers	1933-34	Lesmahagow	1956-57	Carluke Rovers
1898-99	Haywood Wanderers	1934-35	Lesmahagow	1957-58	Carluke Rovers
1899-00	*No Competition*	1935-36	Lesmahagow	1958-59	Lesmahagow
1900-01	Douglas Water Thistle	*1936-37*	*No Competition*	1959-60	Lanark United
1901-02	Douglas Water Thistle	1937-38	Stonehouse Violet	1960-61	Wishaw Juniors
1902-13	*No Competition*	1938-39	Stone house Violet	1961-62	Carluke Rovers
1913-14	Forth Wanderers	*1939-40*	*No Competition*	1962-63	Wishaw Juniors
1914-15	Law Volunteers	1940-41	Burnbank Athletic	1963-64	Shotts Bon Accord
1915-19	*No Competition*	*1941-42*	*No Competition*	1964-65	Larkhall Thistle
1919-20	Wishaw Juniors (YMCA)	1942-43	Armadale Thistle	1965-66	Blantyre Victoria
1920-21	Wishaw Juniors (YMCA)	1943-44	Blantyre Celtic	1966-67	Wishaw Juniors
1921-22	*No Competition*	1944-45	Larkhall Thistle	1967-68	Carluke Rovers
1922-23	Douglas Water Thistle	1945-46	Burnbank Athletic		
1923-24	Lanark United	1946-47	Wishaw Juniors		

Summary: *7 - Carluke Rovers, Douglas Water Thistle; 5 - Haywood Wanderers, Wishaw Juniors; 4 - Lanark United, Lesmahagow; 3 - Coalburn Juniors; 2 - Burnbank Athletic, Carluke (Milton) Rovers, Lanark Athletic, Larkhall Thistle, Law Scotia, Stonehouse Violet, Wishaw Juniors (YMCA); 1 - Armadale Thistle, Blantyre Celtic, Blantyre Victoria, Coltness United, Douglasdale, Forth Wanderers, Glespin Thistle, Law Volunteers, Nethanvale Thistle, Shotts Bon Accord.*

Inglis Cup
(See under Forfarshire Junior Cup)

Intermediate Consolation Cup

1927-28	Irvine Meadow	1929-30	Ashfield
1928-29	Port Glasgow Juniors	1930-31	Pollok

Intermediate Cup

1927-28	Ashfield	1929-30	Clydebank Juniors
1928-29	Ashfield	1930-31	Yoker Athletic

Intermediate League Cup

1927-28	Kirkintilloch Rob Roy	1929-30	Clydebank Juniors
1928-29	Ashfield	1930-31	Pollok

Intermediate North-Eastern Cup

1927-28	Glasgow Perthshire	1929-30	Pollok
1928-29	Bridgeton Waverley	1930-31	St. Roch's

Inveralmond Cup
(See under Winter Cup)

Irvine & District Cup
(See under Ayrshire District Cup)

Irvine & District League

907-08	Kilwinning Rangers	1911-12	Ardrossan Winton Rov.	1916-17	Stevenston Thistle
908-09	Kilwinning Rangers	1912-13	Saltcoats Victoria	*1917-19*	*No Competition*
909-10	Ardrossan Winton Rov.	1913-14	Kilwinning Rangers	1919-20	Irvine Victoria
910-11	Irvine Meadow	*1914-16*	*No Competition*		

Jimmy Gibb Memorial Trophy
(Play-off between winners of Divs. 1 and 2 of the North Regional League East)

980-81	Banks o' Dee	1987-88	Bon Accord	1994-95	FC Stoneywood
981-82	Banks o' Dee	1988-89	Bon Accord	1995-96	Inverurie Loco Works
982-83	Sunnybank	1989-90	Stonehaven	1996-97	Sunnybank
983-84	Banks o' Dee	1990-91	FC Stoneywood	1997-98	Inverurie Loco Works
984-85		1991-92	FC Stoneywood	1998-99	
985-86	Banks o' Dee	1992-93	East End	1999-00	Longside
986-87	East End	1993-94	Longside		

Kiddie Cup
(Also known as the Dundee Junior Charity Cup)

903-04	Fairfield	1928-29	Dundee St. Joseph's	1951-52	Dundee North End
904-05	Dundee Violet	1929-30	East Craigie	1952-53	Dundee North End
905-06	Dundee Violet	1930-31	Lochee Central	1953-54	Lochee Harp
906-07	Lochee Harp	1931-32	East Craigie	1954-55	Osborne
907-08	Dundee Violet	1932-33	Stobswell	1955-56	Dundee North End
908-09	Dundee Violet	1933-34	East Craigie	1956-57	Lochee Harp
909-10	Arnot	1934-35	Stobswell	1957-58	Osborne
910-11	Lochee Harp	1935-36	Lochee Harp	1958-59	Osborne
911-12	Dundee St. Joseph's	1936-37	East Craigie	1959-60	Lochee Harp
912-13	Fairfield	1937-38	Dundee Violet	1960-61	Lochee Harp
913-14	Lochee Harp	1938-39	Stobswell	1961-62	Dundee St. Joseph's
914-15	Dundee North End	*1939-40*	*No Competition*	1962-63	Carnoustie Panmure
915-16	Fairfield/Osborne	1940-41	Anchorage	1963-64	Osborne
916-19	*No Competition*	1941-42	Dundee North End	1964-65	East Craigie
919-20	Dundee Celtic	1942-43	Carnoustie Panmure	1965-66	Dundee Violet
920-21	Dundee North End	*1943-44*	*No Competition*	1966-67	Dundee Violet
921-22	Lochee Harp	1944-45	Anchorage	1967-68	Dundee Violet
922-23	Fairfield	1945-46	Elmwood	1968-69	Dundee North End
923-24	Dundee St. Joseph's	1946-47	Dundee North End	1969-70	Dundee North End
924-25	Osborne	1947-48	Lochee Harp	1970-71	Dundee North End
925-26	Dundee Celtic	1948-49	Lochee Harp	1971-72	Carnoustie Panmure
926-27	East Craigie	1949-50	Dundee North End		
927-28	Dundee North End	1950-51	Carnoustie Panmure		

Summary: *12 - Dundee North End; 11 - Lochee Harp; 8 - Dundee Violet; 6 - Osborne*; 5 - East Craigie; 4 - Carnoustie Panmure, Dundee St. Joseph's, Fairfield*, Stobswell; 2 - Anchorage, Dundee Celtic; 1 - Arnot, Lochee Central, Elmwood.   * includes one shared*

Kilmarnock & Louden District Cup

986-87	Hurlford United	1989-90	Hurlford United	1992-93	Darvel
987-88	Hurlford United	1990-91	Hurlford United	1993-94	Darvel
988-89	Darvel	1991-92	Darvel	1994-95	Darvel

Kirkwood Shield

1893-94	Elderpark	*1926-28*	*No Competition*	1948-49	Rutherglen Glencairn
1894-95	Rangers Ibrox XI	1928-29	Pollok	1949-50	Benburb
1895-96	Moorepark	1929-30	Pollok	1950-51	Vale of Leven
1896-97	Moorepark	1930-31	Kirkintilloch Rob Roy	1951-52	Ashfield
1897-98	Elderpark	1931-32	Yoker Athletic	1952-53	Petershill
1898-99	Co-operative United	1932-33	Pollok	1953-54	Vale of Leven
1899-00	Jordanhill	1933-34	Renfrew	1954-55	Parkhead
1900-01	Co-operative United	1934-35	Clydebank Juniors	1955-56	Petershill
1901-02	Renfrew Victoria	1935-36	Benburb	1956-57	Rutherglen Glencairn
1902-03	Dumbarton Corinthians	1936-37	Renfrew	1957-58	Vale of Leven
1903-04	Strathleven	1937-38	Yoker Athletic	1958-59	Petershill
1904-05	Clydebank Juniors	1938-39	Yoker Athletic	1959-60	St. Roch's
1905-06	Yoker Athletic	1939-40	Petershill	1960-61	Rutherglen Glencairn
1906-19	*No Competition*	1940-41	Kirkintilloch Rob Roy	1961-62	St. Roch's
1919-20	Renfrew/St. Anthony's	1941-42	Morton Juniors	1962-63	Renfrew
1920-21	St. Anthony's	1942-43	Petershill	1963-64	Pollok
1921-22	Pollok	1943-44	St. Anthony's	1964-65	Vale of Leven
1922-23	Ashfield	1944-45	Yoker Athletic	1965-66	Pollok
1923-24	Benburb	1945-46	St. Anthony's/Clydebank	1966-67	Neilston Juniors
1924-25	Renfrew	*1946-47*	*No Competition*	1967-68	Port Glasgow Juniors
1925-26	Yoker Athletic	1947-48	Clydebank Juniors		

Summary: *6 - Pollok, Yoker Athletic*; 5 - Petershill, Renfrew; 4 - Clydebank Juniors*, St. Anthony's**, Vale of Leven; 3 - Benburb, Rutherglen Glencairn; 2 - Ashfield, Co-operative United, Elderpark, Kirkintilloch Rob Roy, Moorepark, St. Roch's; 1 - Dumbarton Corinthians, Jordanhill, Morton Juniors, Neilston Juniors, Parkhead, Port Glasgow Juniors, Rangers Ibrox XI, Renfrew Victoria, Strathleven. * = one shared, ** = two shared.*

Kyle & Carrick District Cup

1986-87	Annbank United	1989-90	Whitletts Victoria	1992-93	Annbank United
1987-88	Annbank United	1990-91	Annbank United	1993-94	Maybole Juniors
1988-89	Whitletts Victoria	1991-92	Maybole Juniors	1994-95	Troon

Laidlaw Shield
(For member clubs of the Fife Junior F.A.)

1981-82	Glenrothes	1985-86	Hill o' Beath Hawthorn	1989-90	Hill o' Beath Hawthorn
1982-83	Glenrothes	1986-87	Kelty Hearts	1990-91	Tulliallan Thistle
1983-84	Kelty Hearts	1987-88	Hill o' Beath Hawthorn	1991-92	Dundonald Bluebell
1984-85	Kelty Hearts	1988-89	St. Andrews United	1992-93	Dundonald Bluebell

Laing Cup
(For member clubs of the Dundee Junior F.A.)

1939-40	Lochee Harp	1949-50	Lochee Harp	1959-60	Dundee North End
1940-41	Stobswell	1950-51	Carnoustie Panmure	1960-61	Lochee United
1941-42	United Juniors	1951-52	Broughty Athletic	1961-62	Lochee United
1942-43	Dundee Violet	1952-53	Carnoustie Panmure	1962-63	Stobswell
1943-44	Jeanfield Swifts	1953-54	Dundee Violet	1963-64	Downfield
1944-45	Anchorage	1954-55	Elmwood	1964-65	Downfield
1945-46	Anchorage	1955-56	Lochee Harp	1965-66	Dundee St. Joseph's
1946-47	Stobswell	1956-57	Dundee North End	1966-67	Downfield
1947-48	Dundee Violet	1957-58	Stobswell	1967-68	Osborne
1948-49	Broughty Ex-S.	1958-59	Dundee North End		

Summary: *4 - Stobswell; 3 - Downfield, Dundee North End, Dundee Violet, Lochee Harp; 2 - Anchorage, Carnoustie Panmure, Lochee United; 1 - Broughty Athletic, Broughty Ex-S, Dundee St. Joseph's, Elmwood, Jeanfield Swifts, Osborne, United Juniors.*

Lanark & Lothians Cup
(Lanarkshire Evening Citizen Cup 1949-59)

949-50	Thorniewood United	1956-57	Douglas Water Thistle	1963-64	Bonnyrigg Rose Athletic
950-51	Burnbank Athletic	1957-58	Carluke Rovers	1964-65	Linlithgow Rose
951-52	Coltness United	1958-59	Douglas Water Thistle	1965-66	Bonnyrigg Rose Athletic
952-53	Larkhall Thistle	1959-60	Tranent Juniors	1966-67	Armadale Thistle
953-54	Thorniewood United	1960-61	Larkhall Thsitle	1967-68	Bo'ness United
954-55	Coltness United	1961-62	Thorniewood United		
955-56	Larkhall Thistle	1962-63	Camelon Juniors		

Lanark & Lothians League
(Wartime competition combining Edinburgh & District and Lanarkshire leagues)

941-42	Polkemmet Juniors	1943-44	Armadale Thistle
942-43	Armadale Thistle	1944-45	Fauldhouse United

Lanarkshire Central Cup

920-21	Cadzow St. Anne's	1936-37	Stonehouse Violet	1954-55	Thorniewood United
921-22	Cleland Juniors	1937-38	Stonehouse Violet	1955-56	Shotts Bon Accord
922-23	Harthill Athletic	1938-42	*No Competition*	1956-57	Blantyre Victoria
923-24	Shieldmuir Celtic	1942-43	Burnbank Athletic	1957-58	Shotts Bon Accord
924-25	Burnbank Athletic	1943-44	Blantyre Victoria	1958-59	Shotts Bon Accord
925-26	Newarthill Thistle	1944-45	Larkhall Thistle	1959-60	Shotts Bon Accord
926-27	Wishaw Juniors	1945-46	Larkhall Thistle	1960-61	Coltness United
927-28	Burnbank Athletic	1946-47	Newarthill Hearts	1961-62	Bellshill Athletic
928-29	Carluke Rovers	1947-48	Larkhall Thistle	1962-63	*No Competition*
929-30	Burnbank Athletic	1948-49	Newarthill Hearts	1963-64	East Kilbride Juniors
930-31	Shotts Battlefield	1949-50	Burnbank Athletic	1964-65	Wishaw Juniors
931-32	Blantyre Victoria	1950-51	Bellshill Athletic	1965-66	Shotts Bon Accord
932-33	Wishaw Juniors	1951-52	Bellshill Athletic	1966-67	Lesmahagow
933-34	Larkhall Thistle	1952-53	Blantyre Celtic		
1934-36	*No Competition*	1953-54	Shotts Bon Accord		

Summary: 6 - Shotts Bon Accord; 5 - Burnbank Athletic; 4 - Larkhall Thistle; 3 - Bellshill Athletic, Blantyre Victoria, Wishaw Juniors; 2 - Newarthill Hearts, Stonehouse Violet; 1 - Blantyre Celtic, Cadzow St. Annes, Carluke Rovers, Cleland Juniors, Coltness United, East Kilbride Juniors, Harthill Athletic, Lesmahagow, Newarthill Thistle, Shieldmuir Celtic, Shotts Battlefield, Thorniewood United.

Lanarkshire Challenge Cup

885-86	Wishaw Thistle	1906-07	Dalziel Rovers	1927-28	Law Scotia
886-87	Wishaw Thistle	1907-08	Larkhall Thistle	1928-29	Maryhill Hibs
887-88	Wishaw Thistle	1908-09	Burnbank Athletic	1929-30	Burnbank Athletic
888-89	Burnbank Swifts	1909-10	Larkhall Thistle	1930-31	Burnbank Athletic
889-90	Carluke Milton Rovers	1910-11	Burnbank Athletic	1931-32	Douglas Water Thistle
890-91	Carluke Milton Rovers	1911-12	Burnbank Athletic	1932-33	Carluke Rovers
891-92	Haywood Wanderers	1912-13	Bellshill Athletic	1933-34	Wishaw Juniors
892-93	Newmains Thistle	1913-14	Blantyre Victoria	1934-35	Lanark United
893-94	Mossend Brigade	1914-15	Mossend Hibs	1935-36	Coltness United
894-95	Cambuslang Hibs	1915-16	Blantyre Victoria	1936-37	Larkhall Thistle
895-96	Mossend Brigade	1916-17	Burnbank Athletic	1937-38	Wishaw Juniors
896-97	Dalziel Rovers	1917-18	Glenboig	1938-39	Lesmahagow
897-98	Dalziel Rovers	1918-19	Bellshill Athletic	1939-40	Blantyre Victoria
898-99	Dalziel Rovers	1919-20	Blantyre Celtic	1940-41	Burnbank Athletic
899-00	Bellhaven Athletic	1920-21	New Steventon United	1941-42	Wishaw Juniors
900-01	Clydesdale Wanderers	1921-22	Cleland Juniors	1942-43	Blantyre Victoria
901-02	Burnbank Athletic	1922-23	Carluke Rovers	1943-44	Polkemmet Juniors
902-03	Burnbank Athletic	1923-24	Blantyre Victoria	1944-45	Fauldhouse United
903-04	Blantyre Victoria	1924-25	Baillieston	1945-46	Blantyre Victoria
904-05	Burnbank Athletic	1925-26	Wishaw Juniors	1946-47	Newarthill Hearts
905-06	Burnbank Athletic	1926-27	Lanark United	1947-48	Lesmahagow

CONTINUED OVERLEAF

1948-49	Blantyre Victoria	1955-56	Larkhall Thistle	1962-63	Shotts Bon Accord
1949-50	Newarthill Hearts	1956-57	Baillieston	1963-64	Thorniewood United
1950-51	Larkhall Thistle	1957-58	Carluke Rovers	1964-65	Thorniewood United
1951-52	Bellshill Athletic	1958-59	Carluke Rovers	1965-66	Wishaw Juniors
1952-53	Newarthill Hearts	1959-60	Forth Wanderers	1966-67	Carluke Rovers
1953-54	Coltness United	1960-61	Shotts Bon Accord	1967-68	Blantyre Victoria
1954-55	Coltness United	1961-62	Carluke Rovers		

Summary: 11 - Burnbank Athletic; 9 - Blantyre Victoria; 6 - Carluke Rovers; 5 - Larkhall Thistle, Wishaw Juniors; 4 - Dalziel Rovers; 3 - Bellshill Athletic, Coltness United, Newarthill Hearts, Wishaw Thistle; 2 - Baillieston, Carluke (Milton) Rovers, Lanark United, Lesmahagow, Mossend Brigade, Shotts Bon Accord, Thorniewood United; 1 - Bellhaven Athletic, Blantyre Celtic, Burnbank Swifts, Cambuslang Hibs, Cleland Juniors, Clydesdale Wanderers, Douglas Water Thistle, Fauldhouse United, Forth Wanderers, Glenboig, Haywood Wanderers, Law Scotia, Maryhill Hibs, Mossend Hibs, Newmains Thistle, New Stevenston United, Polkemmet Juniors.

Lanarkshire League

1891-92	Newmains Thistle	1916-17	Blantyre Victoria	*1940-45*	*No Competition*
1892-93	Blantyre Victoria	1917-18	Cleland Juniors	1945-46	Wishaw Juniors
1893-94	Longriggend	1918-19	Cleland Juniors	1946-47	Burnbank Athletic
1894-95	Mossend Celtic	1919-20	Blantyre Victoria	1947-48	Larkhall Thistle
1895-96	Larkhall Thistle	1920-21	New Stevenston United	1948-49	Newarthill Hearts
1896-97	Burnbank Athletic	1921-22	Cleland Juniors	1949-50	New Stevenston United
1897-98	Dalziel Rovers	1922-23	Carluke Rovers	1950-51	Thorniewood United
1898-99	Dalziel Rovers	1923-24	Shotts United	1951-52	Larkhall Thistle
1899-00	Holytown Thistle	1924-25	Shotts United	1952-53	Lesmahagow
1900-01	Burnbank Athletic	1925-26	Wishaw Juniors	1953-54	Coltness United
1901-02	Burnbank Athletic	1926-27	Blantyre Victoria	1954-55	Douglas Water Thistle
1902-03	Burnbank Athletic	*1927-28*	*No Competition*	1955-56	Thorniewood United
1903-04	Burnbank Athletic	1928-29	Coalburn Juniors	1956-57	Carluke Rovers
1904-05	Bellshill Athletic	1929-30	Coalburn Juniors	1957-58	Shotts Bon Accord
1905-06	Blantyre Victoria	1930-31	Larkhall Thistle	1958-59	Carluke Rovers
1906-07	East Benhar Heatherbell	1931-32	Shotts Battlefield	1959-60	Thorniewood United
1907-08	Quarter Huttonback	1932-33	Douglas Water Thistle	1960-61	Shotts Bon Accord
1908-09	Quarter Huttonback	1933-34	Royal Albert	1961-62	Shotts Bon Accord
1909-10	Lanark United	1934-35	Wishaw Juniors	1962-63	Shotts Bon Accord
1910-11	Blantyre Victoria	1935-36	Royal Albert	1963-64	Thorniewood United
1911-12	Burnbank Athletic	1936-37	Royal Albert	1964-65	Shotts Bon Accord
1912-13	Larkhall Thistle	1937-38	Holytown United	1965-66	Forth Wanderers
1913-14	Larkhall Thistle	1938-39	Stonehouse Violet	1966-67	Larkhall Thistle
1914-16	*No Competition*	1939-40	New Stevenston United	1967-68	Shotts Bon Accord

Summary: 7 - Burnbank Athletic, Larkhall Thistle; 6 - Blantyre Victoria, Shotts Bon Accord; 4 - Thorniewood United; 3 - Carluke Rovers, Cleland Juniors, New Stevenston United, Royal Albert, Wishaw Juniors; 2 - Coalburn Juniors, Dalziel Rovers, Douglas Water Thistle, Quarter Huttonback, Shotts United; 1 - Bellshill Athletic, Coltness United, East Benhar Heatherbell, Forth Wanderers, Holytown Thistle, Holytown United, Larkhall United, Lesmahagow, Longriggend, Mossend Celtic, Newarthill Hearts, Newmains Thistle, Shotts Battlefield, Stonehouse Violet.

Lanarkshire League Cup

1921-22	Fauldhouse United	1932-33	Larkhall Thistle	1948-49	Carluke Rovers
1922-23	Harthill Athletic	1933-34	Royal Albert	1949-50	Newarthill Hearts
1923-24	Cadzow St. Anne's	1934-35	Stonehouse Violet	1950-51	Wishaw Juniors
1924-25	Shotts United	1935-36	Larkhall Thistle	1951-52	Shotts Bon Accord
1925-26	Wishaw Juniors	1936-37	Lesmahagow	1952-53	Larkhall Thistle
1926-27	Shotts United	1937-38	Shieldmuir Celtic	1953-54	Coltness United
1927-28	Motherwell Juniors	1938-39	Stonehouse Violet	1954-55	Carluke Rovers
1928-29	Carluke Rovers	*1939-45*	*No Competition*	1955-56	Douglas Water Thistle
1929-30	Law Scotia	1945-46	Newarthill Hearts	1956-57	Larkhall Thistle
1930-31	Coalburn Juniors	1946-47	Forth Wanderers	1957-58	Shotts Bon Accord
1931-32	Lesmahagow	1947-48	Forth Wanderers	1958-59	Larkhall Thistle

1959-60	Shotts Bon Accord	1962-63	Thorniewood United	1965-66	Thorniewood United
1960-61	Wishaw Juniors	1963-64	Shotts Bon Accord	1966-67	Shotts Bon Accord
1961-62	Larkhall Thistle	1964-65	Shotts Bon Accord	1967-68	Shotts Bon Accord

Summary: *7 - Shotts Bon Accord; 6 - Larkhall Thistle; 3 - Carluke Rovers, Wishaw Juniors; - Forth Wanderers, Lesmahagow, Newarthill Hearts, Shotts United, Stonehouse Violet, Thorniewood United; 1 - Cadzow St. Annes, Coalburn Juniors, Coltness United, Douglas Water Thistle, Fauldhouse United, Harthill Athletic, Law Scotia, Motherwell Juniors, Royal Albert, Shieldmuir Celtic.*

Land O'Burns Cup
(For member clubs of the Ayrshire Junior F.A.)

1949-50	Kilbirnie Ladeside	1953-54	Troon	1957-58	Ardeer Thistle
1950-51	Lugar Boswell Thistle	1954-55	Kello Rovers	1958-59	Kilbirnie Ladeside
1951-52	Ardrossan Winton Rovers	1955-56	Kilwinning Rangers		
1952-53	Dalry Thistle	1956-57	Ardrossan Winton Rovers		

Langbank Charity Cup
(See also under Smyllum Cup)

1929-30	St. Roch's	1930-31	Blantyre Celtic

Linlithgowshire Junior Cup
(Also known as the McLagan Cup and the Usher Cup)

1886-87	Broxburn Emmet	1900-01	Broxburn Athletic	1913-14	Kinneil Ramblers
1887-88	Cardross Swifts	1901-02	Broxburn Athletic	*1914-19*	*No Competition*
1898-99	Armadale Volunteers	1902-03	Vale of Grange	1919-20	Broxburn Athletic
1889-90	East Benhar Heatherbell	1903-04	Vale of Grange	1920-21	Broxburn Athletic
1890-91	East Benhar Heatherbell	1904-05	Linlithgow Rose	1921-22	Livingston United
1891-92	West Benhar Violet	1905-06	Vale of Grange	1922-23	Livingston United
1892-93	West Benhar Violet	1906-07	Bo'ness Our Boys	1923-24	Linlithgow Rose
1893-95	*No Competition*	1907-08	Bo'ness Our Boys	1924-25	Bo'ness Juniors
1895-96	Vale of Grange	1908-09	Bo'ness Our Boys	1925-26	Linlithgow Rose
1896-97	*Not Completed*	1909-10	Vale of Grange	1926-27	Linlithgow Rose
1897-98	Bo'ness Our Boys	1910-11	Vale of Grange	*1927-28*	*No Competition*
1898-99	Vale of Grange	1911-12	Broxburn St. Andrews	1928-29	Armadale Juniors
1899-00	Bo'ness Our Boys	1912-13	Armadale Rangers		

Summary: *7 - Vale of Grange; 5 - Bo'ness Our Boys; 4 - Broxburn Athletic, Linlithgow Rose; - East Benhar Heatherbell, Livingston United, West Benhar Violet; 1 - Armadale Juniors, Armadale Rangers, Armadale Volunteers, Bo'ness Juniors, Broxburn Emmet, Broxburn St. Andrews, Cardross Swifts, Kinneil Ramblers.*

Linlithgowshire Junior League Cup

1940-41	Armadale Thistle	1941-42	Polkemmet Juniors	1942-43	Polkemmet Juniors

Loftus Cup
(For member clubs of the Dundee Junior F.A.)

1948-49	Dundee Violet	1955-56	Carnoustie Panmure	1962-63	Dundee Violet
1949-50	Elmwood	1956-57	Dundee North End	1963-64	Dundee Violet
1950-51	Osborne	1957-58	Osborne	1964-65	Lochee United
1951-52	Carnoustie Panmure	1958-59	Dundee North End	1965-66	Dundee Violet
1952-53	Carnoustie Panmure	1959-60	Lochee Harp	1966-67	Dundee Violet
1953-54	Carnoustie Panmure	1960-61	Lochee Harp	1967-68	Dundee St. Joseph's
1954-55	Dundee Violet	1961-62	Dundee St. Joseph's		

Summary: *5 - Dundee Violet; 4 - Carnoustie Panmure; 2 - Dundee North End, Dundee St. Joseph's, Lochee Harp, Osborne; 1 - Elmwood, Lochee United.*

Lovie Shield
(See under Aberdeen County Trophy)

McLagan Cup
(See under Linlithgowshire Junior Cup)

McLeman Cup
(For Aberdeen & District Clubs. Currently the Gordon Campbell Construction Trophy)

1920-21	Parkvale	1947-48	Hall Russell's	1974-75	Sunnybank
1921-22	Mugiemoss	1948-49	Sunnybank	1975-76	Sunnybank
1922-23	Richmond	1949-50	St. Clement's	1976-77	Mugiemoss
1923-24	Richmond	1950-51	Banks o' Dee	1977-78	Ellon United
1924-25	Banks o' Dee	1951-52	Inverurie Loco Works	1978-79	Banks o' Dee
1925-26	Richmond	1952-53	Sunnybank	1979-80	Parkvale
1926-27	East End	1953-54	Sunnybank	1980-81	Rosemount
1927-28	Hawthorn	1954-55	East End	1981-82	Banks o' Dee
1928-29	Inverurie Loco Works	1955-56	Banks o' Dee	1982-83	FC Stoneywood
1929-30	East End	1956-57	Sunnybank	1983-84	FC Stoneywood
1930-31	Hall Russell's	1957-58	Lewis United	1984-85	Rosslyn Sports
1931-32	Woodside	1958-59	Banks o' Dee	1985-86	Turriff United
1932-33	Hall Russell's	1959-60	South United	1986-87	Banks o' Dee
1933-34	Woodside	1960-61	Banks o' Dee	1987-88	Stonehaven
1934-35	Richmond	1961-62	Sunnybank	1988-89	Culter
1935-36	Hawthorn	1962-63	Lewis United	1989-90	Bon Accord
1936-37	Hall Russell's	1963-64	Sunnybank	1990-91	Banks o' Dee
1937-38	Banks o' Dee	1964-65	Parkvale	1991-92	Lewis United
1938-39	Banks o' Dee	1965-66	East End	1992-93	Culter
1939-40	Hall Russell's	1966-67	Sunnybank	1993-94	F.C. Stoneywood
1940-41	Hall Russell's	1967-68	Banks o' Dee	1994-95	Stonehaven
1941-42	Aberdeen Juniors	1968-69	Inverurie Loco Works	1995-96	Sunnybank
1942-43	I.T.C.	1969-70	Banks o' Dee	1996-97	Sunnybank
1943-44	Mugiemoss	1970-71	Stoneywood Works	1997-98	Sunnybank
1944-45	A. Hall & Co.	1971-72	Lewis United	1998-99	Formartine United
1945-46	Mugiemoss	1972-73	Stonehaven	1999-00	Sunnybank
1946-47	Caledonian	1973-74	Parkvale		

Summary: 13 - Banks o' Dee, Sunnybank; 6 - Hall Russell's; 4 - East End, Lewis United, Mugiemoss, Parkvale, Richmond; 3 - FC Stoneywood, Inverurie Loco Works, Stonehaven; 2 - Culter, Hawthorn, Rosemount/Rosslyn Sports, Woodside; 1 - Aberdeen Juniors, Bon Accord, Caledonian, Ellon United, Formartine United, A. Hall & Co., I.T.C., St. Clement's, Stoneywood Works, Turriff United

McLeod Trophy
(Pintaman Trophy 1968-70)

1968-69	Rutherglen Glencairn	1973-74	Lesmahagow	1978-79	St. Roch's
1969-70	Lesmahagow	1974-75	Lesmahagow	1979-80	Baillieston
1970-71	Kirkintilloch Rob Roy	1975-76	Lesmahagow	1980-81	Larkhall Thistle
1971-72	Larkhall Thistle	1976-77	Arthurlie	1981-82	Larkhall Thistle
1972-73	Dunipace Juniors	1977-78	Glasgow Perthshire		

Marshall Cup
((Initially for member clubs of the East Lothian Junior F.A., later for member clubs of the Edinburgh & District F.A.)

1903-04	Musselburgh Fern	1907-08	Penicuik Juniors	1911-12	Wemyss Athletic
1904-05	Arniston Rangers	1908-09	Penicuik Juniors	1912-13	Penicuik Athletic
1905-06	Newtongrange Star	1909-10	Arniston Rangers	1913-14	Bonnyrigg Rose Athletic
1906-07	Newtongrange Star	1910-11	Dalkeith Thistle	1914-15	Musselburgh Athletic

1915-19	*No Competition*	1923-24	Tranent Juniors
1919-20	Tranent Juniors	*1924-27*	*No Competition*
1920-21	Musselburgh Bruntonians	1927-28	Newtongrange Star
1921-22	Newtongrange Star	*1928-29*	*No Competition*
1922-23	Arniston Rangers	1929-30	Rosewell Rosedale

1930-31	Tranent Juniors
1931-32	Linlithgow Rose
1932-33	Bo'ness Cadora
1933-34	Blackburn Athletic

Summary: 4 - Newtongrange Star; 3 - Arniston Rangers, Tranent Juniors; 2 - Penicuik Juniors; 1 - Blackburn Athletic, Bo'ness Cadora, Bonnyrigg Rose Athletic, Dalkeith Thistle, Linlithgow Rose, Musselburgh Athletic, Musselburgh Bruntonians, Musselburgh Fern, Penicuik Athletic, Rosewell Rosedale, Wemyss Athletic.

Martin & Johnson Trophy
(For North Regional League East Clubs)

1973-74	Banks o' Dee	1975-76	Sunnybank
1974-75	East End	1976-77	Banks o' Dee

Martin-White Cup
(For clubs in the St. Andrews district)

1893-94	Ancient City Athletic	1904-05	Anstruther Rangers	1919-20	Cupar Juniors
1894-95	Anstruther Rangers	1905-06	Anstruther Rangers	1920-21	St. Andrews United
1895-96	Ancient City Athletic	1906-07	St. Andrews City	1921-22	St. Andrews United
1896-97	Ancient City Athletic	1907-08	Anstruther Rangers	1922-23	Pittenweem Hearts
1897-98	Ancient City Athletic	1908-09	St. Andrews City	1923-24	Cupar Juniors
1898-99	Ancient City Athletic	1909-10	St. Andrews City	1924-25	St. Andrews United
1899-00	Wormit	1910-11	St. Andrews City	1925-26	St. Andrews United
1900-01	Crail Union	1911-12	Anstruther Rangers	1926-27	St. Andrews United
1901-02	Anstruther Rangers	1912-13	Cupar Violet	1927-28	St. Andrews United
1902-03	Cellardyke Bluejackets	1913-14	Cupar Violet		
1903-04	St. Andrews City	*1914-19*	*No Competition*		

Summary: 6 - Anstruther Rangers, St. Andrews United; 5 - Ancient City Athletic, St. Andrews City; 2 - Cupar Juniors, Cupar Violet; 1 - Cellardyke Bluejackets, Crail Union, Pittenweem Hearts, Wormit.

Maryhill Charity Cup

1887-88	Maryhill	1914-15	Ashfield	1941-42	Maryhill
1888-89	Northern F.C.	1915-16	Petershill	1942-43	Petershill
1889-90	Northern F.C.	1916-17	Petershill	1943-44	Glasgow Perthshire
1890-91	Minerva	1917-18	Ashfield	1944-45	Maryhill
1891-92	Minerva	1918-19	Maryhill	1945-46	Glasgow Perthshire
1892-93	Myrtle	1919-20	Ashfield	1946-47	Ashfield
1893-94	Ashfield	1920-21	Ashfield	1947-48	Petershill
1894-95	Ashfield	1921-22	Maryhill	1948-49	Petershill
1895-96	Jordanhill	1922-23	Glasgow Perthshire	1949-50	Ashfield
1896-97	Maryhill	1923-24	Ashfield	1950-51	Petershill
1897-98	Ashfield	1924-25	Ashfield	1951-52	Ashfield
1898-99	Ashfield	1925-26	Ashfield	1952-53	Maryhill
1899-00	Maryhill	1926-27	Ashfield	1953-54	Petershill
1900-01	Glasgow Perthshire	1927-28	Ashfield	1954-55	Petershill
1901-02	Maryhill	1928-29	Ashfield	1955-56	Ashfield
1902-03	Glasgow Perthshire	1929-30	Petershill	1956-57	Maryhill
1903-04	Ashfield	1930-31	Glasgow Perthshire	1957-58	Petershill
1904-05	Ashfield	1931-32	Ashfield	1958-59	Ashfield
1905-06	Maryhill	1932-33	Ashfield	1959-60	Ashfield
1906-07	Ashfield	1933-34	Petershill	1960-61	Ashfield
1907-08	Maryhill	1934-35	Petershill	1961-62	Maryhill
1908-09	Petershill	1935-36	Glasgow Perthshire	1962-63	Ashfield
1909-10	Ashfield	1936-37	Ashfield	1963-64	Maryhill
1910-11	Ashfield	1937-38	Ashfield	1964-65	Glasgow Perthshire
1911-12	Petershill	1938-39	Petershill	1965-66	Ashfield
1912-13	Ashfield	1939-40	Glasgow Perthshire	1966-67	Glasgow Perthshire
1913-14	Petershill	1940-41	Maryhill	1967-68	Petershill

CONTINUED OVERLEAF

the winners

1968-69	Ashfield	1977-78	Glasgow Perthshire	1986-87	Ashfield
1969-70	Petershill	1978-79	Petershill	1987-88	Glasgow Perthshire
1970-71	Ashfield	1979-80	Glasgow Perthshire	1988-89	Petershill
1971-72	Petershill	1980-81	Maryhill	1989-90	Glasgow Perthshire
1972-73	Maryhill	1981-82	Maryhill	1990-91	Maryhill
1973-74	Maryhill	1982-83	Petershill	1991-92	Glasgow Perthshire
1974-75	Ashfield	1983-84	Ashfield	1992-93	Maryhill
1975-76	Maryhill	1984-85	Petershill	1993-94	Glasgow Perthshire
1976-77	Glasgow Perthshire	1985-86	Petershill		

Summary: *38 - Ashfield; 24 - Petershill; 22 - Glasgow Perthshire, Maryhill; 2 - Minerva, Northern F.C.; 1 - Jordanhill, Myrtle.*

Matthew Cup
(For North Regional League North Clubs)

1950-51	Bishopmill United	1967-68	Buckie Rovers	1984-85	Deveronside
1951-52	Lossiemouth United	1968-69	Buckie Rovers	1985-86	Fochabers
1952-53	RAF Kinloss	1969-70	Buckie Rovers	1986-87	Islavale
1953-54	New Elgin	1970-71	New Elgin	1987-88	Deveronside
1954-55	Lossiemouth United	1971-72	Burghead Thistle	1988-89	Bishopmill United
1955-56	RNAS Lossiemouth	1972-73	Burghead Thistle	1989-90	Lossiemouth United
1956-57	RAF Kinloss	1973-74	Bishopmill United	1990-91	Deveronside
1957-58	Losiemouth United	1974-75	Burghead Thistle	1991-92	Islavale
1958-59	Burghead Thistle	1975-76	Buckie Rovers	1992-93	Deveronside
1959-60	New Elgin	1976-77	Bishopmill United	1993-94	Buckie Rovers
1960-61	New Elgin	1977-78	Buckie Rovers	1994-95	New Elgin
1961-62	Islavale	1978-79	New Elgin	1995-96	R.A.F. Lossiemouth
1962-63	Buckie Rovers	1979-80	Rothes Decimals	1996-97	Lossiemouth United
1963-64	Buckie Rovers	1980-81	Rothes Decimals	1997-98	Nairn St. Ninian
1964-65	Buckie Rovers	1981-82	New Elgin	1998-99	Buckie Rovers
1965-66	Islavale	1982-83	Cabar Feidh	1999-00	New Elgin
1966-67	Buckie Rovers	1983-84	Deveronside		

Summary: *11 - Buckie Rovers; 8 - New Elgin; 5 - Deveronside, Lossiemouth United; 4 - Bishopmill United, Burghead Thistle, Islavale; 2 - RAF Kinloss, Rothes Decimals; 1 - Cabar Feidh, Fochabers, Nairn St. Ninian, RAF Lossiemouth, RNAS Lossiemouth.*

Midland League
(Wartime competition for Dundee, Perthshire and Angus clubs)

1939-40	Dundee Violet	1942-43	Carnoustie Panmure	1945-46	Jeanfield Swifts
1940-41	Stobswell	1943-44	Jeanfield Swifts	1946-47	Jeanfield Swifts
1941-42	Dundee Violet	1944-45	Carnoustie Panmure		

Midlothian Junior League

1893-94	Arniston Rangers	1903-04	Arniston Rangers	1913-14	Bonnyrigg Rose Athletic
1894-95	Arniston Rangers	1904-05	Arniston Rangers	1914-15	
1895-96	Arniston Rangers	1905-06	Newtongrange Star	1915-16	
1896-97		1906-07	Newtongrange Star	1916-17	
1897-98		1907-08	Newtongrange Star	1917-18	Winchburgh Violet
1898-99		1908-09	Arniston Rangers	1918-19	
1899-00		1909-10	Penicuik Juniors	1919-20	Newtongrange Star
1900-01	Arniston Rangers	1910-11	Arniston Rangers	1920-21	Newtongrange Star
1901-02	Arniston Rangers	1911-12	Arniston R/Wemyss Ath.	1921-22	Newtongrange Star
1902-03	Edinburgh Myrtle	1912-13	Wemyss Athletic		

Mitchell Cup
(For member clubs of the Fife Junior F.A. Also known as the Fife League Cup, 1951-3 and the Fife Consolation Cup, 1953-6.)

1937-38	Lochore Welfare	*1939-47*	*No Competition*	1948-49	Dundonald Bluebell
1938-39	Hearts of Beath	1947-48	Dundonald Bluebell	1949-50	Lochgelly Albert

1950-51	Steelend Victoria	1956-57	St. Andrews United	1962-63	Lochore Welfare
1951-52	Thornton Hibs	1957-58	Lochgelly Albert	1963-64	Newburgh
1952-53	St. Andrews United	1958-59	Thornton Hibs	1964-65	Newburgh
1953-54	Glencraig Colliery	1959-60	Thornton Hibs	1965-66	St. Andrews
1954-55	Newburgh	1960-61	Newburgh		U/Valleyfield
1955-56	Lochore Welfare	1961-62	Lochore Welfare	1966-67	Valleyfield

Summary: *4 - Lochore Welfare, Newburgh; 3 - St. Andrews United*, Thornton Hibs; 2 - Dundonald Bluebell, Lochgelly Albert, Valleyfield*; 1 - Glencraig Colliery, Hearts of Beath, Steelend Victoria. * includes one shared*

Montrave Cup
(See under East Fife Cup)

Moore Trophy
(For Ayrshire Junior Clubs)

1927-28	Kilwinning Rangers	1937-38	Johnstone Athletic	1947-48	Auchinleck Talbot
1928-29	Irvine Meadow	1938-39	Irvine Meadow	1948-49	Kilbirnie Ladeside
1929-30	Irvine Meadow	1939-40	Hurlford United	1949-50	Lugar Boswell Thistle
1930-31	Ardrossan Winton Rovers	1940-41	Ardeer Recreation	1950-51	Lugar Boswell Thistle
1931-32	Ardrossan Winton Rovers	1941-42	Ardeer Recreation	1951-52	Lugar Boswell Thistle
1932-33	Irvine Meadow	*1942-43*	*No Competition*	1952-53	Cumnock Juniors
1933-34	Darvel Juniors	1943-44	Hurlford United	1953-54	Cumnock Juniors
1934-35	Kilbirnie Ladeside	1944-45	Hurlford United	1954-55	Annbank United
1935-36	Saltcoats Victoria	1945-46	Annbank United	1955-56	Lugar Boswell Thistle
1936-37	Irvine Victoria	1946-47	Ardeer Recreation		

Summary: *4 - Irvine Meadow, Lugar Boswell Thistle; 3 - Ardeer Recreation, Hurlford United; 2 - Annbank United, Ardrossan Winton Rovers, Cumnock Juniors, Kilbirnie Ladeside; 1 - Auchinleck Talbot, Darvel Juniors, Irvine Victoria, Johnstone Athletic, Kilwinning Rangers, Saltcoats Victoria.*

Morayshire Junior Cup
(From 1968 to 1998 awarded to League runners-up)

1919-20	Elgin Hearts	1950-51	New Elgin	1975-76	Burghead Thistle
1920-21	Fochabers	1951-52	45 MU Kinloss	1976-77	New Elgin
1921-22	Fochabers	1952-53	Burghead Thistle	1977-78	Forres Thistle
1922-23	Fochabers	1953-54	Forres Thistle	1978-79	Bishopmill United
1923-24	Fochabers	1954-55	RAF Kinloss	1979-80	Nairn St. Ninian
1924-25	Rothes Victoria	1955-56	New Elgin	1980-81	Islavale
1925-26	Forres Thistle	1956-57	Fochabers	1981-82	Buckie Rovers
1926-27	Lossiemouth Rangers	1957-58	RAF Kinloss	1982-83	Cabar Feidh
1927-28	Lossiemouth Rangers	1958-59	Lossiemouth United	1983-84	Fochabers
1928-29		1959-60	New Elgin	1984-85	Deveronside
1929-30		1960-61	Islavale	1985-86	Fochabers
1930-31	Forres Thistle	1961-62	Burghead Thistle	1986-87	Deveronside
1931-32	Burghead Thistle	1962-63	Bishopmill United	1987-88	Fochabers
1932-33	Lossiemouth Rangers	1963-64	Bishopmill United	1988-89	Bishopmill United
1933-34	Keith Territorials	1964-65	Islavale	1989-90	Lossiemouth United
1934-35	Dufftown	1965-66	Fulmar	1990-91	Fochabers
1935-36	Rothes Victoria	1966-67	Buckie Rovers	1991-92	Forres Thistle
1936-37		1967-68	Buckie Rovers	1992-93	Deveronside
1937-38		1968-69	Nairn St. Ninian	1993-94	Lossiemouth United
1938-39		1969-70	Burghead Thistle	1994-95	Deveronside
1939-46	*No Competition*	1970-71	Forres Thistle	1995-96	Islavale
1946-47	Buckie Rovers	1971-72	Islavale	1996-97	Buckie Rovers
1947-48	Royal Engineers	1972-73	RAF Kinloss	1997-98	Nairn St. Ninian
1948-49	Bishopmill United	1973-74	Forres Thistle	1998-99	Islavale
1949-50	RNAS Lossiemouth	1974-75	Burghead Thistle	1999-00	Forres Thistle

Summary: *9 - Fochabers; 8 - Forres Thistle; 6 - Burghead Thistle, Islavale; 5 - Bishopmill United, Buckie Rovers; 4 - Deveronside, New Elgin; 3 - Lossiemouth Rangers, Lossiemouth United, Nairn St. Ninian, RAF Kinloss; 2 - Rothes Victoria; 1 - Cabar Feidh, Dufftown, Elgin Hearts, 45 MU Kinloss, Fulmar, Keith Territorials, RNAS Lossiemouth, Royal Engineers.*

Morayshire Junior League

1919-20	Lossiemouth Rangers	1934-35	Rothes Victoria	1955-56	Lossiemouth United
1920-21	Federation	1935-36	Deveron Valley	1956-57	New Elgin
1921-22	Territorials	1936-37		1957-58	New Elgin
1922-23	Fochabers	1937-38		1958-59	Lossiemouth United
1923-24	Bishopmill United	1938-39		1959-60	New Elgin
1924-25	Elgin City 'A'	*1939-46*	*No Competition*	1960-61	Fochabers
1925-26	Newmill	1946-47	RNAS Lossiemouth	1961-62	Islavale
1926-27	Forres Thistle	1947-48	New Elgin	1962-63	Buckie Rovers
1927-28	Lossiemouth Rangers	1948-49	RNAS Lossiemouth	1963-64	New Elgin
1928-29	Lossiemouth Rangers	1949-50	Lossiemouth United	1964-65	Buckie Rovers
1929-30	Forres Thistle	1950-51	New Elgin	1965-66	Buckie Rovers
1930-31	Elgin Thistle	1951-52	New Elgin	1966-67	New Elgin
1931-32	Burghead Thistle	1952-53	Lossiemouth United	1967-68	Buckie Rovers
1932-33	Keith Territorials	1953-54	New Elgin		
1933-34	Hopeman	1954-55	New Elgin		

Summary: 10 - New Elgin; 4 - Buckie Rovers, Lossiemouth; 3 - Lossiemouth Rangers; 2 - Fochabers, Forres Thistle, RNAS Lossiemouth; 1 - Bishopmill United, Burghead Thistle, Deveron Valley, Elgin City 'A', Elgin Thistle, Federation, Hopeman, Islavale, Keith Territorials, Newmill, Rothes Victoria, Territorials.

Morrison Trophy
(For member clubs of the North Regional Junior F.A. (East))

1971-72	Sunnybank	1981-82	Stonehaven	1991-92	Lewis United
1972-73	Parkvale	1982-83	Parkvale	1992-93	Lewis United
1973-74	Parkvale	1983-84	Parkvale	1993-94	Longside
1974-75	East End	1984-85	Stonehaven	1994-95	Banchory St. Ternan
1975-76	Mugiemoss	1985-86	Banks o' Dee	1995-96	Banchory St. Ternan
1976-77	Parkvale	1986-87	Rosslyn Sports	1996-97	Hermes
1977-78	Ellon United	1987-88	FC Stoneywood	1997-98	Cruden Bay
1978-79	Formartine United	1988-89	Buchanhaven Hearts	1998-99	East End
1979-80	Fraserburgh United	1989-90	Longside	1999-00	Cruden Bay
1980-81	Sunnybank	1990-91	FC Stoneywood		

Summary: 5 - Parkvale; 2 - Banchory St. Ternan, Cruden Bay, East End, FC Stoneywood, Lewis United, Longside, Stonehaven, Sunnybank; 1 - Banks o' Dee, Buchanhaven Hearts, Ellon United, Formartine United, Fraserburgh United, Hermes, Mugiemoss, Rosslyn Sports.

Murray Cup
(For member clubs of the Edinburgh & District Junior F.A.)

1950-51	Newtongrange Star	1954-55	Newtongrange Star	1958-59	West Calder United
1951-52	Newtongrange Star	*1955-56*	*No Competition*	1959-60	Broxburn Athletic
1952-53	Newtongrange Star	1956-57	Dalkeith Thistle	1960-61	Bonnybridge Juniors
1953-54	Newtongrange Star	1957-58	West Calder United		

Musselburgh Cup
(For member clubs of the Midlothian Junior F.A.)

1901-02	Niddrie Bluebell	1912-13	Wemyss Athletic	1927-28	Musselburgh Bruntonians
1902-03	Arniston Rangers	1913-14	Tranent Juniors	1928-29	Musselburgh Bruntonians
1903-04	Musselburgh Fern	*1914-19*	*No Competition*	1929-30	Wemyss Athletic
1904-05	Arniston Rangers	1919-20	Tranent Juniors	1930-31	Arniston Rangers
1905-06	Newtongrange Star	1920-21	Dalkeith Thistle	1931-32	Tranent Juniors
1906-07	Newtongrange Star	1921-22	Tranent Juniors	1932-33	Tranent Juniors
1907-08	Arniston Rangers	1922-23	Dalkeith Thistle	1933-34	Musselburgh Bruntonians
1908-09	Penicuik Juniors	1923-24	Portobello Thistle	1934-35	Thorntree United
1909-10	Bonnyrigg Rose Athletic	1924-25	Bonnyrigg Rose Athletic	1935-36	Musselburgh Athletic
1910-11	Arniston Rangers	1925-26	Newtongrange Star		
1911-12	Arniston Rangers	1926-27	Newtongrange Star		

National Drybrough Cup

970-71	Cambuslang Rangers	*1976-77*	*No Competition*	1982-83	Sauchie Juniors
971-72	Larkhall Thistle	1977-78	(Lothian Region) *	1983-84	Ormiston Primrose
972-73	Irvine Meadow	1978-79	(Fife Region) *	1984-85	Ormiston Primrose
973-74	Lochgelly Albert	1979-80	Baillieston	1985-86	Bonnyrigg Rose Athletic
974-75	Newtongrange Star	1980-81	Pollok	1986-87	Auchinleck Talbot
975-76	Kilbirnie Ladesde	*1981-82*	*No Competition*		

Played for by Regional presentative teams.

National Steeplejacks Club
(See under Brown Cup)

Nicholson Cup
(For North Regional League North Clubs)

921-22	Fochabers	1958-59	New Elgin	1979-80	Nairn St. Ninian
922-23	Fochabers	1959-60	New Elgin	1980-81	Nairn St. Ninian
923-24	Bishopmill United	1960-61	Fochabers	1981-82	Buckie Rovers
924-25	Elgin City 'A'	1961-62	Buckie Rovers	1982-83	Nairn St. Ninian
925-26	Lossiemouth Rangers	1962-63	Buckie Rovers	1983-84	Deveronside
926-27	Forres Thistle	1963-64	Buckie Rovers	1984-85	Fochabers
927-28	Lossiemouth Rangers	1964-65	Buckie Rovers	1985-86	Buckie Rovers
928-29	Lossiemouth Rangers	1965-66	Buckie Rovers	1986-87	Cabar Feidh
929-30	Lossiemouth Rangers	1966-67	Buckie Rovers	1987-88	Fochabers
930-47	No Competition	1967-68	New Elgin	1988-89	Deveronside
947-48	RNAS Lossiemouth	1968-69	Lossiemouth United	1989-90	Deveronside
948-49	Burghead Thistle	1969-70	Buckie Rovers	1990-91	Bishopmill United
949-50	Lossiemouth United	1970-71	Islavale	1991-92	Lossiemouth United
950-51	Lossiemouth United	1971-72.	R.A.F. Kinloss	1992-93	Deveronside
951-52	New Elgin	1972-73	Forres Thistle	1993-94	Deveronside
952-53	RAF Kinloss	1973-74	Lossiemouth United	1994-95	Deveronside
953-54	RAF Kinloss	1974-75	Burghead Thistle	1995-96	Burghead Thistle
954-55	Fochabers	1975-76	Buckie Rovers	1996-97	New Elgin
955-56	Lossiemouth United	1976-77	Cabar Feidh	1997-98	Nairn St. Ninian
956-57	Fochabers	1977-78	Bishopmill United	1998-99	Burghead Thistle
957-58	Burghead Thistle	1978-79	Bishopmill United	1999-00	Burghead Thistle

North Ayrshire Cup

995-96	Kilwinning Rangers	1997-98	Kilwinning Rangers	1999-00	Kilwinning Rangers
996-97	Irvine Meadow	1998-99	Irvine Victoria		

North Drybrough Cup

968-69	Inverurie Loco Works	1975-76	Sunnybank	1982-83	Sunnybank
969-70	Banks o' Dee	1976-77	Banks o' Dee	1983-84	Banks o' Dee
970-71	Banks o' Dee	1977-78	St. Machar	1984-85	Banks o' Dee
971-72	Formartine United	1978-79	Banks o' Dee	1985-86	Deveronside
972-73	Forres Thistle	1979-80	Sunnybank	1986-87	Turriff United
973-74	Banks o' Dee	1980-81	Banks o' Dee		
974-75	Lewis United	1981-82	Banks o' Dee		

North End Centenary Cup
(See under Concept Group Cup)

North End Challenge Cup
(For member clubs of Tayside Regional Junior F.A.)

1999-00   Tayport

North of Scotland Cup
(For member clubs of the Morayshire Junior F.A.)

1949-50	Bishopmill United	1962-63	Burghead Thistle	1975-76	Forres Thistle
1950-51	Lossiemouth United	1963-64	Bishopmill United	1976-77	Islavale
1951-52	45 MU Kinloss	1964-65	New Elgin	1977-78	Buckie Rovers
1952-53	Forres Thistle	1965-66	New Elgin	1978-79	
1953-54	New Elgin	1966-67	Islavale	1979-80	Bishopmill United
1954-55	Fochabers	1967-68	Buckie Rovers	1980-81	Nairn St. Ninian
1955-56	Fochabers	1968-69	Forres Thistle	1981-82	Rothes Decimals
1956-57	RAF Kinloss	1969-70	Buckie Rovers	1982-83	RAF Lossiemouth
1957-58	Forres Thistle	1970-71	Islavale	1983-84	Burghead Thistle
1958-59	Forres Thistle	1971-72	Islavale	1984-85	Forres Thistle
1959-60	New Elgin	1972-73	RAF Kinloss	1985-86	Forres Thistle
1960-61	Fochabers	1973-74	Forres Thistle	1986-87	Islavale
1961-62	Buckie Rovers	1974-75	Forres Thistle		

Summary: *9 - Forres Thistle; 5 - Islavale; 4 - Buckie Rovers, New Elgin; 3 - Bishopmill United, Fochabers; 2 - Burghead Thistle, RAF Kinloss; 1 - 45 MU Kinloss, Lossiemouth United, Nairn St. Ninian, RAF Lossiemouth, Rothes Decimals.*

North Regional League (East) - DIVISION 1

1968-69	Banks o' Dee	1979-80	Fraserburgh United	1990-91	FC Stoneywood
1969-70	Banks o' Dee	1980-81	Banks o' Dee	1991-92	FC Stoneywood
1970-71	Banks o' Dee	1981-82	Banks o' Dee	1992-93	Inverurie Loco Works
1971-72	Sunnybank	1982-83	Sunnybank	1993-94	Stonehaven
1972-73	Banks o' Dee	1983-84	Banks o' Dee	1994-95	FC Stoneywood
1973-74	Parkvale	1984-85	FC Stoneywood	1995-96	Inverurie Loco Works
1974-75	Sunnybank	1985-86	Banks o' Dee	1996-97	Sunnybank
1975-76	Sunnybank	1986-87	Banks o' Dee	1997-98	Inverurie Loco Works
1976-77	Banks o' Dee	1987-88	Rosslyn Sports	1998-99	Sunnybank
1977-78	East End	1988-89	Bon Accord	1999-00	Longside
1978-79	Banks o' Dee	1989-90	Stonehaven		

Summary: *11 - Banks o' Dee; 6 - Sunnybank; 4 - FC Stoneywood; 3 - Inverurie Loco Works; 2 - Stonehaven; 1 - Bon Accord, East End, Fraserburgh United, Longside, Parkvale, Rosslyn Sports.*

North Regional League (East) - DIVISION 2

1973-74	Mugiemoss	1982-83	Parkvale	1991-92	Buchanhaven Hearts
1974-75	Stoneywood Works	1983-84	Ellon United	1992-93	East End
1975-76	Lads Club	1984-85	East End	1993-94	Longside
1976-77	Mugiemoss	1985-86	Cove Rangers	1994-95	Hermes
1977-78	Cuminestown	1986-87	East End	1995-96	Banks o' Dee
1978-79	Rosemount	1987-88	Bon Accord	1996-97	Lewis United
1979-80	Buchanhaven Hearts	1988-89	Stonehaven	1997-98	Cruden Bay
1980-81	Rosemount	1989-90	Hall Russell United	1998-99	Banks o' Dee
1981-82	FC Stoneywood	1990-91	Fraserburgh United	1999-00	Cruden Bay

Summary: *3 - East End; 2 - Banks o' Dee, Buchanhaven Hearts, Cruden Bay, Mugiemoss, Rosemount; 1 - Bon Accord, Cove Rangers, Cuminestown, Ellon United, FC Stoneywood, Fraserburgh United, Hall Russell United, Hermes, Lads Club, Lewis United, Longside, Parkvale, Stonehaven, Stoneywood Works.*

North Regional League (East) League Cup
(Currently the Grill League Cup)

1968-69	Banks o' Dee	1979-80	Banks o' Dee	1990-91	FC Stoneywood
1969-70	Banks o' Dee	1980-81	Sunnybank	1991-92	Inverurie Loco Works
1970-71	Banks o' Dee	1981-82	Sunnybank	1992-93	Sunnybank
1971-72	Banks o' Dee	1982-83	Banks o' Dee	1993-94	Sunnybank
1972-73	Lewis United	1983-84	Banks o' Dee	1994-95	FC Stoneywood
1973-74	Banks o' Dee	1984-85	Turriff United	1995-96	Bon Accord
1974-75	Lewis United	1985-86	FC Stoneywood	1996-97	Sunnybank
1975-76	Sunnybank	1986-87	Inverurie Loco Works	1997-98	FC Stoneywood
1976-77	Lewis United	1987-88	Bon Accord	1998-99	Formartine United
1977-78	St. Machar	1988-89	Inverurie Loco Works	1999-00	Sunnybank
1978-79	Sunnybank	1989-90	East End		

Summary: *8 - Banks o' Dee, Sunnybank; 4 - FC Stoneywood; 3 - Inverurie Loco Works, Lewis United; 2 - Bon Accord; 1 - East End, Formartine United, St. Machar, Turriff United.*

North Regional League (North)

1968-69	Formartine United	1979-80	Forres Thistle	1990-91	Deveronside
1969-70	Buckie Rovers	1980-81	Bishopmill United	1991-92	Lossiemouth United
1970-71	Islavale	1981-82	Nairn St. Ninian	1992-93	Buckie Rovers
1971-72	Forres Thistle	1982-83	Buckie Rovers	1993-94	Deveronside
1972-73	Burghead Thistle	1983-84	Deveronside	1994-95	Lossiemouth United
1973-74	Burghead Thistle	1984-85	Fochabers	1995-96	Deveronside
1974-75	Buckie Rovers	1985-86	Deveronside	1996-97	Islavale
1975-76	Nairn St. Ninian	1986-87	Cabar Feidh	1997-98	Islavale
1976-77	Burghead Thistle	1987-88	Deveronside	1998-99	New Elgin
1977-78	Nairn St. Ninian	1988-89	Deveronside	1999-00	Deveronside
1978-79	Nairn St. Ninian	1989-90	Deveronside		

Summary: *9 - Deveronside; 4 - Buckie Rovers, Nairn St. Ninian; 3 - Burghead Thistle, Islavale; 2 - Forres Thistle, Lossiemouth United; 1 - Bishopmill United, Cabar Feidh, Fochabers, Formartine United, New Elgin.*

P.A. Cup
(The first of two cups presented by the Perthshire Advertiser, this one was always known as the P.A. Cup, and was for clubs in the Perthshire Junior F.A. For the second cup, see under Perthshire Advertiser Cup.)

1936-37	Perth YMCA	1949-50	Newburgh	1962-63	Errol
1937-38	Perth Craigie	1950-51	St. Johnstone YMCA	1963-64	Luncarty
1938-39	Coupar Angus	1951-52	Comrie Rovers	1964-65	Alyth United
1939-40	St. Johnstone YMCA	1952-53	Blairgowrie	1965-66	Alyth United
1940-41	Jeanfield Swifts	1953-54	Newburgh	1966-67	Jeanfield Swifts
1941-42	Jeanfield Swifts	1954-55	Newburgh	1967-68	Kinnoull
1942-43	Jeanfield Swifts	1955-56	Blairgowrie	1968-69	Jeanfield Swifts
1943-44	St. Johnstone YMCA	1956-57	Alyth United	1969-70	Kinnoull
1944-45	Jeanfield Swifts	1957-58	Newburgh	1970-71	Jeanfield Swifts
1945-46	Jeanfield Swifts	1958-59	Newburgh	1971-72	Luncarty
1946-47	Jeanfield Swifts	1959-60	Kinnoull	1972-73	Crieff Earngrove
1947-48	Jeanfield Swifts	1960-61	Kinnoull		
1948-49	Coupar Angus	1961-62	Kinnoull		

Summary: *10 - Jeanfield Swifts; 5 - Kinnoull, Newburgh; 3 - Alyth United, St. Johnstone YMCA; 2 - Blairgowrie, Coupar Angus, Luncarty; 1 - Comrie Rovers, Crieff Earngrove, Errol, Perth Craigie, Perth YMCA.*

Peddie Smith Malocco (PSM) Cup
(See under Fife Cup)

Perthshire Advertiser Cup

(The second of the cups presented by the Perthshire Adveritiser, this was for member clubs of the Tayside Regional Junior F.A. For the first cup, see under P.A. Cup.)

1988-89	Downfield	1991-92	Jeanfield Swifts	1994-95	Dundee St. Joseph's
1989-90	Dundee North End	1992-93	Dundee North End	1995-96	Tayport
1990-91	Tayport	1993-94	Downfield		

Perthshire Junior Consolation Cup

(See under Constitutional Cup)

Perthshire Junior Cup

1901-02	Perth Celtic	1928-29	Scone Thistle	1951-52	Luncarty
1902-03	Perth Craigie	1929-30	Scone Thistle	1952-53	Blairgowrie
1903-04	Perth Craigie	1930-31	Scone Thistle	1953-54	Jeanfield Swifts
1904-05	Perth Roselea	1931-32	Perth YMCA	1954-55	Jeanfield Swifts
1905-06	Perth Roselea	1932-33	Perth YMCA	1955-56	Blairgowrie
1906-07	St. Leonards	1933-34	Perth Craigie	1956-57	Blairgowrie
1907-08	St. Leonards	1934-35	Perth Celtic	1957-58	Blairgowrie
1908-09	Perth Roselea	1935-36	Scone Thistle	1958-59	Blairgowrie
1909-10	Alyth Thistle	1936-37	St. James	1959-60	Blairgowrie
1910-11	Perth Violet	1937-38	Crieff Earngrove	1960-61	Coupar Angus
1911-12	Perth Violet	1938-39	Coupar Angus	1961-62	Alyth United
1912-13	Perth Craigie	1939-40	Perth YMCA	1962-63	Blairgowrie
1913-14	Perth Craigie	1940-41	Luncarty	1963-64	Luncarty
1914-19	*No Competition*	1941-42	Crieff Earngrove	1964-65	Jeanfield Swifts
1919-20	St. Leonards	1942-43	Jeanfield Swifts	1965-66	Jeanfield Swifts
1920-21	St. Leonards	1943-44	Jeanfield Swifts	1966-67	Alyth United
1921-22	Perth Violet	1944-45	Jeanfield Swifts	1967-68	Alyth United
1922-23	Perth Caledonian	1945-46	Jeanfield Swifts	1968-69	Blairgowrie
1923-24	Auchterarder Fairmuir	1946-47	Jeanfield Swifts	*1969-70*	*No Competition*
1924-25	Auchterarder Fairmuir	1947-48	Blairgowrie	1970-71	Kinnoull
1925-26	Scone Thistle	1948-49	Blairgowrie	1971-72	Blairgowrie
1926-27	Perth YMCA	1949-50	Blairgowrie	1972-73	Jeanfield Swifts
1927-28	Scone Thistle	1950-51	Auchterarder Primrose		

Summary: *12 - Blairgowrie; 10 - Jeanfield Swifts; 6 - Scone Thistle; 5 - Perth Craigie; 4 - Perth YMCA, St. Leonards; 3 - Alyth United, Luncarty, Perth Roselea, Perth Violet; 2 - Auchterarder Fairmuir, Coupar Angus, Crieff Earngrove, Perth Celtic; 1 - Alyth Thistle, Auchterarder Primrose, Kinnoull, Perth Caledonain, St. James.*

Perthshire Junior League

1899-00	Perth Celtic	1920-21	Scone Thistle	1936-37	Perth Craigie
1900-01	St. Leonards	1921-22	Perth Violet	1937-38	Crieff Earngrove
1901-02	Perth Celtic	1922-23	Vale of Earn	1938-39	Perth Craigie
1902-03	St. Leonards	1923-24	Scone Thistle	1939-40	St. Johnstone YMCA
1903-04	Perth Roselea	1924-25	St. Johnstone YMCA	1940-41	St. Johnstone YMCA
1904-05	St. Leonards	1925-26	St. Johnstone YMCA	1941-42	Jeanfield Swifts
1905-06	Perth Roselea	1926-27	Vale of Earn	*1942-46*	*No Competition*
1906-07	Perth Roselea	1927-28	Vale of Earn	1946-47	Newburgh
1907-08	Perth Roselea	1928-29	Vale of Earn*	1947-48	Jeanfield Swifts
1908-09	St. Leonards		Luncarty*	1948-49	Jeanfield Swifts
1909-10	Perth Roselea	1929-30	St. Johnstone YMCA	1949-50	Luncarty
1910-11	Perth Violet	1930-31	St. Johnstone YMCA	1950-51	Comrie Rovers
1911-12	Perth Violet	1931-32	Luncarty	1951-52	Blairgowrie
1912-13	Perth Violet	1932-33	Scone Thistle	1952-53	Blairgowrie
1913-14	Perth Violet	1933-34	Perth Celtic	1953-54	Newburgh
1914-19	*No Competition*	1934-35	Scone Thistle	1954-55	Newburgh
1919-20	Perth Celtic	1935-36	Scone Thistle	1955-56	Newburgh

956-57	Newburgh	1961-62	Blairgowrie	1966-67	Jeanfield Swifts
957-58	Blairgowrie	1962-63	Coupar Angus	1967-68	Jeanfield Swifts
958-59	Blairgowrie	1963-64	Jeanfield Swifts	1968-69	Jeanfield Swifts
959-60	Blairgowrie	1964-65	Luncarty		
960-61	Blairgowrie	1965-66	Jeanfield Swifts		

* For one season only, the League was played in two sections - Perth & District (Luncarty) and Perthshire Vale of Earn).

ummary: 8 - Jeanfield Swifts; 7 - Blairgowrie; 6 - St. Johnstone YMCA; 5 - Newburgh, Perth oselea, Perth Violet, Scone Thistle; 4 - Luncarty, Perth Celtic, St. Leonards, Vale of Earn; 2 - Perth raigie; 1 - Comrie Rovers, Coupar Angus, Crieff Earngrove.

Perthshire Rosebowl

948-49	Jeanfield Swifts	1955-56	Blairgowrie	1962-63	Luncarty
949-50	Jeanfield Swifts	1956-57	Newburgh	1963-64	Coupar Angus
950-51	Blairgowrie	1957-58	Kinnoull	1964-65	Errol
951-52	Blairgowrie	1958-59	Jeanfield Swifts	1965-66	Blairgowrie
952-53	Blairgowrie	1959-60	Jeanfield Swifts	1966-67	Jeanfield Swifts
953-54	Blairgowrie	1960-61	Kinnoull	1967-68	Jeanfield Swifts
954-55	Newburgh	1961-62	Jeanfield Swifts		

ummary: 7 - Jeanfield Swifts; 6 - Blairgowrie; 2 - Kinnoull, Newburgh; 1 - Coupar Angus, Errol, uncarty.

Peter Craigie Cup
(For member clubs of the East of Scotland Junior F.A.)

989-90	Newtongrange Star	1991-92	Newtongrange Star	1993-94	Livingston United
990-91	Armadale Thistle	1992-93	Bonnyrigg Rose Athletic		

Pintaman Cup
(See under **McLeod Trophy**)

Pompey Cup

949-50	Duntocher Hibs	1954-55	Baillieston	1959-60	Ashfield
950-51	Dennistoun Waverley	1955-56	Rutherglen Glencairn	1960-61	Clydebank Juniors
951-52	Clydebank Juniors	1956-57	Kilsyth Rangers	1961-62	Pollok
952-53	Baillieston	1957-58	Kilsyth Rangers	1962-63	*No Competition*
953-54	Baillieston	1958-59	Pollok	1963-64	Johnstone Burgh

Renfrewshire-Dunbartonshire Junior Cup

927-28	*Not Completed*	1938-39	Morton Juniors	1952-53	Neilston Juniors
928-29	Clydebank Juniors	1939-40	Clydebank Juniors	1953-54	Vale of Leven
929-30	Neilston Victoria	1940-44	*No Competition*	1954-55	Arthurlie
930-31	Renfrew	1944-45	Vale of Leven	1955-56	Duntocher Hibs
931-32	Yoker Athletic	1945-46	Renfrew	1956-57	Arthurlie
932-33	Clydebank Juniors	1946-47	*No Competition*	1957-58	Renfrew
933-34	Arthurlie	1947-48	Duntocher Hibs	1958-59	Renfrew
934-35	Morton Juniors	1948-49	Renfrew	1959-60	Arthurlie
935-36	Dumbarton Harp	1949-50	Clydebank Juniors	1960-61	Johnstone Burgh
936-37	Morton Juniors	1950-51	Arthurlie		
937-38	Johnstone	1951-52	Clydebank Juniors		

ummary: 5 - Arthurlie, Clydebank Juniors, Renfrew; 3 - Morton Juniors; 2 - Duntocher Hibs, Vale f Leven; 1 - Dumbarton Harp, Johnstone, Johnstone Burgh, Neilston Juniors, Neilston Victoria, oker Athletic.

Renfrewshire Junior Cup

1885-86	Cartvale	1913-14	Neilston Victoria	1941-42	Morton Juniors
1886-87	Abercorn Blackstoun XI	1914-15	Port Glasgow Athletic	1942-43	Renfrew
1887-88	Abercorn Blackstoun XI	1915-16	Port Glasgow Athletic	1943-44	Gourock Juniors
1888-89	Southside	1916-17	Renfrew	1944-45	Arthurlie
1889-90	Blackstoun Rangers	1917-18	Renfrew	1945-46	Renfrew
1890-91	Jordanhill	1918-19	St. Mirren Juniors	1946-47	Neilston Juniors
1891-92	Ferguslie Athletic	1919-20	Renfrew	1947-48	Neilston Juniors
1892-93	Greenock Volunteers	1920-21	Paisley Vulcan	1948-49	Dunoon Athletic
1893-94	Greenock Volunteers	1921-22	Neilston Victoria	1949-50	Arthurlie
1894-95	Jordanhill	1922-23	Port Glasgow Athletic	1950-51	Arthurlie
1895-96	Overton	1923-24	Cartvale Juniors	1951-52	Neilston Juniors
1896-97	St. Mirren Westmarch XI	1924-25	Overton Athletic	1952-53	Port Glasgow Juniors
1897-98	Port Glasgow Juniors	1925-26	Overton Athletic	1953-54	Gourock Juniors
1898-99	Abercorn Westmarch XI	1926-27	Renfrew	1954-55	Arthurlie
1899-00	Morton 'A'	1927-28	Rothesay Royal Victoria	1955-56	Arthurlie
1900-01	Overton	1928-29	Maryhill Hibs	1956-57	Arthurlie
1901-02	Overton	1929-30	Maryhill Hibs	1957-58	Johnstone Burgh
1902-03	Ferguslie	1930-31	Dumbarton Harp United	1958-59	Johnstone Burgh
1903-04	Renfrew Victoria	1931-32	Renfrew	1959-60	Greenock Juniors
1904-05	Port Glasgow Juniors	1932-33	Renfrew	1960-61	Greenock Juniors
1905-06	Neilston Victoria	1933-34	Arthurlie	1961-62	Johnstone Burgh
1906-07	Neilston Victoria	1934-35	Morton Juniors	1962-63	Greenock Juniors
1907-08	Port Glasgow Juniors	1935-36	Morton Juniors	1963-64	Greenock Juniors
1908-09	Port Glasgow Juniors	1936-37	Morton Juniors	1964-65	Neilston Juniors
1909-10	Neilston Victoria	1937-38	Arthurlie	1965-66	Renfrew
1910-11	Port Glasgow Juniors	1938-39	Johnstone Athletic	1966-67	Greenock Juniors
1911-12	Port Glasgow Juniors	1939-40	Morton Juniors		
1912-13	Neilston Victoria	1940-41	Renfrew		

Summary: 10 - Renfrew; 8 - Arthurlie; 7 - Port Glasgow Juniors; 6 - Neilston Victoria; 5 - Greenock Juniors, Morton Juniors; 4 - Neilston Juniors; 3 - Johnstone Burgh, Overton, Port Glasgow Athletic Juniors; 2 - Abercorn Blackstoun XI, Gourock Juniors, Greenock Volunteers, Jordanhill, Maryhill Hibs, Overton Athletic; 1 - Abercorn Westmarch XI, Blackstoun Rangers, Cartvale, Cartvale Juniors, Dumbarton Harp United, Dunoon Athletic, Ferguslie, Ferguslie Athletic, Johnstone Athletic, Morton 'A', Paisley Vulcan, Renfrew Victoria, Rothesay Royal Victoria, St. Mirren Juniors, St. Mirren Westmarch XI, Southside.

R.L. Rae Cup
(For Edinburgh & District League Clubs)

1952-53	Broxburn Athletic	1959-60	Whitburn	1969-70	Newtongrange Star
1953-54	Bo'ness United	1960-61	Arniston Rangers	1970-71	Dalkeith Thistle
1954-55	Broxburn Athletic	1961-65	*No Competition*	1971-72	Arniston Rangers
1955-56	Dunbar United	1965-66	Bathgate Thistle	1972-73	Sauchie
1956-57	Dalkeith Thistle	1966-67	Dalkeith Thistle	1973-74	Camelon
1957-58	Bo'ness United	1967-68	Linlithgow Rose	1974-75	Bonnyrigg Rose Athletic
1958-59	Bo'ness United	1968-69	Dalkeith Thistle		

Summary: 4 - Dalkeith Thistle; 3 - Bo'ness United; 2 - Arniston Rangers, Broxburn Athletic; 1 - Bathgate Thistle, Bonnyrigg Rose Athletic, Camelon, Dunbar United, Linlithgow Rose, Newtongrange Star, Sauchie, Whitburn.

Robbie Nicol Cup
(For member clubs of the North regional Junior F.A. North Section. Formerly the Tom Gordon Cup)

1975-76	Burghead Thistle	1980-81	RAF Kinloss	1985-86	Cabar Feidh
1976-77		1981-82	Lossiemouth United	1986-87	Deveronside
1977-78	Bishopmill United	1982-83	Lossiemouth United	1987-88	Deveronside
1978-79		1983-84	Fochabers	1988-89	Nairn St. Ninian
1979-80	Bishopmill United	1984-85	Cabar Feidh	1989-90	Fochabers

1990-91	Fochabers	1994-95	Lossiemouth United	1998-99	Strathspey Thistle
1991-92	Bishopmill United	1995-96	Nairn St. Ninian	1999-00	Deveronside
1992-93	Forres Thistle	1996-97	New Elgin		
1993-94	Deveronside	1997-98	Portgordon United		

Summary: 4 - Deveronside; 3 - Bishopmill United, Fochabers, Lossiemouth United; 2 - Cabar Feidh, Nairn St. Ninian; 1 - Burghead Thistle, Forres Thistle, New Elgin, Portgordon United, Strathspey Thistle.

Robertson Cup

(For member clubs of the North regional Junior F.A. North Section)

1926-27	Lossiemouth Rangers	1960-61	Forres Thistle	1980-81	Nairn St. Ninian
1927-28	Lossiemouth Rangers	1961-62	New Elgin	1981-82	Bishopmill United
1928-29	Lossiemouth Rangers	1962-63	Buckie Rovers	1982-83	Nairn St. Ninian
1929-30	Aberlour	1963-64	Bishopmill United	1983-84	Buckie Rovers
1930-31	Forres Thistle	1964-65	New Elgin	1984-85	Deveronside
1931-46	*No Competition*	1965-66	Buckie Rovers	1985-86	Deveronside
1946-47	RNAS Lossiemouth	1966-67	Islavale	1986-87	Cabar Feidh
1947-48	New Elgin	1967-68	Forres Thistle	1987-88	Deveronside
1948-49	RAF Kinloss	1968-69	Forres Thistle	1988-89	Forres Thistle
1949-50	Lossiemouth United	1969-70	Nairn St. Ninian	1989-90	Islavale
1950-51	New Elgin	1970-71		1990-91	Deveronside
1951-52	45 MU Kinloss	1971-72		1991-92	Lossiemouth United
1952-53	RAF Kinloss	1972-73		1992-93	Islavale
1953-54	New Elgin	1973-74	Burghead Thistle	1993-94	Deveronside
1954-55	RAF Kinloss	1974-75		1994-95	Lossiemouth United
1955-56	RAF Kinloss	1975-76		1995-96	Buckie Rovers
1956-57	New Elgin	1976-77		1996-97	Islavale
1957-58	RAF Kinloss	1977-78	Burghead Thistle	1997-98	Deveronside
1958-59	New Elgin	1978-79		1998-99	Islavale
1959-60	Forres Thistle	1979-80	New Elgin	1999-00	Islavale

Summary: 9 - New Elgin; 6 - Forres Thistle; 5 - Deveronside, RAF Kinloss; 4 - Islavale, Nairn St. Ninian; 3 - Bishopmill United, Buckie Rovers, Lossiemouth Rangers, Lossiemouth United; - Burghead Thistle; 1 - Aberlour, Cabar Feidh, 45 MU Kinloss, Portgordon United, RNAS Lossiemouth, Strathspey Thistle.

Robertson Homes Cup

(See under Brown Cup)

Rollstud Archibald Cup

(See under Archibald Cup)

Rosebank C.C. Cup

(Formerly the Intersport Cup. In 1995-96 took over from the Winter Cup as the competition for Tayside Regional League Division 2 Clubs.)

1987-88	Jeanfield Swifts	1992-93	Dundee St. Joseph's	1997-98	Broughty Athletic
1988-89	Dundee North End	1993-94	Tayport	1998-99	Montrose Roselea
1989-90	Lochee United	1994-95	Carnoustie Panmure	1999-00	Blairgowrie
1990-91	Tayport Juniors	1995-96	Jeanfield Swifts		
1991-92	Dundee Violet	1996-97	Montrose Roselea		

Roseberry Cup (Junior)

(Edinburgh & District clubs. Cup presented by Lord Roseberry.)

1911-12	Wemyss Athletic	1918-19	Winchburgh Violet	1924-25	Newtongrange Star
1912-13	Broxburn St. Andrew's	*1919-22*	*No Competition*	1925-26	Wallyford Bluebell
1913-17	*No Competition*	1922-23	Broxburn United	1926-27	Tranent Juniors
1917-18	Leith Benburb	1923-24	Musselburgh Bruntonians	*1927-31*	*No Competition*

CONTINUED OVERLEAF

1931-32	Dalkeith Thistle	1934-35	Stoneyburn Junors	1937-38	Bonnyrigg Rose Athletic
1932-33	Dalkeith Thistle	1935-36	Bo'ness Cadora	1938-39	Stoneyburn Juniors
1933-34	Stoneyburn Juniors	1936-37	Tranent Juniors	1939-40	Armadale Thistle

Rothesay-Dunoon Cup

1937-38	Rothesay Royal Victoria	1938-39	Bute Athletic

St. Johnstone Y.M. Cup

1961-62	Jeanfield Swifts	1963-64	Blairgowrie	1965-66	Jeanfield Swifts
1962-63	Blairgoowrie	1964-65	Blairgowrie	1966-67	Jeanfield Swifts

St. Michael Cup
(Originally for West Lothian junior clubs, later for all Edinburgh & District League clubs)

1907-08	Vale of Grange	1943-44	Carluke Rovers	1966-67	Musselburgh Athletic
1908-09	Armadale Thistle	1944-45	Wishaw Juniors	1967-68	Linlithgow Rose
1909-10	Linlithgow Rose	1945-46	Tranent Juniors	1968-69	Linlithgow Rose
1910-11	Linlithgow Rose	1946-47	Whitburn	1969-70	Whitburn
1911-12	Seafield Athletic	1947-48	Arniston Rangers	1970-71	Bonnyrigg Rose Athletic
1912-18	*No Competition*	1948-49	Stoneyburn Juniors	1971-72	Sauchie
1918-19	Seafield Athletic	1949-50	Haddington Athletic	1972-73	Linlithgow Rose
1919-20	Seafield Athletic	1950-51	Arniston Rangers	1973-74	Sauchie
1920-21	Livingston United	1951-52	Newtongrange Star	1974-75	Bonnyrigg Rose Athletic
1921-22	Winchburgh Thistle	1952-53	Armadale Thistle	1975-76	Bonnyrigg Rose Athletic
1922-23	Linlithgow Rose	1953-54	Bo'ness United	*1976-84*	*No Competition*
1923-24	Linlithgow Rose	1954-55	Bo'ness United	1984-85	Linlithgow Rose
1924-25	Vale of Grange	1955-56	Bo'ness United	1985-86	Dalkeith Thistle
1925-27	*No Competition*	1956-57	Dalkeith Thistle	1986-87	Ormiston Primrose
1927-28	Newtongrange Star	1957-58	Arniston Rangers	1987-88	Ormiston Primrose
1928-36	*No Competition*	1958-59	Haddington Athletic	1988-89	Linlithgow Rose
1936-37	Musselburgh Athletic	1959-60	Bathgate Thistle	*1989-96*	*No Competition*
1937-38	Musselburgh Athletic	1960-61	Arniston Rangers	1996-97	Linlithgow Rose
1938-39	Winchburgh Juniors	1961-62	Newtongrange Star	1997-98	Whitburn
1939-40	Stoneyburn Juniors	1962-63	Armadale Thistle	1998-99	Linlithgow Rose
1940-41	Bathgate Thistle	1963-64	Bo'ness United	1999-00	Armadale Thistle
1941-42	Armadale Thistle	1964-65	Armadale Thistle		
1942-43	Newarthill Hearts	1965-66	Bonnyrigg Rose Athletic		

Summary: *9 - Linlithgow Rose; 6 - Armadale Thistle; 5 - Seafield Athletic; 4 - Arniston Rangers, Bo'ness United, Bonnyrigg Rose Athletic; 3 - Musselburgh Athletic, Newtongrange Star, Whitburn; 2 - Bathgate Thistle, Dalkeith Thistle, Haddington Athletic, Ormiston Primrose, Sauchie, Stoneyburn Juniors, Vale of Grange; 1 - Carluke Rovers, Livingston United, Newarthill Hearts, Tranent Juniors, Winchburgh Juniors, Winchburgh Thistle, Wishaw Juniors.*

Scottish Junior Cup

1886-87	Fairfield (Govan)	1899-00	Maryhill	1912-13	Inverkeithing United
1887-88	Wishaw Thistle	1900-01	Burnbank Athletic	1913-14	Larkhall Thistle
1888-89	Burnbank Swifts	1901-02	Glencairn	1914-15	Parkhead
1889-90	Burnbank Swifts	1902-03	Parkhead	1915-16	Petershill
1890-91	Vale of Clyde	1903-04	Vale of Clyde	1916-17	St. Mirren Juniors
1891-92	Minerva	1904-05	Ashfield	1917-18	Petershill
1892-93	Vale of Clyde	1905-06	Dunipace Juniors	1918-19	Rutherglen Glencairn
1893-94	Ashfield	1906-07	Strathclyde	1919-20	Parkhead
1894-95	Ashfield	1907-08	Larkhall Thistle	1920-21	Kirkintilloch Rob Roy
1895-96	Cambuslang Hibs	1908-09	Kilwinning Rangers	1921-22	St. Roch's
1896-97	Strathclyde	1909-10	Ashfield	1922-23	Musselburgh Bruntonians
1897-98	Dalziel Rovers	1910-11	Burnbank Athletic	1923-24	Parkhead
1898-99	Parkhead	1911-12	Petershill	1924-25	Saltcoats Victoria

925-26	Strathclyde	1950-51	Petershill	1975-76	Bo'ness United
926-27	Rutherglen Glencairn	1951-52	Kilbirnie Ladeside	1976-77	Kilbirnie Ladeside
927-28	Maryhill Hibs	1952-53	Vale of Leven	1977-78	Bonnyrigg Rose Athletic
928-29	Dundee Viloet	1953-54	Sunnybank	1978-79	Cumnock Juniors
929-30	Newtongrange Star	1954-55	Kilsyth Rangers	1979-80	Baillieston
930-31	Denny Hibs	1955-56	Petershill	1980-81	Pollok
931-32	Glasgow Perthshire	1956-57	Banks o' Dee	1981-82	Blantyre Victoria
932-33	Yoker Athletic	1957-58	Shotts Bon Accord	1982-83	East Kilbride Thistle
933-34	Benburb	1958-59	Irvine Meadow	1983-84	Bo'ness United
934-35	Tranent Juniors	1959-60	St. Andrews United	1984-85	Pollok
935-36	Benburb	1960-61	Dunbar United	1985-86	Auchinleck Talbot
936-37	Arthurlie	1961-62	Kirkintilloch Rob Roy	1986-87	Auchinleck Talbot
937-38	Cambuslang Rangers	1962-63	Irvine Meadow	1987-88	Auchinleck Talbot
938-39	Rutherglen Glencairn	1963-64	Johnstone Burgh	1988-89	Cumnock Juniors
939-40	Maryhill	1964-65	Linlithgow Rose	1989-90	Hill o' Beath Hawthorn
940-41	Glasgow Perthshire	1965-66	Bonnyrigg Rose Athletic	1990-91	Auchinleck Talbot
941-42	Clydebank Juniors	1966-67	Kilsyth Rangers	1991-92	Auchinleck Talbot
942-43	Kirkintilloch Rob Roy	1967-68	Johnstone Burgh	1992-93	Glenafton Athletic
943-44	Glasgow Perthshire	1968-69	Cambuslang Rangers	1993-94	Largs Thistle
944-45	Burnbank Athletic	1969-70	Blantyre Victoria	1994-95	Camelon Juniors
945-46	Fauldhouse United	1970-71	Cambuslang Rangers	1995-96	Tayport
946-47	Shawfield	1971-72	Cambuslang Rangers	1996-97	Pollok
947-48	Bo'ness United	1972-73	Irvine Meadow	1997-98	Arthurlie
948-49	Auchinleck Talbot	1973-74	Cambuslang Rangers	1998-99	Kilwinning Rangers
949-50	Blantyre Victoria	1974-75	Glenrothes	1999-00	Whitburn

ummary: *6 - Auchinleck Talbot; 5 - Cambuslang Rangers, Parkhead, Petershill; 4 - Ashfield; - Blantyre Victoria, Bo'ness United, Burnbank Athletic, Glasgow Perthshire, Irvine Meadow, irkintilloch Rob Roy, Pollok, Rutherglen Glencairn, Strathclyde, Vale of Clyde; 2 - Arthurlie, Benburb, onnyrigg Rose Athletic, Burnbank Swifts, Cumnock Juniors, Johnstone Burgh, Kilbirnie Ladeside, ilsyth Rangers, Kilwinning Rangers, Larkhall Thistle, Maryhill; 1 - Baillieston, Banks o' Dee, ambuslang Hibs, Camelon Juniors, Clydebank Juniors, Dalziel Rovers, Denny Hibs, Dunbar United, undee Violet, Dunipace Juniors, East Kilbride Thistle, Fairfield, Fauldhouse United, Glenafton thletic, Glencairn, Glenrothes, Hill o' Beath Hawthorn, Inverkeithing United, Largs Thistle, Linlithgow ose, Maryhill Hibs, Minerva, Musselburgh Bruntonians, Newtongrange Star, St. Andrews United, t. Mirren Juniors, St. Roch's, Saltcoats Victoria, Shawfield, Shotts Bon Accord, Sunnybank, Tayport, ranent Juniors, Vale of Leven, Whitburn, Wishaw Thistle, Yoker Athletic.*

Scottish Junior League

892-93	Baillieston Thistle	1914-15	Renfrew	1928-29	Alva Albion Rangers
893-94	Baillieston Thistle	1915-16	Renfrew	1929-30	Port Glasgow Juniors
894-00	*No Competition*	1916-17	St. Anthony's	1930-31	Dumbarton Harp United
900-01	Kirkintilloch Rob Roy	1917-18	Burnbank Athletic	1931-32	Rothesay Royal Victoria
901-02	Kilsyth Emmet	1918-19	St. Anthony's	1932-33	Maryhill Hibs
902-03	Milngavie	1919-20	St. Anthony's	1933-34	Milngavie
903-04	Kilbirnie Ladeside	1920-21	St. Anthony's	1934-35	Bute Athletic
904-08	*No Competition*	1921-22	St. Roch's	1935-36	Rothesay Royal Victoria
908-09	Bellshill Athletic	1922-23	Duntocher Hibs	1936-37	Rothesay Royal Victoria
909-10	Port Glasgow Athletic	1923-24	Baillieston	1937-38	Port Glasgow Juniors
910-11	Port Glasgow Athletic	1924-25	Baillieston	1938-39	Johnstone Juniors
911-12	Vale of Grange	1925-26	Kilsyth Rangers	1939-40	Forth Rangers
912-13	Neilston Victoria	1926-27	Croy Celtic	*1940-46*	*No Competition*
913-14	Port Glasgow Athletic	1927-28	Maryhill Hibs	1946-47	Dunoon Athletic

ummary: *4 - St. Anthony's; 3 - Port Glasgow Athletic Juniors, Rothesay Royal Victoria; - Baillieston, Baillieston Thistle, Maryhill Hibs, Milngavie, Port Glasgow Juniors, Renfrew; 1 - Alva lbion Rangers, Bellshill Athletic, Burnbank Athletic, Bute Athletic, Croy Celtic, Dumbarton Harp nited, Dunoon Athletic, Duntocher Hibs, Forth Rangers, Johnstone Juniors, Kilbirnie Ladeside, ilsyth Emmet, Kilsyth Rangers, Kirkintilloch Rob Roy, Neilston Victoria, St. Roch's, Vale of Grange.*

Scottish Junior League Victory Consolation Cup

1919-20	Duntocher Hibs	1925-26	Vale of Leven Juniors	1931-32	Cumbernauld Thistle
1920-21	St. Roch's	1926-27	Cleansing Juniors	1932-33	Milngavie
1921-22	Condorrat Rovers	1927-28	Maryhill Hibs	1933-34	Baillieston
1922-23	Dumbarton Juniors	1928-29	Coats Juniors	1934-35	St. Francis
1923-24	Vale of Leven Juniors	1929-30	Port Glasgow Athletic J.	1935-36	Twechar United
1924-25	Duntocher Hibs	1930-31	Grange Rovers	1936-37	Kilsyth Rangers

Scottish Junior League Victory Cup

1918-19	St. Anthony's	1926-27	Yoker Athletic	1934-35	Rothesay Royal Victoria
1919-20	Wishaw YMCA	1927-28	Dunipace Juniors	1935-36	Cumbernauld Thistle
1920-21	Kilsyth Emmet	1928-29	Dunblane Rovers	1936-37	Forth Rangers
1921-22	St. Anthony's	1929-30	Dunblane Rovers	1937-38	Grange Rovers
1922-23	Dumbarton Juniors	1930-31	Kilsyth Rangers	1938-39	Dunipace Juniors
1923-24	Paisley Juniors	1931-32	Camelon Juniors	1939-40	
1924-25	Bridgeton Waverley	1932-33	Bute Athletic	1940-41	Maryhill Harp
1925-26	Port Glasgow Athletic J.	1933-34	Baillieston		

Scottish Road Services Cup
(Also known as the British Road Services Cup)

1989-90	Carnoustie Panmure	1990-91	Forfar Albion	1991-92	Forfar Albion

Simpson Shield
(For member clubs of the East Lothian Junior F.A.)

1892-93	Niddrie Bluebell	1902-03	Bo'ness Our Boys	1911-12	Musselburgh Athletic
1893-94	Musselburgh Windsor	1903-04	Arniston Rangers	1912-13	Wemyss Athletic
1894-95		1904-05	Arniston Rangers	1913-14	Musselburgh Athletic
1895-96	Niddrie Bluebell	1905-06	Bonnyrigg Rose Athletic	1914-15	Musselburgh Athletic
1897-98	Arniston Rangers	1906-07	Newtongrange Star	1915-19	*No Competition*
1898-99	Edinburgh Renton	1907-08	Arniston Rangers	1919-20	Newtongrange Star
1899-00		1908-09	Penicuik Juniors	1920-21	Penicuik Juniors
1900-01	Bo'ness Our Boys	1909-10	Edinburgh Roseberry	1921-22	Tranent Juniors
1901-02	Arniston Rangers	1910-11	Arniston Rangers		

Summary: *6 - Arniston Rangers; 3 - Musselburgh Athletic; 2 - Bo'ness Our Boys, Newtongrange Star, Niddrie Bluebell; 1 - Bonnyrigg Rose Athletic, Edinburgh Renton, Edinburgh Roseberry, Musselburgh Windsor, Tranent Juniors, Wemyss Athletic.*

Smyllum Charity Cup
(Smyllum-Langbank Cup from 1935-36 to 1947-48)

1919-20	Vale of Clyde	1930-31	St. Roch's	1948-50	*No Competition*
1920-21	Rutherglen Glencairn	1931-32	Shawfield	1950-51	St. Roch's
1921-22	Parkhead	1932-33	Shawfield	1951-52	St. Anthony's
1922-23	Strathclyde	1933-34	St. Anthony's	1952-53	Blantyre Celtic
1923-24	Strathclyde	1934-35	St. Francis	1953-54	Blantyre Celtic
1924-25	Strathclyde	1935-36	St. Anthony's	1954-55	Maryhill Harp
1925-26	St. Anthony's	1936-37	St. Anthony's	1955-56	St. Anthony's
1926-27	Strathclyde	1937-38	Maryhill Hibs	1956-57	Maryhill Harp
1927-28	Strathclyde	1938-39	St. Roch's	1957-58	Duntocher Hibs
1928-29	Bridgeton Waverley	1939-47	*No Competition*	1958-59	Burnbank Athletic
1929-30	Bridgeton Waverley	1947-48	Blantyre Celtic		

Summary: *6 - St. Anthony's; 5 - Strathclyde; 3 - Blantyre Celtic, St. Roch's; 2 - Bridgeton Waverley, Maryhill Harp, Shawfield; 1 - Burnbank Athletic, Duntocher Hibs, Maryhill Hibs, Parkhead, Rutherglen Glencairn, St. Francis, Vale of Clyde.*

South Ayrshire Cup

95-96	Maybole Juniors	1997-98	Annbank United	1999-00	Troon
96-97	Troon	1998-99	Troon		

South Ayrshire Junor League

20-21	Auchinleck Talbot	1924-25	Muirkirk Athletic	*1928-31*	*No Competition*
21-22	New Cumnock United	1925-26	Cumnock Juniors	1931-32	Glenafton Athletic
22-23	New Cumnock United	1926-27	Lugar Boswell Thistle		
23-24	New Cumnock United	1927-28	Cronberry Eglinton		

Stewart Memorial Cup

(For member clubs of the North Regional Junior F.A. North Section)

54-55	RAF Kinloss	1970-71	Nairn St. Ninian	1986-87	Deveronside
55-56	Fochabers	1971-72	Forres Thistle	1987-88	Nairn St. Ninian
56-57	New Elgin	1972-73	Buckie Rovers	1988-89	Deveronside
57-58	Lossiemouth United	1973-74	Burghead Thistle	1989-90	Deveronside
58-59	Fochabers	1974-75	Burghead Thistle	1990-91	Islavale
59-60	Fochabers	1975-76	Burghead Thistle	1991-92	Islavale
60-61	Lossiemouth United	1976-77		1992-93	Deveronside
61-62	Islavale	1977-78	Nairn St. Ninian	1993-94	Deveronside
62-63	New Elgin	1978-79	Rothes Decimals	1994-95	Deveronside
63-64	New Elgin	1979-80	Burghead Thistle	1995-96	Nairn St. Ninian
64-65	Buckie Rovers	1980-81	Nairn St. Ninian	1996-97	Islavale
65-66	Buckie Rovers	1981-82	Buckie Rovers	1997-98	Lossiemouth United
66-67	New Elgin	1982-83	RAF Kinloss	1998-99	New Elgin
67-68	Buckie Rovers	1983-84	Deveronside	1999-00	Forres Thistle
68-69	RAF Kinloss	1984-85	Cabar Feidh		
69-70	Burghead Thistle	1985-86	Cabar Feidh		

Summary: *7 - Deveronside; 5 - Buckie Rovers, Burghead Thistle, Nairn St. Ninian, New Elgin; - Islavale; 3 - Fochabers, Lossiemouth United, RAF Kinloss; 2 - Cabar Feidh, Forres Thistle; - Rothes Decimals.*

Stirling & District Junior Cup

(For member clubs of the Stirlingshire Junior F.A.)

97-98	Bannockburn	1911-12	Denny Athletic	1928-29	Kilsyth Emmet
98-99	Dunipace Juniors	1912-13	Dunipace Juniors	1929-30	Forth Rangers
99-00	Dunipace Juniors	1913-14	Kilsyth Emmet	1930-31	Denny Hibs
00-01	Dunipace Juniors	*1914-18*	*No Competition*	1931-32	Grange Rovers
01-02	Dunipace Juniors	1918-19	Cowie	1932-33	St. Ninians Thistle
02-03	Dunipace Juniors	1919-20	Dunipace Juniors	1933-34	Dunipace Juniors
03-04	Stenhousemuir Hearts	1920-21	Dunipace Juniors	1934-35	Dunipace Juniors
04-05	Dunipace Juniors	1921-22	Dunipace Juniors	1935-36	Camelon Juniors
05-06	Dunipace Juniors	1922-23	Dunipace Juniors	1936-37	Forth Rangers
06-07	St. Ninians Thistle	1923-24	St. Ninians Thistle	1937-38	Forth Rangers
07-08	Dunipace Juniors	1924-25	Kilsyth Rangers	1938-39	Grange Rovers
08-09	St. Ninians Thistle	1925-26	Dunipace Juniors	1939-40	Forth Rangers
09-10	Denny Athletic	1926-27	Camelon Juniors		
10-11	Denny Hibs	1927-28	Grange Rovers		

Summary: *16 - Dunipace Juniors; 4 - Forth Rangers, St. Ninians Thistle; 3 - Grange Rovers; - Camelon Juniors, Denny Athletic, Denny Hibs, Kilsyth Emmet; 1 - Bannockburn, Cowie, Kilsyth Rangers, Stenhousemuir Hearts.*

Stirlingshire Junior Consolation Cup

02-03	Vale of Carron	1905-06	Bonnybridge Athletic	1908-09	St. Ninians Thistle
03-04	Stenhousemuir Hearts	1906-07	Cowie Wanderers	1909-10	Denny Athletic
04-05	Vale of Carron	1907-08	East Plean United		

Stirlingshire Junior Cup

1891-92	Campsie Black Watch	1913-14	Grange Rovers	1936-37	St. Ninians Thistle
1892-93	Slamannan Swifts	1914-15	Cowie Wanderers	1937-38	Kilsyth Rangers
1893-94	Slamannan Swifts	1915-16	Denny Hibs	1938-39	Forth Rangers
1894-95	Kilsyth Rangers	*1916-18*	*No Competition*	1939-40	Grange Rovers
1895-96	Campsie Black Watch	1918-19	Kilsyth Rangers	*1940-45*	*No Competition*
1896-97	Campsie Black Watch	1919-20	Dunipace Juniors	1945-46	Kilsyth Rangers
1897-98	Gairdoch Juniors	1920-21	Grange Rovers	1946-47	Forth Rangers
1898-99	Campsie Minerva	1921-22	Denny Hibs	1947-48	Grange Rovers
1899-00	Hawthorn	1922-23	St. Ninians Thistle	1948-49	Camelon Juniors
1900-01	Grange Rovers	1923-24	Grange Rovers	1949-50	Grange Rovers
1901-02	Dunipace Juniors	1924-25	Grange Rovers	1950-51	Camelon Juniors
1902-03	Dunipace Juniors	1925-26	Camelon Juniors	1951-52	Camelon Juniors
1903-04	Dunipace Juniors	1926-27	Dunblane Rovers	1952-53	Kilsyth Rangers
1904-05	Dunipace Juniors	1927-28	Grange Rovers	1953-54	Kilsyth Rangers
1905-06	Dunipace Juniors	1928-29	Grange Rovers	1954-55	Kilsyth Rangers
1906-07	St. Ninians Thistle	1929-30	Dunblane Rovers	1955-56	Kilsyth Rangers
1907-08	St. Ninians Thistle	1930-31	Dunblane Rovers	1956-57	Kilsyth Rangers
1908-09	Dunipace Juniors	1931-32	Denny Hibs	1957-58	Kilsyth Rangers
1909-10	Grange Rovers	1932-33	St. Ninians Thistle	1958-59	Kilsyth Rangers
1910-11	Dunipace Juniors	1933-34	St. Ninians Thistle	1959-60	Kilsyth Rangers
1911-12	Dunipace Juniors	1934-35	Dunipace Juniors	1960-61	Grangemouth
1912-13	Dunipace Juniors	1935-36	Camelon Juniors	1961-62	Kilsyth Rangers

Summary: *13 - Kilsyth Rangers; 11 - Dunipace Juniors, Grange Rovers; 6 - St. Ninian's Thistle; 5 - Camelon Juniors; 3 - Campsie Black Watch, Denny Hibs, Dunblane Rovers; 2 - Forth Rangers, Slamannan Swifts; 1 - Campsie Minerva, Cowie Wanderers, Gairdoch Juniors, Grangemouth, Hawthorn*

Stirlingshire Junior League

1900-01	Dunipace Juniors	1910-11	Denny Hibs	1922-23	Dunipace Juniors
1901-02	Dunipace Juniors	1911-12	Kilsyth Emmet	1923-24	Dunipace Juniors
1902-03	Dunipace Juniors	1912-13	Dunipace Juniors	1924-25	Alva Albion Rangers
1903-04	Dunipace Juniors	1913-14	Dunipace Juniors	1925-26	Grange Rovers
1904-05	Dunipace Juniors	1914-15	California Celtic	1926-27	Grange Rovers
1905-06	Vale of Carron	1915-16	California Celtic	1927-28	Camelon Juniors
1906-07	Dunipace Juniors	*1916-19*	*No Competition*	*1928-32*	*No Competition*
1907-08	Dunipace Juniors	1919-20	Dunipace Juniors	1932-33	Clackmannan Juniors
1908-09	Dunipace Juniors	1920-21	Dunipace Juniors		
1909-10	Kilsyth Emmet	1921-22	Dunipace Juniors		

Summary: *15 - Dunipace Juniors; 2 - California Celtic, Grange Rovers, Kilsyth Emmet; 1 - Alva Albion Rangers, Camelon Juniors, Clackmannan Juniors, Denny Hibs, Vale of Carron.*

Stirlingshire Junior League Cup

1920-21	Dunipace Juniors	1925-26	Denny Hibs	1930-31	Alva Albion Rangers
1921-22	Dunipace Juniors	1926-27	Dunipace Juniors	1931-32	Camelon Juniors
1922-23	Dunipace Juniors	1927-28	Kilsyth Rangers	1932-33	Clackmannan Juniors
1923-24	Dunipace Juniors	1928-29	Grange Rovers		
1924-25	Grange Rovers	1929-30	Grange Rovers		

Taycars Trophy
(Fife & Tayside Regions' Junior Clubs)

1995-96	Hill o' Beath Hawthorn	1997-98	Kelty Hearts	1999-00	Tayport
1996-97	Dundee St. Joseph's	1998-99	Tayport		

Tayside Drybrough Cup

73-74	Blairgowrie	1978-79	Lochee United	1983-84	Dundee North End
74-75	Arbroath Victoria	1979-80	Kirrie Thistle	1984-85	Kinnoull
75-76	Carnoustie Panmure	1980-81	Lochee United	1985-86	Dundee North End
76-77	Jeanfield Swifts	1981-82	Lochee United	1986-87	Downfield
77-78	Carnoustie Panmure	1982-83	Lochee Harp		

Tayside Regional League Cup
(Currently the Downfield S.C. Cup)

68-69	Jeanfield Swifts	1978-79	Osborne	1988-92	No Competition
69-70	Carnoustie Panmure	1979-80	Downfield	1992-93	Dundee St. Joseph's
70-71	Blairgowrie	1980-81	Arbroath S.C.	1993-94	Montrose Roselea
71-72	East Craigie	1981-82	Downfield	1994-95	East Craigie
72-73	Dundee North End	1982-82	Downfield	1995-96	Kirriemuir Thistle
73-74	Arbroath Victoria	1983-84	Lochee United	1996-97	Kirriemuir Thistle
74-75	Broughty Athletic	1984-85	Jeanfield Swifts	1997-98	Lochee Harp
75-76	Blairgowrie	1985-86	Kirriemuir Thistle	1998-99	Bankfoot Athletic
76-77	Kinnoull	1986-87	Downfield	1999-00	East Craigie
77-78	Kirriemuir Thistle	1987-88	Downfield		

Summary: 5 - Downfield; 4 - Kirriemuir Thistle; 3 - East Craigie; 2 - Blairgowrie, Jeanfield Swifts; 1 - Arbroath S.C., Arbroath Victoria, Bankfoot Athletic, Broughty Athletic, Carnoustie Panmure, Dundee North End, Dundee St. Joseph's, Kinnoull, Lochee Harp, Lochee United, Montrose Roselea, Osborne.

Tayside Regional League - Division 1

69-70	Blairgowrie	1980-81	Carnoustie Panmure	1991-92	Tayport
70-71	Blairgowrie	1981-82	Lochee United	1992-93	Tayport
71-72	Blairgowrie	1982-83	Kinnoull	1993-94	Tayport
72-73	Jeanfield Swifts	1983-84	Kinnoull	1994-95	Tayport
73-74	Kirrie Thistle	1984-85	Lochee Harp	1995-96	Tayport
74-75	Blairgowrie	1985-86	Lochee Harp	1996-97	Dundee St. Joseph's
75-76	Carnoustie Panmure	1986-87	Lochee United	1997-98	Dundee North End
76-77	Carnoustie Panmure	1987-88	Downfield	1998-99	Tayport
77-78	Carnoustie Panmure	1988-89	Downfield	1999-00	Tayport
78-79	Carnoustie Panmure	1989-90	Downfield		
79-80	Lochee United	1990-91	Forfar West End		

Summary: 7 - Tayport; 5 - Carnoustie Panmure; 4 - Blairgowrie; 3 - Downfield, Lochee United; 2 - Kinnoull, Lochee Harp; 1 - Dundee North End, Dundee St. Joseph's, Forfar West End, Jeanfield Swifts, Kirrie Thistle.

Tayside Regional League - Division 2

69-70	Broughty Athletic	1980-81	Kinnoull	1991-92	Carnoustie Panmure
70-71	Carnoustie Panmure	1981-82	Forfar Albion	1992-93	Dundee St. Joseph's
71-72	Dundee St. Joseph's	1982-83	Forfar West End	1993-94	Lochee United
72-73	Luncarty	1983-84	Bankfoot Athletic	1994-95	Scone Thistle
73-74	Alyth United	1984-85	East Craigie	1995-96	Jeanfield Swifts
74-75	Crieff Earngrove	1985-86	Broughty Athletic	1996-97	Kirrie Thistle
75-76	Dundee Violet	1986-87	Blairgowrie	1997-98	Lochee Harp
76-77	Jeanfield Swifts	1987-88	Forfar Albion	1998-99	Bankfoot Athletic
77-78	Forfar Albion	1988-89	Kinnoull	1999-00	Jeanfield Swifts
78-79	Dundee North End	1989-90	Luncarty		
79-80	Broughty Athletic	1990-91	Tayport		

Summary: 3 - Broughty Athletic, Forfar Albion, Jeanfield Swifts; 2 - Bankfoot Athletic, Carnoustie Panmure, Dundee St. Joseph's, Kinnoull, Luncarty; 1 - Alyth United, Blairgowrie, Crieff Earngrove, Dundee North End, Dundee Violet, East Craigie, Forfar West End, Kirrie Thistle, Lochee Harp, Lochee United, Scone Thistle, Tayport.

Telegraph Cup
(For member clubs of the Dundee Junior F.A.)

1901-02	Edenbank	1925-26	Dundee Celtic	1949-50	Osborne
1902-03	Fairfield	1926-27	Forthill	1950-51	Carnoustie Panmure
1903-04	Stobswell	1927-28	Logie	1951-52	Dundee North End
1904-05	Stobswell	1928-29	Dundee Violet	1952-53	Dundee North End
1905-06	Dundee Violet	1929-30	Logie	1953-54	Elmwood
1906-07	Dundee North End	1930-31	Fairfield	1954-55	Dundee St. Joseph's
1907-08	Lochee Harp	1931-32	East Craigie	1955-56	Dundee St. Joseph's
1908-09	Dundee Violet	1932-33	Dundee North End	1956-57	Dundee North End
1909-10	East Craigie	1933-34	Downfield	1957-58	Osborne
1910-11	Arnot	1934-35	Lochee Harp	1958-59	Stobswell
1911-12	Forthill	1935-36	Arnot	1959-60	Lochee Harp
1912-13	Fairfield	1936-37	Broughty Ex-S	1960-61	Lochee United
1913-14	Arnot	1937-38	Dundee Violet	1961-62	Dundee St. Joseph's
1914-15	Dundee St. Joseph's	1938-39	Broughty Ex-S	1962-63	Lochee United
1915-16	Fairfield	1939-40	Dundee Violet	1963-64	Downfield
1916-17	*No Competition*	1940-41	Stobswell	1964-65	Carnoustie Panmure
1917-18	Fairfield	1941-42	Carnoustie Panmure	1965-66	Osborne
1918-19	*No Competition*	1942-43	Dundee Violet	1966-67	Dundee St. Joseph's
1919-20	Osborne	1943-44	Dundee North End	1967-68	Carnoustie Panmure
1920-21	*No Competition*	*1944-45*	*No Competition*	1968-69	Lochee Harp
1921-22	Dundee Violet	1945-46	Dundee Violet	1969-70	Lochee Harp
1922-23	Anchorage	1946-47	Dundee North End	1970-71	Osborne
1923-24	Fairfield	1947-48	Stobswell	1971-72	Dundee St. Joseph's
1924-25	Dundee Celtic	1948-49	Arnot	1972-73	Dundee St. Joseph's

Summary: *8 - Dundee Violet; 7 - Dundee North End, Dundee St. Joseph's; 6 - Fairfield, 5 - Lochee Harp, Osborne, Stobswell; 4 - Arnot, Carnoustie Panmure; 2 - Broughty Ex-S, Downfield, Dundee Celtic, East Craigie, Forthill, Lochee United, Logie; 1 - Anchorage, Edenbank, Elmwood.*

Thistle Cup
(For member clubs of the East Regional Junior F.A.)

1960-61	Armadale Thistle	1966-67	Bonnyrigg Rose Athletic	1972-73	Musselburgh Athletic
1961-62	Whitburn	1967-68	Newtongrange Star	1973-74	Tranent Juniors
1962-63	Newtongrange Star	1968-69	Newtongrange Star	1974-75	Newtongrange Star
1963-64	Whitburn	1969-70	Pumpherston Juniors	1975-76	Dunbar United
1964-65	Bonnyrigg Rose Athletic	1970-71	Broxburn Athletic	1976-77	Newtongrange Star
1965-66	Bonnyrigg Rose Athletic	1971-72	Whitburn		

Summary: *5 - Newtongrange Star; 3 - Bonnyrigg Rose Athletic, Whitburn; 1 - Armadale Thistle, Broxburn Athletic, Dunbar United, Musselburgh Athletic, Pumpherston Juniors, Tranent Juniors.*

Thornton Shield
(For member clubs of the Edinburgh & District Junior F.A.)

1923-24	Newtongrange Star	1935-36	Dalkeith Thistle	1947-48	Armadale Thistle
1924-25	Portobello Thistle	1936-37	Dalkeith Thistle	1948-49	Tranent Juniors
1925-26	Linlithgow Rose	1937-38	Stoneyburn Juniors	1949-50	Grange Rovers
1926-27	Musselburgh Bruntonians	1938-39	Dunbar United	1950-51	Newtongrange Star
1927-28	Newtongrange Star	1939-40	Haddington Athletic	1951-52	Newtongrange Star
1928-29	Newtongrange Star	1940-41	Haddington Athletic	1952-53	Newtongrange Star
1929-30	Musselburgh Bruntonians	1941-42	Armadale Thistle	1953-54	Linlithgow Rose
1930-31	Tranent Juniors	1942-43	Polkemmet Juniors	1954-55	Newtongrange Star
1931-32	Newtongrange Star	1943-44	Bathgate Thistle	1955-56	Bonnyrigg Rose Athletic
1932-33	Newtongrange Star	1944-45	Bathgate Thistle	1956-57	Pumpherston Juniors
1933-34	Wallyford Bluebell	1945-46	Fauldhouse United	1957-58	West Calder United
1934-35	Thorntree United	1946-47	Haddington Athletic	1958-59	West Calder United

Summary: *9 - Newtongrange Star; 3 - Haddington Athletic; 2 - Armadale Thistle, Bathgate Thistle, Dalkeith Thistle, Linlithgow Rose, Musselburgh Bruntonians, Tranent Juniors, West Calder United; 1 - Bonnyrigg Rose Athletic, Dunbar United, Fauldhouse United, Grange Rovers, Polkemmet Juniors, Portobello Thistle, Pumpherston Juniors, Stoneyburn Juniors, Thorntree United, Wallyford Bluebell.*

Thornton Sports Cup

| 81-82 | Newtongrange Star | 1982-83 | Newtongrange Star | 1983-84 | Newtongrange Star |

Tom Gordon Cup
(See under Robbie Nicol Cup)

Usher Cup
(See under Linlithgowshire Junior Cup)

Vernon Trophy
(for Ayrshire Clubs)

36-37	Cumnock Juniors	1948-49	Ardrossan Winton Rovers	1956-57	Ardeer Thistle
37-38	Kilwinning Rangers	1949-50	Irvine Meadow	1957-58	Darvel Juniors
38-39	Johnstone Athletic	1950-51	Cumnock Juniors	1958-59	Glenafton Athletic
39-40	Ardeer Recreation	1951-52	Annbank United	1959-60	Darvel Juniors
40-45	*No Competition*	1952-53	Irvine Meadow	1960-61	Irvine Meadow
45-46	Annbank United	1953-54	Largs Thistle	1961-62	Saltcoats Victoria
46-47	Ardeer Recreation	1954-55	Auchinleck Talbot	1962-63	Maybole Juniors
47-48	Kello Rovers	1955-56	Annbank United		

Summary: *3 - Annbank United, Irvine Meadow; 2 - Ardeer Recreation, Cumnock Juniors, Darvel Juniors; 1 - Ardeer Thistle, Ardrossan Winton Rovers, Auchinleck Talbot, Glenafton Athletic, Johnstone Athletic, Kello Rovers, Kilwinning Rangers, Largs Thistle, Maybole Juniors, Saltcoats Victoria.*

Western League

19-20	Ardrossan Winton Rovers	1936-37	Cumnock Juniors	1953-54	Lugar Boswell Thistle
20-21	Kilwinning Rangers	1937-38	Johnstone Athletic	1954-55	Irvine Meadow
21-22	Irvine Meadow	1938-39	Saltcoats Victoria	1955-56	Lugar Boswell Thistle
22-23	Kilwinning Rangers	1939-40	Johnstone Athletic	1956-57	Irvine Meadow
23-24	Saltcoats Victoria	1940-41	Ardeer Recreation	1957-58	Irvine Meadow
24-25	Ardeer Thistle	1941-42	Ardeer Recreation	1958-59	Glenafton Athletic
25-26	Saltcoats Victoria	1942-43	Ardeer Recreation	1959-60	Ardeer Thistle
26-27	Saltcoats Victoria	1943-44	Ardeer Recreation	1960-61	Irvine Meadow
27-28	Kilwinning Rangers	1944-45	Ardeer Recreation	1961-62	Glenafton Athletic
28-29	Irvine Meadow	1945-46	Saltcoats Victoria	1962-63	Glenafton Athletic
29-30	Kilwinning Eglinton	1946-47	Neilston Juniors	1963-64	Glenafton Athletic
30-31	Kilwinning Rangers	1947-48	Kilbirnie Ladeside	1964-65	Beith Juniors
31-32	Kilwinning Rangers	1948-49	Irvine Meadow	1965-66	Kilwinning Rangers
32-33	Irvine Meadow	1949-50	Kilbirnie Ladeside	1966-67	Darvel Juniors
33-34	Ardrossan Winton Rovers	1950-51	Irvine Meadow	1967-68	Kilbirnie Ladeside
34-35	Glenafton Athletic	1951-52	Kilbirbie Ladeside		
35-36	Cumnock Juniors	1952-53	Cumnock Juniors		

Summary: *9 - Irvine Meadow; 6 - Kilwinning Rangers; 5 - Ardeer Recreation, Glenafton Athletic, Saltcoats Victoria; 4 - Kilbirnie Ladeside; 3 - Cumnock Juniors; 2 - Ardeer Thistle, Ardrossan Winton Rovers, Johnstone Athletic, Lugar Boswell Thistle; 1 - Beith Juniors, Darvel Juniors, Kilwinning Eglinton, Neilston Juniors.*

Western League Cup

22-23	Dreghorn Juniors	1928-29	Irvine Meadow	1934-35	Glenafton Athletic
23-24	Kilbirnie Ladeside	1929-30	Kilwinning Rangers	1935-36	Ardrossan Winton Rov.
24-25	Ardeer Thistle	1930-31	Darvel Juniors	1936-37	Cumnock Juniors
25-26	Ardeer Thistle	1931-32	Kilbirnie Ladeside	1937-38	Saltcoats Victoria
26-27	Saltcoats Victoria	1932-33	Saltcoats Victoria	1938-39	Kilbirnie Ladeside
27-28	Irvine Meadow	1933-34	Dalry Thistle	1939-40	Ardeer Recreation

1940-41	Hurlford United	1950-51	Irvine Meadow	1960-61	Ardeer Thistle
1941-42	Ardeer Recreation	1951-52	Irvine Victoria	1961-62	Irvine Meadow
1942-43	Annbank United	1952-53	Cumnock Juniors	1962-63	Glenafton Athletic
1943-44	Annbank United	1953-54	Irvine Victoria	1963-64	Craigmark Burntonians
1944-45	Hurlford United	1954-55	Irvine Meadow	1964-65	Craigmark Burntonians
1945-46	Saltcoats Victoria	1955-56	Irvine Meadow	1965-66	Glenafton Athletic
1946-47	Neilston Juniors	1956-57	Beith Juniors	1966-67	Cumnock Juniors
1947-48	Auchinleck Talbot	1957-58	Largs Thistle	1967-68	Darvel Juniors
1948-49	Cumnock Juniors	1958-59	Glenafton Athletic		
1949-50	Auchinleck Talbot	1959-60	Ardeer Thistle		

Summary: *6 - Irvine Meadow; 4 - Ardeer Thistle, Cumnock Juniors, Glanafton Athletic, Saltcoats Victoria; 3 - Kilbirnie Ladeside; 2 - Annbank United, Ardeer Recreation, Auchinleck Talbot, Craigmark Burntonians, Darvel Juniors, Hurlford United, Irvine Victoria; 1 - Ardrossan Winton Rovers, Beith Juniors, Dalry Thistle, Dreghorn Juniors, Kilwinning Rangers, Largs Thistle, Neilston Juniors.*

West Fife Cup
(Formerly the Dunfermline Cup)

1892-93	Crossgates Thistle	*1917-19*	*No Competition*	1950-51	Kelty Rangers
1893-94	Dunfermline Ath. Juniors	1919-20	Hearts of Beath	1951-52	Thornton Hibs
1894-95	Dunfermline Ath. Juniors	1920-21	Hearts of Beath	1952-53	Glencraig Colliery
1895-96	Kingseat Athletic	1921-22	Hearts of Beath	1953-54	Lochore Welfare
1896-97	Leven Thistle	1922-23	Kelty Rangers	1954-55	Lochore Welfare
1897-98	Leven Thistle	1923-24	Rosyth Recreation	1955-56	Lochgelly Albert
1898-99	Dunfermline Ath. Juniors	*1924-27*	*No Competition*	1956-57	Lochgelly Albert
1899-00	Buckhaven United	1927-28	Lochgelly Celtic	1957-58	Crossgates Primrose
1900-01	Lochgelly Rangers	1928-29	St. Leonards	1958-59	St. Andrews United
1901-02	Buckhaven United	*1929-30*	*No Competition*	1959-60	Thornton Hibs
1902-03	Lassodie	1930-31	Bowhill Rovers	1960-61	St. Andrews United
1903-04	Kelty Rangers	1931-32	Inverkeithing Juniors	1961-62	St. Andrews United
1904-05	Dunnikier Athletic	1932-33	Inverkeithing Juniors	1962-63	Lochore Welfare
1905-06	Sauchie	1933-34	Inverkeithing Juniors	1963-64	St. Andrews United
1906-07	Townhill United	1934-35	Lochgelly Albert	1964-65	Comrie Colliery
1907-08	Vale of Wemyss	1935-36	Kirkford Juniors	1965-66	Valleyfield
1908-09	Buckhaven	1936-37	Lochgelly Albert	1966-67	Clackmannan Juniors
1909-10	Glencraig Celtic	1937-38	Lochore Welfare	1967-68	Tulliallan Thistle
1910-11	Denbeath Star	1938-39	Lochore Welfare	1968-69	Oakley United
1911-12	Glencraig Celtic	1939-40	Bowhill Rovers	1969-70	Valleyfield
1912-13	Glencraig Celtic	1940-41	Bowhill Rovers	1970-71	Valleyfield
1913-14	Hearts of Beath	*1941-47*	*No Competition*	1971-72	Lochgelly Albert
1914-15	Kelty Rangers	1947-48	Crossgates Primrose	1972-73	Oakley United
1915-16	Glencraig Celtic	1948-49	Lochore Welfare		
1916-17	Denbeath Star	1949-50	Comrie Colliery		

Summary: *6 - Lochore Welfare; 5 - Lochgelly Albert; 4 - Glencraig Celtic, Hearts of Beath, Kelty Rangers, St. Andrews United; 3 - Bowhill Rovers, Dunfermline Athletic Juniors, Inverkeithing Junior, Valleyfield; 2 - Buckhaven United, Comrie Colliery, Crossgates Primrose, Denbeath Star, Leven Thistle, Oakley United, Thornton Hibs; 1 - Buckhaven, Clackmannan Juniors, Crossgates Thistle, Dunnikier Athletic, Glencraig Colliery, Kingseat Athletic, Kirkford Juniors, Lassodie, Lochgelly Celtic, Lochgelly Rangers, Rosyth Recreation, St. Leonards, Sauchie, Townhill United, Tulliallan Thistle, Vale of Wemyss.*

West of Scotland Consolation Cup

1931-32	Wishaw/Kilwinning R.	1933-34	Petershill	1935-36	Ardrossan Winton Rovers
1932-33	Cambuslang Rangers	1934-35	Saltcoats Victoria	1936-37	Wishaw Juniors

West of Scotland Cup
(Currently the Whyte & MacKay Cup)

31-32	Irvine Meadow	1954-55	Maryhill Harp	1977-78	Arthurlie
32-33	Strathclyde	1955-56	Irvine Meadow	1978-79	Auchinleck Talbot
33-34	Wishaw	1956-57	Lesmahagow	1979-80	Auchinleck Talbot
34-35	Ardrossan Winton Rovers	1957-58	Petershill	1980-81	Auchinleck Talbot
35-36	Bridgeton Waverley	1958-59	Johnstone Burgh	1981-82	Auchinleck Talbot
36-37	Parkhead	1959-60	Cambuslang Rangers	1982-83	Benburb
37-38	St. Anthony's	1960-61	Kirkintilloch Rob Roy	1983-84	Auchinleck Talbot
38-39	Shawfield	1961-62	Irvine Meadow	1984-85	Auchinleck Talbot
39-40	Glasgow Perthshire	1962-63	Kirkintilloch Rob Roy	1985-86	Auchinleck Talbot
40-41	Benburb	1963-64	Shotts Bon Accord	1986-87	Pollok
41-42	Benburb	1964-65	Johnstone Burgh	1987-88	Auchinleck Talbot
42-43	Arthurlie	1965-66	Beith Juniors	1988-89	Auchinleck Talbot
43-44	Blantyre Victoria	1966-67	Beith Juniors	1989-90	Irvine Meadow
44-45	Pollok	1967-68	Kilsyth Rangers	1990-91	Largs Thistle
45-46	Saltcoats Victoria	1968-69	Petershill	1991-92	Pollok
46-47	Saltcoats Victoria	1969-70	Irvine Meadow	1992-93	Shettleston
47-48	Auchinleck Talbot	1970-71	Irvine Meadow	1993-94	Kilwinning Rangers
48-49	Newarthill Hearts	1971-72	Cambuslang Rangers	1994-95	Shettleston
49-50	Clydebank	1972-73	Cambuslang Rangers	1995-96	Petershill
50-51	Irvine Meadow	1973-74	East Kilbride Thistle	1996-97	Arthurlie
51-52	Petershill	1974-75	Shettleston	1997-98	Pollok
52-53	Baillieston	1975-76	Arthurlie	1998-99	Kilwinning Rangers
53-54	Kilsyth Rangers	1976-77	Lanark United	1999-00	Pollok

ummary: *10 - Auchinleck Talbot; 7 - Irvine Meadow; 5 - Pollok; 4 - Arthurlie, Petershill; - Benburb, Cambuslang Rangers, Shettleston; 2 - Beith Juniors, Johnstone Burgh, Kilsyth Rangers, Jwinning Rangers, Kirkintilloch Rob Roy, Saltcoats Victoria; 1 - Ardrossan Winton Rovers, aillieston, Blantyre Victoria, Bridgeton Waverley, Clydebank Juniors, East Kilbride Thistle, Glasgow rthshire, Lanark United, Largs Thistle, Lesmahagow, Maryhill Harp, Newarthill Hearts, Parkhead, . Anthony's, Shawfield, Shotts Bon Accord, Strathclyde, Wishaw Juniors.*

Whitbread Cup
(For member clubs of the Fife Junior F.A.)

96-97	Glenrothes	1998-99	Glenrothes
97-98	Hill o' Beath Hawthorn	1999-00	Hill o' Beath Hawthorn

White Horse Cup
(For Morayshire Junior Clubs)
After 1977 awarded to the team scoring most League goals

29-30	Forres Thistle	1949-50	Bishopmill United	1963-64	Bishopmill United
30-31	Elgin Thistle	1950-51	New Elgin	1964-65	RAF Kinloss
31-32	Burghead Thistle	1951-52	Bishopmill United	1965-66	Islavale
32-33		1952-53	Forres Thistle	1966-67	Buckie Rovers
33-34	Keith Territorials	1953-54	Lossiemouth United	1967-68	Fulmar
34-35	Rothes Victoria	1954-55	RAF Kinloss	1968-69	Forres Thistle
35-36		1955-56	Lossiemouth United	1969-70	
36-37	Forres Thistle	1956-57	RAF Kinloss	1970-71	
37-38		1957-58	Burghead Thistle	1971-72	New Elgin
38-39		1958-59	New Elgin	1972-73	New Elgin
39-46	*No Competition*	1959-60	New Elgin	1973-74	Burghead Thistle
46-47	RNAS Lossiemouth	1960-61	New Elgin	1974-75	Nairn St. Ninian
47-48	Buckie Rovers	1961-62	Buckie Rovers	1975-76	Buckie Rovers
48-49	RNAS Lossiemouth	1962-63	New Elgin	1976-77	Forres Thistle

ammary: *7 - New Elgin; 5 - Forres Thistle; 4 - Buckie Rovers; 3 - Bishopmill United, Burghead histle, RAF Kinloss; 2 - Lossiemouth United, RNAS Lossiemouth; 1 - Elgin Thistle, Fulmar, Islavale, ith Territorials, Nairn St. Ninian, Rothes Victoria.*

Whyte & MacKay Cup (1)
(See under Currie Cup)

Whyte & MacKay Cup (2)
(See under West of Scotland Cup)

Wick Allan Shield
(Play-off between champions of North Regional League North and East Sections)

1969-70	Banks o' Dee	1980-81	Banks o' Dee	1991-92	FC Stoneywood
1970-71	Banks o' Dee	1981-82	Banks o' Dee	1992-93	Buckie Rovers
1971-72	Sunnybank	1982-83	Sunnybank	1993-94	Stonehaven
1972-73	Banks o' Dee	1983-84	Banks o' Dee	1994-95	FC Stoneywood
1973-74	Burghead Thistle	1984-85	FC Stoneywood	1995-96	Inverurie Loco Works
1974-75	Sunnybank	1985-86	Banks o' Dee	1996-97	Sunnybank
1975-76	Sunnybank	1986-87	Banks o' Dee	1997-98	Inverurie Loco Works
1976-77	Banks o' Dee	1987-88	Deveronside	1998-99	Sunnybank
1977-78	East End	1988-89	Bon Accord	1999-00	Deveronside
1978-79	Banks o' Dee	1989-90	Deveronside		
1979-80	Fraserburgh United	1990-91	FC Stoneywood		

Summary: *10 - Banks o' Dee; 6 - Sunnybank; 4 - FC Stoneywood; 3 - Deveronside; 2 - Inverurie Loco Works; 1 - Bon Accord, Buckie Rovers, Burghead Thistle, East End, Fraserburgh United, Stonehaven.*

Winter Cup
(Formerly the Inveralmond Cup. For Tayside Region Division 2 Clubs)

1977-78	Forfar Albion	1983-84	East Craigie	1989-90	Blairgowrie
1978-79	Dundee North End	1984-85	Downfield	1990-91	Kirriemuir Thistle
1979-80	Arbroath S.C.	1985-86	Forfar Albion	1991-92	Broughty Athletic
1980-81	Arbroath S.C.	1986-87	Blairgowrie	1992-93	Dundee St. Joseph's
1981-82	Stobswell	1987-88	Kirriemuir Thistle	1993-94	Bankfoot Athletic
1982-83	Forfar West End	1988-89	East Craigie	1994-95	Broughty Athletic

W.T. Menswear Cup
(For member clubs of the Fife Regional Junior F.A.)

1993-94	Hill o' Beath Hawthorn	1994-95	Glenrothes

Zamoyski Cup
(See under Concept Group Cup)

Special 'One-Off' Competitions

Exhibition Cup	1907-08	Newtongrange Star
Haddow Silver Jubilee Cup	1976-77	Kirkintilloch Rob Roy
Robert Lawson Shield	1997-98	Carnoustie Panmure
V.E. Day Commerorative Cup	1994-95	Kilsyth Rangers
West Lothian Millennium Cup	1999-2000	Fauldhouse United

(Competitions, both Junior and Senior, where starting and finishing dates are not generally known and (presumably) only some of the winners have been found. Where starting and/or finishing dates are known they are marked thus +)

Aberdeen Challenge Cup
1929-30	Waterloo

Aberdeenshire Junior Charity Cup
1898-99	East End
1901-02	East End
1903-04	Abergeldie
1904-05	East End
1905-06	Mugiemoss
1908-09	Mugiemoss
1909-10	Mugiemoss
1910-11	Parkvale
1912-13	Not Completed
1919-20	Mugiemoss
1920-21	Hawthorn
1922-23	Hawthorn
1923-24	Mugiemoss
1924-25	Richmond
1927-28	Banks o' Dee
1928-29	Banks o' Dee
1929-30	Banks o' Dee
1930-31	Banks o' Dee
1931-32	Mugiemoss
1932-33	Mugiemoss
1933-34	Hall Russell's
1934-35	Not Completed

Aberdeenshire Junior Consolation Cup
1920-21	Dyce
1921-22	Argyle
1923-24	Banks o' Dee
1924-25	Parkvale
1927-28	Inverurie Loco Works
1947-48	Lewis United
1958-59	Woodside
1959-61	No Competition
1961-62	Stonehaven
1962-63	Lads' Club
1964-65	Formartine United

Aberdeenshire Junior Shield
1934-35	Hall Russell's
1937-38	Hall Russell's

Aberdeen & District Victory Cup
1945-46	St. Clement's

Adams Cup
1900-01	Arbroath Ardenlea

Ainsworth Cup
1922-23	Lochgilphead
1929-30	Campbelltown United

Alloa & District Cup
1909-10	Sauchie

Angus & Kincardine League
1946-47	St. Laurence
1947-48	Montrose Roselea
1949-50	Montrose Roselea
1950-51	Bervie United
1951-52	St. Laurence
1952-53	Gourdon Selbie
1953-54	Luthermuir

Angus Supplementary League
1963-64	Brechin Matrix
1964-65	Alyth United
1966-67	Arbroath Victoria

Annandale Junior Cup
1913-14	Kello Rangers
1922-23	Nithbank

Arbroath League
1951-52	Anchorage
1952-53	Anchorage
1954-55	Arbroath Victoria

Armitage Cup
1906-07	Markinch Albion
1909-10	Markinch Albion
1910-11	Leslie Hearts

Ayr & District Junior Cup
1911-12	Auchinleck Talbot
1912-13	Auchinleck Talbot
1921-22	New Cumnock United
1923-24	New Cumnock United
1924-25	Cumnock Juniors
1930-31	Auchinleck Talbot

Ayr & District Shield
1923-24	New Cumnock United
1924-25	Benquhat Heatherbell

Ayrshire Gold Watch Tournament
1930-31	Kilwinning Rangers

Bain Cup
1991-92	Whitburn

Banffshire Cup
1919-20	Buckie Thistle
1929-30	Buckie Thistle

Begg Cup
1940-41	Hillside United

Bon Accord League
1902-03	Victoria Thistle
1905-06	Parkvale

Bo'ness Cup
1898-99	Bo'ness Our Boys

Brae Cup
1927-28	Fraserburgh
1931-32	Fraserburgh

Brechin-America Cup
1903-04	Brechin Harp
1949-50	Brechin Victoria

Brechin Shield
1926-27	Arbroath Roselea

Brotherhood Cup
1929-30	Crieff Earngrove

Broxburn Charity Cup
1900-01	Broxburn Athletic
1908-09	Vale of Grange

Buckie Junior Cup
1921-22	Portgordon
1928-29	Buckie Rovers
1932-33	Buckpool Celtic

Buteshire Junior Cup
1901-02	St. Blane's
1902-03	St. Blane's
1904-05	Rothesay Royal Victoria
1905-06	Rothesay Royal Victoria
1919-20	Bute Comrades
1923-24	Bute Athletic
1924-25	Bute Athletic
1926-27	Bute Athletic
1927-28	Rothesay Royal Victoria
1928-29	Bute Athletic
1929-30	Bute Athletic
1930-31	Rothesay Royal Victoria
1931-32	Bute Athletic
1933-34	Bute Athletic
1934-35	Rothesay Royal Victoria

Calder Cup
1920-21	Bo'ness Juniors
1923-24	Broxburn

Cambuslang & District Cup
1895-96	Westburn Hopehill
1900-01	Rutherglen Glencairn

Cambuslang & District League
1897-98	Rutherglen Glencairn

Cambuslang District Cup
1898-99	Burnbank Athletic

Carmichael Trophy
1894-95	Newtongrange Star
1899-00	West Calder
1905-06	Newtongrange Star

1906-07	Newtongrange Star
1914-15	Newtongrange Star
1919-20	Newtongrange Star
1920-21	Newtongrange Star
1921-22	Newtongrange Star
1922-23	Newtongrange Star

Carry Cup
1897-98	Forfar Athletic
1901-02	Dundee 'A'
1903-04	Forfar Athletic

Central League Cup
1919-20	Hearts 'A'
1920-21	Bathgate

Clydebank & District Cup
1922-23	Duntocher Hibs
1923-24	Duntocher Hibs

Cyledsdale District Challenge Cup
1990-91	Lesmahagow

Commercial Cup
1932-33	Keith
1937-38	Portgordon
1946-47	Buckie Thistle

Cowal Cup
1924-25	Kirn Thistle

Coylton & District Cup
1919-20	Cumnock Juniors
1920-21	New Cumnock United
1921-22	Ayr Fort
1922-23	Auchinleck Talbot
1923-24	Dalmellington Thistle
1924-25	Cumnock Juniors
1926-27	Auchinleck Talbot
1927-28	Kello Rovers
1928-29	Cronberry Eglinton
1929-30	Cronberry Eglinton
1931-32	Lugar Boswell Thistle

Cumnock Cup
1911-12	Auchinleck Talbot
1919-20	Cumnock Juniors
1922-23	Annbank Primrose
1923-24	Cumnock Juniors
1924-25	Muirkirk Athletic
1925-26	Cumnock Juniors
1927-28	Kello Rovers
1928-29	Lugar Boswell Thistle
1931-32	Cumnock Juniors
1932-33	Muirkirk Juniors
1933-34+	Muirkirk Juniors

Daily Record Cup
1937-38	Grange Rovers

Dalmellington Charity Shield
1923-24	New Cumnock United

Dalrymple Cup
1901-02	Penicuik Bluebell

Darvel Centenary Cup
1989-90   Auchinleck Talbot

Davidson Cup
1903-04   St. Andrews City
1904-05   St. Andrews City

Dawson Cup
1923-24   Edzell

Denny & District Cottage Hospital Shield
1899-00   Denny Athletic
1901-02   Dunipace Juniors
1904-05   Dunipace Juniors
1905-06   Dunipace Juniors
1906-07   Dunipace Juniors
1907-08   Dunipace Juniors
1908-09   Dunipace Juniors
1909-10   Dunipace Juniors
1913-14   Denny Athletic
1915-16   Denny Hibs

Dickson Junior Cup
1936-37   Montrose Roselea
1937-38   Hillside United

Dow Cup
1911-12   Broxburn St. Andrews
1912-13   Armadale Rangers
1913-14   Bo'ness Our Boys
1922-23   Stoneyburn Bluebell
1924-25   Linlithgow Rose
1925-26   Vale of Grange

Dudley Cup
1921-22   Cumledge Mills
1923-24   Coldstream 'A'
1924-25   Civil Service Strollers
1925-26   Civil Service Strollers

Dunbartonshire Jubilee Cup
1925-26   Dumbarton Harp
1944-45   Yoker Athletic

Duncan Shield
1953-54   Arbroath Victoria

Dundee Charity Shield
1897-98   Arbroath

Eastern Consolation Cup
1900-01   Cowdenbeath

Eastern Cup
1915-16   Armadale

East Fife League
1897-98   Leven Thistle
1916-17   Denbeath Star

East Lothian League
1901-02   Tranent United

East of Scotland Junior Consolation Cup
1924-25   Tranent Juniors

East of Scotland Junior League
1913-14   Pumpherston Rangers
1914-15   Pumpherston Rangers

Edinburgh Cup
1904-05   Edinburgh Roseberry

Elgin & District Cup
1900-01   Forres Mechanics
1901-02   Buckie
1919-20   Nairn County
1920-21   Elgin City
1922-23   Elgin City
1926-27   Forres Mechanics
1928-29   Elgin City
1929-30   Keith
1930-31   Elgin City
1931-32   Nairn County
1932-33   Forres Mechanics
1934-35   Elgin City

Elginshire Cup
1898-99   Nairn
1901-02   Forres Thistle
1905-06   Elgin City 'A'

Express Cup
1936-37   Montrose Roselea

Falkirk Hospital Cup
1901-02   Vale of Carron

Falkirk Junior Charity Shield
1907-08   Forth Rangers

Farquhar Cup
1937-38   Rothes

Fernandini Cup
1919-20   St. Andrews United

Fife & Stirlingshire Cup
1956-57   Blairhall Colliery

Fife Consolation Cup
1924-25   Rosslyn Juniors
1925-26   Anstruther Rangers
1927-28   Anstruther Rangers
1929-30   St. Andrews Athletic
1931-32   Rosslyn Juniors

Fife Junior Charity Cup
1905-06   Ladybank Violet
1922-23   Inverkeithing Juniors
1924-25   East Fife Juniors
1936-37   Lochgelly Violet

Figaro Cup
1899-00   East End
1900-01   East End

CONTINUED OVERLEAF

1901-02	East End
1902-03	East End

Fleming Charity Shield
1919-20	Fraserburgh

Forfar Rosebowl
1920-21	Hawthorn

Fowler Cup
1928-29	Inverurie Loco Works

Fraser Cup
1918-19	Clydebank

Galloway Cup
1895-96	Castle Douglas
1902-03	Stranraer

Glasgow Clothing Cup
1899-00	Dundee Violet
1900-01	Dundee Violet

Gourock & District Cup
1894-95	Roseberry
1918-19	Kilbarchan Athletic
1919-20	Kilbarchan Athletic

Greenock & District Cup
1897-98	Morton Juniors
1898-99	Greenock Overton
1902-03	Port Glasgow Juniors
1904-05	Gourock Juniors
1922-23	Port Glasgow Athletic
1926-27	Overton Athletic
1959-60	Greenock Juniors
1961-62	Greenock Juniors

Harry Johnston Trophy
1982-83	Parkvale
1988-89	Fraserburgh United
1989-90	Longside
1990-91	Fraserburgh United

Hay Cup
1941-42	St. Clement's
1943-44	St. Clement's

Henderson Cup
1922-23	Shotts United

Herschell Trophy
1988-89	Downfield
1989-90	Downfield
1990-91	Downfield
1991-92	Tayport
1998-99	Dundee North End
1999-00	Tayport

Hope Charity Cup
1912-13	Bonnyrigg Rose Athletic
1914-15	Loanhead Mayflower

Hundred Guineas Cup
1930-31	Kirkintilloch Rob Roy
1939-40	Benburb

1947-48	Duntocher Hibs

Hunt Cup
1911-12	Dundee St. Joseph's

Huntly & District Cup
1919-20	Keith

Inter-City League
1900-01	Third Lanark
1901-02	Hearts
1902-03	Hearts

Inter County League
1906-07	Tayside
1907-08	Ardmere
1908-09	Dundee Celtic
1909-10	Panmure
1910-11	Lochee Central

James Kerr Cup
1989-90	Newtongrange Star

Jamieson Cup
1959-60	Forfar Celtic
1961-62	Alyth United
1962-63	Alyth United
1963-64	Brechin Matrix
1964-65	Alyth United
1966-67	Forfar East End
1967-68	Alyth United

John Masson Cup
1973-74+	Bankfoot
1974-75	Crieff Earngrove

John Stirling Cup
1929-30	Saltcoats Victoria
1930-31	Kilwinning Rangers

Johnstone Charity Cup
1937-38	Arthurlie
1938-39	Arthurlie

Johnstone Junior Cup
1894-95	Johnstone Rangers
1899-00	Cartside Juniors

Jubilee Cup
1935-36	Morton Juniors

Kelso Cup
1929-30	Bo'ness Cadora

Kilbarchan Charity Cup
1957-58	Kilbirnie Ladeside

Kilmarnock Junior League
1899-00	Crosshouse

Kilmarnock Shield
1913-14	Auchinleck Talbot

Kingdom Cup
1991-92	Kelty Hearts
1994-95	Newburgh

Kinnabar Cup

1937-38	Montrose Roselea

Kirkintilloch & District Cup

1919-20	Twechar Rangers
1921-22	Kirkintilloch Rob Roy
1923-24	Kirkintilloch Rob Roy
1925-26	Kilsyth Rangers

Knockdow Charity Cup

1920-21	Rothesay Royal Victoria
1926-27	Rothesay Royal Victoria
1929-30	Rothesay Royal Victoria
1930-31	Rothesay Royal Victoria
1931-32	Rothesay Royal Victoria
1932-33	Rothesay Royal Victoria
1933-34	Bute Athletic

Lanarkshire Charity Cup

1917-18	Motherwell
1918-19	Albion Rovers

Lanarkshire Consolation Cup

1921-22	Fauldhouse United
1923-24	Law Scotia
1926-27	Law Scotia
1929-30	Law Scotia
1934-35	Larkhall Thistle
1935-36	Royal Albert
1937-38	Holytown

Larkhall Charity Cup

1889-90	Royal Albert
1890-91	Airdrieonians
1891-92	Albion Rovers
1892-93	No Competition
1893-94	Royal Albert
1894-95	Royal Albert
1908-09	Hamilton Academical

Laurie Cup

1959-60	Bo'ness United

Leith Burghs Cup

1898-99	Leith Ivanhoe
1900-01	Leith Ivanhoe
1904-05	Leith Ivanhoe
1905-06	Edinburgh Rosebery
1906-07	Edinburgh Rosebery
1907-08	Kinleith Thistle
1908-09	Musselburgh Athletic
1909-10	Queensferry St. Andrews
1910-11	Royal Field Artillery
1911-12	Niddrie Bluebell
1913-14	Pumpherston Rangers
1917-18	Leith Benburb
1918-19	Leith Benburb
1922-23	Edinburgh Emmet
1923-24	Tranent Juniors
1925-26	Portobello Thistle
1926-27	Tranent Juniors
1927-28	Ormiston Primrose
1928-29	Ormiston Primrose
1936-37	Armadale Thistle

Lindsay Cup

1929-30	Perth Craigie

Linton Cup

1905-06	Stratheden United

Loanhead & District Cup

1913-14	Penicuik Juniors

Loftus Cup

1911-12	Dunfermline Athletic

Longmuir Junior Cup

1920-21	Dumfries
1921-22	Tayleurians

Lorne Shield

1899-00	Arbroath Ardenlea
1900-01	Arbroath Ardenlea

Lumley Cup

1912-13	Pumpherston Rangers
1913-14	Linlithgow Rose
1916-17	Leith Benburb
1917-18	Leith Benburb
1918-19	Broxburn Athletic
1921-22	West Calder
1922-23	Stow Amateurs
1926-27	Duns
1938-39	Murrayfield Amateurs

McAllister Charity Cup

1922-23	Dunoon Athletic
1923-24	Sandbank

McArthur Cup

1905-06	St. Andrews City
1906-07	St. Andrews City
1911-12	Tayport

Macbeth Cup

1929-30	Crieff Earngrove

McIvor Cup

1942-43	Burnbank Athletic

MacRae Cup

1978-79	Ardrossan Winton Rovers

Mather Cup

1942-43	Brechin Victoria
1943-44	RAF XI

Mauchline Cup

1911-12	Auchinleck Talbot
1918-19	Burnfoothill Primrose
1920-21	Auchinleck Talbot
1921-22	New Cumnock United
1923-24	Glenbuck Cherrypickers
1924-25	Muirkirk Athletic
1925-26	Lugar Boswell Thistle
1927-28	Kello Rovers
1930-31	New Cumnock

Melvin League

1898-99	Arbroath Rovers
1899-00	Arbroath Rovers
1900-01	Arbroath Rovers
1909-10	Arbroath Ardenlea

Merchants Trophy

| 1973-74 | Shettleston |

Mid-Argyll Possil Cup

| 1922-23 | Tarbert |
| 1923-24 | Tarbert |

Midland Junior League

| 1899-00 | Smithston Albion |

Midlothian Cup

1892-93	West Calder Wanderers
1893-94	West Calder Wanderers
1904-05	Arniston Rangers

Montrose & District Junior Cup

1896-97	Ashfield
1897-98	Ashfield
1904-05	Union
1921-22	Arbroath Woodside
1922-23	Arbroath Woodside

Montrose & Kincardine League

| 1936-37 | Montrose Roselea |

Montrose Junior League

| 1904-05 | Rosevale |

Morayshire Charity Cup

1919-20	Lossiemouth
1923-24	Keith
1924-25	Nairn County
1925-26	Forres Thistle
1930-31	Forres Thistle

Morayshire District Cup

| 1927-28 | Keith |

Motherwell Charity Cup

| 1917-18 | Motherwell |

M.R.S. Cup

| 1986-87 | Ormiston Primrose |

Munro Cup

| 1919-20 | Invergordon |

Musselburgh Junior League

| 1898-99 | Edinburgh Renton |

Nairn District Cup

| 1945-46 | Inverness Thistle |

Nelson Cup

| 1989-90 | Newtongrange Star |
| 1990-91 | Newtongrange Star |

Newgate Cup

| 1911-12 | Arbroath Fairfield |

1912-13	Arbroath Ardenlea
1913-14	Arbroath Parkhead
1920-21	Arbroath Victoria
1921-22	Arbroath Woodside
1922-23	Arbroath Ardenlea

Nicol Charity Cup

| 1909-10 | Arbroath Parkhead |

Nithsdale Cup

| 1923-24 | Sanquhar United |

North-Eastern Cup

1909-10+	Hearts
1910-11	Hibernian
1911-12	Falkirk
1913-14	Aberdeen

North-East Fife League

| 1899-00 | Anstruther Rangers |
| 1921-22 | Pittenweem Hearts |

Paisley & District Cup

1900-01	Renfrew Victoria
1919-20	St. Anthony's
1921-22	Duntocher Hibs
1922-23	Duntocher Hibs

Paisley Charity Cup

| 1900-01 | Renfrew Victoria |

Pattison Cup

| 1932-33 | Golspie |

Peden Cup

| 1926-27 | Longniddry |

Perthshire Junior Charity Cup

1906-07	St. Leonards
1909-10	St. Leonards
1921-22	Perth Violet
1929-30	Perth Roselea
1931-32	Kinnoull
1940-41	Jeanfield Swifts
1960-61	Perth Celtic

Perthshire Consolation Cup

1910-11	Scone
1911-12	Morrisonians
1922-23	Dunkeld
1927-28	Killin
1929-30	Vale of Atholl
1934-35	Killin

Perthshire League

1897-98	Scone
1898-99	Huntingtower
1899-00	Dunblane
1902-03	Stanley
1904-05	Scone
1907-08	Stanley
1911-12	Scone
1913-14	Tulloch
1914-19	No Competition
1921-22	Not Completed

Perthshire League Cup
| 1910-11 | Scone |

Premier Talent Trophy
| 1988-89 | Coltness United |
| 1994-95 | Port Glasgow Juniors |

Prudential Charity Cup
| 1987-88 | Auchinleck Talbot |

Radio Forth Cup
1984-85	Linlithgow Rose
1986-87	Whitburn
1987-88	Newtongrange Star

R & B Fabrications Cup
| 1987-88 | Forfar Albion |

Reid Sports Cup
| 1981-82 | Irvine Meadow |

Renfrewshire County Cup
| 1955-56 | Dunoon Athletic |

Renfrewshire Junior Consolation Cup
1910-11	Port Glasgow Juniors
1912-13	Inkerman Rangers
1914-15	Neilston Victoria
1915-16	Neilston Victoria
1923-24	Renfrew
1924-25	Millport
1932-33	Renfrew
1935-36	Rothesay Royal Victoria
1937-38	Dunoon Milton Rovers
1938-39	Morton Juniors
1949-50	Renfrew
1951-52	Renfrew
1952-53	Gourock Juniors

Renfrewshire Junior League
| 1926-27 | Bute Athletic |

Renfrewshire Shield
| 1921-22 | Port Glasgow Athletic |

Renfrewshire Victory Cup
1917-18	Arthurlie
1919-20	Johnstone
1922-23	Arthurlie
1923-24	Arthurlie
1926-27	Overton Athletic
1930-31	Moorpark Amateurs

Renton Cup
1885-86+	
1895-96	Dalry Primrose
1904-05	Edinburgh Rosebery
1907-08	Kinleith Thistle
1908-09	Hearts Tynecastle XI
1909-10	Arniston Rangers
1910-11	Granton Gasworks
1911-12	Niddrie Bluebell

1913-14	Pumpherston Rangers
1922-23	Edinburgh Emmet
1934-35	Arniston Rangers

Reserve Cup
| 1913-14 | Falkirk |

Roseberry Shield
1900-01	Bathgate Thistle
1905-06	Vale of Grange
1908-09	Vale of Grange

Rossshire Cup
| 1932-33 | Invergordon |
| 1938-39 | Invergordon |

Rothesay Charity Cup
| 1932-33 | Rothesay Royal Victoria |

St. Vincent de Paul Charity Cup
1923-24	Saltcoats Victoria
1925-26	Saltcoats Victoria
1926-27	Saltcoats Victoria
1935-36	Ardrossan Winton Rovers
1936-37	Largs Thistle

Salvesan Shield
1928-29	Bute Athletic
1929-30	Rothesay Royal Victoria
1931-32	Bute Athletic
1932-33	Bute Athletic
1934-35	Bute Athletic

Scottish Junior League - Division 2
1911-12	Croy Celtic
1913-14	Thornliebank
1920-21	St. Roch's

Scottish Junior League Consolation Cup
1920-21	Kilsyth Emmet
1923-24	Vale of Leven
1927-28	Maryhill Hibs
1928-29	Coats Juniors
1934-35	St. Francis
1936-37	Kilsyth Rangers
1937-38	Baillieston
1938-39	Twechar United

Scottish Junior League Cup
1929-30	Clydebank Juniors
1930-31	Denny Hibs
1933-34	St. Ninians Thistle
1938-39	Dunipace Juniors
1939-40	Baillieston
1946-47+	Dunoon Athletic

Scottish League 'C' Division Cup
| 1946-47 | Stirling Albion |

Simpson Sports Cup
| 1989-90 | Culter |
| 1991-92 | FC Stoneywood |

Sinagoga Cup

1934-35	Denbeath Star
1937-38	Not Completed

South Side Cup

1894-95	Ibrox XI
1895-96	Ibrox XI
1896-97	Rutherglen Glencairn
1899-00	Benburb
1901-02	Ibrox Juniors
1903-04	Cambuslang Rangers

Stafford Cup

1925-26	Brora
1926-27	Brora
1928-29	Brora Rangers
1929-30	Brora Rangers

Stirlingshire Consolation Cup

1913-14	Falkirk
1923-24	King's Park
1924-25	King's Park
1925-26	Larbert Amateurs

Stirlingshire Jubilee Cup

1937-38	Dunipace Juniors
1938-39	Kilsyth Rangers

Stirlingshire Junior Charity Cup

1907-08	St. Ninians Thistle
1920-21	Dunipace Juniors
1924-25	Alva Albion Rangers
1925-26	Camelon Juniors
1926-27	St. Ninians Thistle
1928-29	Grange Rovers
1929-30	Alva Albion Rangers

Stirlingshire Junior League - Division 2

1905-06	Bannockburn

Stirlinshire Victory Cup

1919-20	Dunipace Juniors

Swan Cup

1984-85	Linlithgow Rose

Tayside Cup

1988-89	Kinnoull

Thomson Cup

1937-38	Mosstodloch

Torrance Cup

1925-26	Arrochar

Tramway Junior Cup

1920-21	Maryhill

Victoria Cup

1903-04	Thornliebank
1911-12	Abercorn
1912-13	St. Mirren

Walker Cup

1909-10	Pumpherston Rangers

Weekly Record Cup

1917-18	St. Anthony's

Western Cup

1917-18	Dumbarton Harp
1918-19	Dumbarton Harp
1919-20	Vale of Leven
1922-23	Royal Albert
1923-24	Arthurlie

West Lothian League

1906-07	Armadale Th./Our Boys
1922-23	Linlithgow Rose
1924-25	Linlithgow Rose
1928-29	Stoneyburn Juniors

West of Scotland Consolation Cup

1932-33	Cambuslang Rangers
1934-35	Saltcoats Victoria
1935-36	Ardrossan Winton Rovers

Whitbread Trophy

1973-74	Broxburn Athletic
1975-76	Shettleston

Wick League Cup

1922-23	Wick Thistle
1929-30	Wick Thistle

Wilkinson Cup

1900-01	Lochgelly Rangers
1901-02	Lochgelly Juniors

Williamson Cup

1938-39	Rosslyn Juniors

Wilson Charity Cup

1936-37	Lochgelly Violet
1937-38	Lochgelly Albert
1993-94	Lochgelly Albert

Wishaw & District Cup

1907-08	Larkhall Thistle

Livingston

Livingston started life as **Ferranti Thistle** and became **Meadowbank Thistle** on admission to the Scottish League. They changed again to their present name when they moved from Edinburgh to Livingston.

Dyce Juniors

Dyce Juniors are an amalgamation of **Rosslyn Sports** and **Mugiemoss**. Rosslyn Sports were previously known as **Rosemount**.

Inverness Caledonian Thistle

Inverness Caledonian Thistle were formed by the merger of **Inverness Caledonian** and **Inverness Thistle**. At first the club was called simply Caledonian Thistle, but added the Inverness at the request of the local council when their new stadium was provided.

Rosyth Recreation

Rosyth Recreation were formerly **Jubilee Athletic**. As far as is known, they are not connected to the original Rosyth Recreation club.

Edinburgh City

Edinburgh City were formerly **Postal United**. They are, however, connected to the original Edinburgh City through inheriting the former club's Social Club.

Lochore Welfare

Lochore Welfare became Lochore Miners' Welfare in 1998, but reverted to their former name in July 2000.

St. Bernards

St. Bernards first saw light of day as the **3rd Edinburgh Rifle Volunteers**. The early change was, in fact to St. Bernard, but within a few years the addition of the "s" became common practice. The name itself relates to St. Bernard's well, a local landmark which is situated close to the club's birthplace.

Pencaitland & Ormiston

Pencaitland & Ormiston were formed by the amalgamation of the Senior club **Pencaitland** with the **Junior Ormiston Primrose**.

Dumfries High School F.P.

Dumfries High School F.P. are changing their name to **Dumfries** at the start of the 2000-01 season.

Ayr United

Ayr United were formed as a result of the merger between **Ayr F.C.** and **Ayr Parkhouse**.

Dundee United

Dundee United originally started life as **Dundee Hibernian**.

Maryhill Harp

Maryhill Harp were founded as **Maryhill Hibernian**.

Bo'ness United

Bo'ness United were formed by the merging of the old **Bo'ness** Senior club with the Junior **Bo'ness Cadora**.

Edinburgh Athletic

Edinburgh Athletic were known as **Manor Thistle** until 1996.

Forfar Albion

Forfar Albion came into being by the combination of **Forfar Celtic** and **Forfar East End**.

There have been two separate and distinct **Clydebank** clubs in the Scottish League. The first, founded in 1914, were members from that season until they went defunct in 1931. The second came into being as the result of the move of **East Stirlingshire** from Falkirk to Clydebank and merging with **Clydebank Juniors** to form **E.S. Clydebank**.

After one season, as a result of court action by former 'Shire directors and fans, the 'Shire returned to Falkirk and Clydebank became a club in its own right.

Vale Ocoba

Vale Ocoba obtained their suffix from th acronym of **Our Church Old Boys Association**.

Third Lanark

Third Lanark derived their name by th contraction of the name of their founder - the 3rd Lanarkshire Rifle Volunteers.

Despite its popularity in the rest of th U.K., not one Scottish Junior or Senio club bears the suffix "Town" Furthermore, during the whole of m research for this book, I have not foun one single instance of a club called ... Town having ever been in existence i Senior or Junior football.

SECTION 5 - ADDITIONAL PUBLICATIONS

(Special offers on relevant books on the Scottish football game.)

Publications available from

Stewart Davidson

84 Gallowhill Road, Paisley PA3 4TJ

(Tel 0141 562 5721)   E-Mail - jsdavidson@tinyworld.co.uk

Scottish Non League Review'

The review of 1999/2000 is the thirteenth consecutive annual and like the previous twelve gives all the league tables and results and cup results from each of the six Junior regions, the Highland, East and South of Scotland Leagues as well as details from many minor leagues. This invaluable guide, often referred to elsewhere as the 'bible' of the Scottish non-league scene, should not be missed. The following back issues are still available, several reduced in price:

1987/88 (first issue - reprinted) £1.50.

1993/94 £1 (half price)

1995/96 £1.25 (half price)

1996/97 £1.25 (half price)

1997/98 £1.50 (half price)

1998/99 £1.50 (half price).

1999-2000 £3.

Add 40p postage per edition.

**SPECIAL OFFER
93/94, 96/97, 97/98, 98/99 for £4.75
post free.**

Scottish Non League Histories'

A sister publication to the 'Review', appearing on a less regular basis - approximately every two years.   It contains, as the title suggests, historical articles on the game in Scotland, many of which are short histories of clubs, both past and present, as well as histories of cup competitions etc.   Each has around 50 pages.

Volume 1 (reprint) £1.50

Volumes 2 and **3** at £1.50 each

Volumes 4 and **5** at £2 each

(40p postage each).   ****Vols 2-5** for £5.50 post free.

'Past Members of the Scottish League'

Although there are currently 42 clubs in the Scottish League, there are a similar number of ex-members.   These range from those clubs which lasted one season to the likes of Third Lanark who were members for over 70 years.   This series of 5 books looks at these clubs, giving the following details where known: grounds (including the first match played on each of them), club colours, other leagues competed in, honours (including local competitions), their Scottish League year-by-year performance, and a list of players capped.   The main part of each club's section contains ALL their League results, divided into each opponent i.e. Abercorn v Aberdeen, v Airdrie, v Albion

CONTINUED OVERLEAF

Rovers, etc. Each part costs £2 (Parts 2-5 were originally £3 each). 40p postage for each part should be added. The total series has around 350 pages, an average of 70 pages for each volume.

Volume One - Abercorn, Armadale, Ayr, Ayr Parkhouse.

Volume Two - Bathgate, Beith, Bo'ness, Broxburn United, Cambuslang, Clackmannan, Clydebank, Cowlairs, Dumbarton Harp, Dundee Hibernian, Dundee Wanderers, Dykehead.

Volume Three - Edinburgh City, ES Clydebank, Galston, Helensburgh, Johnstone, King's Park, Leith, Leith Athletic.

Volume Four - Linthouse, Lochgelly United, Mid-Annandale, Nithsdale Wanderers, Northern, Peebles Rovers, Port Glasgow Athletic, Renton, Royal Albert.

Volume Five - St. Bernards, Solway Star, Thistle, Third Lanark, Vale of Leven.

Volume 5 only is available for £1 - largely on Third Lanark.

Special Offer - Parts 2,3,4 and 5 for £6 post free

'Scottish Qualifying Cup 1895-1995'

Published May 1995, this contains ALL the results for the Qualifying Cup in its various formats over the years, including cup final scorers etc. Additionally, the results of the preliminary rounds of the Scottish Cup (early 1890s), Scottish Consolation Cup and Victory Cup are also detailed. This impressive statistical book (210 pages) is vital to any historian. Now £5.00 (originally £6.95)(90p postage). An update since 1995 as well as some additions and corrections will be sent with each order.

'History of Cowlairs Football Club 1876-1896'

This is a 56 page history of one of th Scottish League's founder members an is the most in depth history writte (published 1991) of any pre-1900 Scottis Club. The club finished up appearing i court almost as often as they played football match! Originally priced at £ now reduced to 75p (40p postage)

'Senior Non-League Football in South West Scotland'

The first book to cover League football i this area. Leagues have been i operation in the South for 100 years an there are many long running cu competitions. As well as all the fin tables and cup winners, individual clu histories of all current and past membe clubs and results of all Scottish Cup tie are given. An invaluable addition to th history of Scottish football. Now £4 (wa £5.95)(65p postage.

Renfrewshire FA Cup - The First 50 Years'

This is the first book published on Scottish County Cup competition an contains all the results in the cup for th period 1879 to 1929 as well as the cu final line ups and scorers etc. as well as commentary on a competition whic attracted almost 100 different clubs in i first 50 years. Now £1.50 (was £2.25)(40 postage)

'School's Out - A History of School's Football in Glasgow's East End'

Written by retired teacher Walter Ewin who was involved with schools footba for over 20 years, this booklet cove many of the ups and downs of th schools game, as well as Walter's ow xperiences. There are few books on cottish schools football, and this elcome addition gives statistical cords of the league and cup winners in e Glasgow East Association. Reduced om £1.50 to only 70p (40p postage)

Other Publications

The Juniors - 100 Years'

he definitive history of the Junior game ublished 1986) and contains over 300 ages listing league and cup winners, the istory of the game, a large section on e Scottish Junior Cup, a club directory nd much, much more. £4.95 (£1.50 ostage).

Scottish Junior Football - The arly Years'

riginally published in 1991, this 28 page ooklet looks at the pre-1900 Junior otball scene, with listings of clubs, etc. eprinted copies now available. £1.25 5p postage)

'Fields of Fife'

Over 70 large size pages with narrative details, photos, drawings etc. of the county of Fife's football grounds, both past and present. £4 (£1.20 postage)

'Renfrew Football Club - A Brief History'

Published 1990 - 16 pages. 50p (30p postage)

'The Central League'

Originally published in 1991, this has been reprinted and contains details on each club as well as who has competed over the years and much, much more. £2.50 (50p postage) An update is also sent with each order.

All the above publications available from
Stewart Davidson
84 Gallowhill Road, Paisley PA3 4TJ
(Tel 0141 562 5721) E-Mail - jsdavidson@tinyworld.co.uk

Ian Spittal holds aloft the Scottish Junior Cup after Pollock's triumph in 1997

Paul Wright and Ray Montgomerie celebrate Kilmarnock's Scottish Cup win in 1997

Competition	Section	Competition	Section
Aberdeen and District Junior League	2	Barrie Consolation Cup	2
Aberdeen and District Junior League Cup	2	Begg Cup	3
Aberdeen and District Victory Cup	3	Birks Cup	1
Aberdeen Cable TV Cup	2	Blenheim Cup	1
Aberdeen Challenge Cup	3	Bo'ness Cup	3
Aberdeen County Trophy	2	Bon Accord League	3
Aberdeenshire Charity Cup	1	Border Cup	1
Aberdeenshire Cup	1	Brae Cup	3
Aberdeenshire Junior Charity Cup	2	Brechin Rosebowl	2
Aberdeenshire Junior Consolation Cup	2	Brechin Shield	3
Aberdeenshire Junior Shield	3	Brechin-America Cup	3
Aberdeenshire Shield	1	British Legion Cup	1
Acorn Heating Cup	2	British Road Services Cup	2
Adams Cup	3	Brotherhood Cup	3
Ainsworth Cup	3	Brown Cup	2
Airdrie Charity Cup	1	Broxburn Charity Cup	3
Alex Jack Trophy	1	Buckie Junior Cup	3
Alloa and District Cup	3	Buteshire Junior Cup	3
Angus and Kincardine League	3		
Angus Junior League	2	Cafolla Cup	1
Angus Supplementary League	3	Calder Cup	2
Annandale Cup	1	Calder Cup (2)	3
Annandale Junior Cup	2	Cambuslang and District Cup	3
Arbroath and District Cup	2	Cambuslang and District League	3
Arbroath League	3	Cambuslang District Cup	3
Archibald Cup	2	Candida Casa Cup	1
Armitage Cup	3	Carmichael Trophy	3
Atholl Cup	1	Carry Cup	3
Ayr and District Junior Cup	3	Central League (Senior)	1
Ayr and District Shield	3	Central League Cup	2
Ayr Charity Cup	1	Central League Cup (Senior)	3
Ayrshire Charity Cup	2	Central Regional League	2
Ayrshire Combination	1	Central Regional League Sectional League Cup	2
Ayrshire Consolation Cup	2	Cherry Video Cup	2
Ayrshire Cup (Junior)	2	Chic Allan Memorial Trophy	1
Ayrshire Cup (Senior)	1	Churchill Cup	1
Ayrshire District Cup	2	City Cup	1
Ayrshire Gold Watch Tournament	3	Clackmannanshire Charity Cup (Junior)	2
Ayrshire Junior League	2	Clackmannanshire Charity Cup (Senior)	1
Ayrshire League Cup	2	Clackmannanshire Junior Challenge Cup	2
Ayrshire Qualifying Cup	1	Clackmannanshire Junior League	2
Ayrshire Regional League	2	Clark Beckett Cup	2
Ayrshire Super Cup	2	Clive Williamson Trophy	2
		Clydebank and District Cup	3
Bain Cup	3	Clydesdale District Challenge Cup	3
Banffshire Cup	3	Commercial Cup	3

Concept Group Cup	2
Connon Cup	2
Constitutional Cup	2
Coronation Cup	2
Coronation Cup (Senior)	1
Courier Cup	2
Cowal Cup	3
Cowdenbeath Cup	2
Coylton and District Cup	3
Craig Stephen Cup	2
Cream of the Barley Trophy	2
Cree Lodge Cup	1
Cumnock and Doon Valley Cup	2
Cumnock Cup	3
Cunningham District Cup	2
Currie Cup	2
D.J. Laing Homes Cup	2
Daily Record Cup	3
Dalkeith Glazing Cup	2
Dalmellington Charity Shield	3
Dalmeny Cup	2
Dalrymple Cup	3
Darvel Centenary Cup	3
Davidson Cup	3
Dawson Cup	3
Denny and District Cottage Hospital Shield	3
Dewar Shield	1
Dickson Junior Cup	3
Dow Cup	3
Downfield S.C. Cup	2
Drybrough Cup	1
Dudley Cup	3
Dumfries and District Junior Cup	2
Dumfries and District Junior League	2
Dumfries and District Junior Shield	2
Dumfries and Galloway Cup	1
Dunbartonshire Charity Cup (Senior)	1
Dunbartonshire Cup (Senior)	1
Dunbartonshire Jubilee Cup	3
Dunbartonshire Junior Charity Cup	2
Dunbartonshire Junior Cup	2
Duncan Shield	3
Dundee Charity Cup	1
Dundee Charity Shield	3
Dundee Junior Charity Cup	2
Dundee Junior League	2
Dunedin Cup	1
Dunfermline Cottage Hospital Cup	1
Dunfermline Cup	2
Dunfermline Shield	2
Duthie Cup	2
East Ayrshire Cup	2
East Coast Windows Cup	2

East Fife Cup	2
East Fife League	3
East Lothian Cup	2
East Lothian League	3
East of Scotland (City) Cup	1
East of Scotland Consolation Cup	1
East of Scotland Junior Consolation Cup	3
East of Scotland Junior Cup	2
East of Scotland Junior League	2
East of Scotland League	1
East of Scotland League Cup	1
East of Scotland Qualifying Cup	1
East of Scotland Shield	1
East Regional League	2
East Regional League Cup	2
Eastern Consolation Cup	3
Eastern Cup	3
Eastern League (Senior)	1
Edinburgh and District Junior League	2
Edinburgh and District League (Senior)	1
Edinburgh Cup	3
Elder Cottage Hospital Cup	2
Elgin and District Cup	3
Elginshire Cup	3
Erskine Charity Cup	2
Evening Times Cup Winners Cup	2
Exhibition Cup (Junior)	2
Exhibition Cup (Senior)	1
Express Cup (1)	2
Express Cup (2)	3
Falkirk and District Charity Cup	1
Falkirk and District Junior Cup	2
Falkirk Hospital Cup	3
Falkirk Infirmary Shield	1
Falkirk Junior Charity Cup	3
Farquhar Cup	2
Fernandini Cup	3
Fife and Lothians Cup	2
Fife and Stirlingshire Cup	3
Fife Consolation Cup	3
Fife County League	2
Fife Cup (Junior)	2
Fife Cup (Senior)	1
Fife Drybrough Cup	2
Fife Junior Charity Cup	3
Fife Regional League	2
Fife Shield	2
Fifeshire Charity Cup	1
Figaro Cup	3
Findlay and Co. Cup	2
Fleming Charity Shield	3
Football Times Cup	1
Forfar and District Cup	2
Forfar and District Junior Charity Cup	2

Forfar Businessman's Trophy	2
Forfar Rosebowl	3
Forfarshire Charity Cup (Senior)	1
Forfarshire Cup (Senior)	1
Forfarshire Junior Consolation Cup	2
Forfarshire Junior Cup	2
Fowler Cup	3
Fraser Cup	3
Galloway Cup	3
Gardeners Cup	1
Glasgow and District Intermediate Cup	2
Glasgow Charity Cup (Junior)	2
Glasgow Charity Cup (Senior)	1
Glasgow Clothing Cup	3
Glasgow Cup (Senior)	1
Glasgow Eastern Charity Cup	2
Glasgow Intermediate Consolation Cup	2
Glasgow Intermediate North-Eastern Cup	2
Glasgow Junior Consolation Cup	2
Glasgow Junior Cup	2
Glasgow Junior League	2
Glasgow Junior League Cup	2
Glasgow North-Eastern Cup	2
GNT North Regional Cup	2
Gordon Campbell Construction Trophy	2
Gordon Williamson Cup	2
Gourock and District Cup	3
Greenock and District Charity Cup	1
Greenock and District Cup	3
Grill League Cup	2
Guide Cup	2
Haddow Silver Jubilee Cup	2
Haig Gordon Memorial Trophy	1
Harry Johnston Trophy	3
Hay Cup	3
Heineken Cup	2
Henderson Cup	3
Herschell Trophy	3
Highland League	1
Highland League Cup	1
Hope Charity Cup	3
Hozier Cup	2
Hundred Guineas Cup	3
Hunt Cup	3
Huntly and District Cup	3
Inglis Cup	2
Inter County League	3
Inter-City League	3
Intermediate Consolation Cup	2
Intermediate Cup	2
Intermediate League	2
Intermediate League Cup	2

Intermediate North-Eastern Cup	2
Inveralmond Cup	2
Inverness Cup	1
Irvine and District League	2
James Kerr Cup	3
Jamieson Cup	3
Jimmy Gibb Memorial Trophy	2
John Masson Cup	3
John Stirling Cup	3
Johnstone Charity Cup	3
Johnstone Junior Cup	3
Johnstone-Currie Cup	1
Jubilee Cup	3
Kelso Cup	3
Kiddie Cup	2
Kilbarchan Charity Cup	3
Kilmarnock and Loudon District Cup	2
Kilmarnock Charity Cup	1
Kilmarnock Junior League	3
Kilmarnock Shield	3
King Cup	1
Kingdom Cup	3
Kinnabar Cup	3
Kirkcaldy Cottage Hospital Cup	1
Kirkintilloch and District Cup	3
Kirkwood Shield	2
Knockdow Charity Cup	3
Kyle and Carrick District Cup	2
Laidlaw Shield	2
Laing Cup	2
Lanark and Lothians Cup	2
Lanark and Lothians League	2
Lanarkshire Central Cup	2
Lanarkshire Challenge Cup	2
Lanarkshire Charity Cup	3
Lanarkshire Consolation Cup	3
Lanarkshire Cup	1
Lanarkshire Express Cup	1
Lanarkshire League	2
Lanarkshire League Cup	2
Land o' Burns Cup	2
Langbank Charity Cup	2
Larkhall Charity Cup	3
Laurie Cup	3
Law-Galloway Cup	1
Leith Burghs Cup	3
Lindsay Cup	3
Linlithgowshire Cup (Senior)	1
Linlithgowshire Junior Cup	2
Linlithgowshire Junior League Cup	2
Linlithgowshire Second Eleven Cup	1
Linton Cup	3

Loanhead and District Cup	3	Newgate Cup	
Loftus Cup	2	Nicholson Cup	
Loftus Cup (Senior)	3	Nicol Charity Cup	
Longmuir Junior Cup	3	Nithsdale Cup	
Lorne Shield	3	North Ayrshire Cup	
Lovie Shield	2	North Caledonian Cup	
Lumley Cup	3	North Caledonian League	
		North Drybrough Cup	
M.R.S. Cup	3	North End Centenary Cup	
MacBeth Cup	3	North End Challenge Cup	
MacNichol Trophy	1	North of Scotland Cup (Junior)	
MacRae Cup	3	North of Scotland Cup (Senior)	
Marshall Cup	2	North Regional League (East)	
Martin and Johnson Trophy	2	North Regional League (East) League Cup	
Martin-White Cup	2	North Regional League (North)	
Maryhill Charity Cup	2	North-East Fife League	
Mathers Cup	3	North-Eastern Cup (1)	
Matthew Cup	2	North-Eastern Cup (2)	
Mauchline Cup	3	North-Eastern League	
McAllister Charity Cup	3	North-Eastern League Supplementary Cup	
McArthur Cup	3	Northern League	
McIvor Cup	3		
McLagan Cup	2	P.A. Cup	
McLeman Cup	2	Paisley and District Cup	
McLeod Trophy	2	Paisley Charity Cup	
Melvin League	3	Paisley Charity Cup (Junior)	
Merchants Trophy	3	Pattison Cup	
Mid-Argyll Possil Cup	3	Peden Cup	
Midland Junior League	3	Penman Cup	
Midland League (Junior)	2	Perthshire Advertiser Cup	
Midland League (Senior)	1	Perthshire Consolation Cup (Senior)	
Midlothian Cup	3	Perthshire Cup (Senior)	
Midlothian Junior League	2	Perthshire Junior Charity Cup	
Mitchell Cup (Junior)	2	Perthshire Junior Consolation Cup	
Mitchell Cup (Senior)	1	Perthshire Junior Cup	
Montrose and District Junior Cup	3	Perthshire Junior League	
Montrose and Kincardine League	3	Perthshire League Cup	
Montrose Junior League	3	Perthshire Rosebowl	
Moore Trophy	2	Perthshire League (Senior)	
Morayshire Charity Cup	3	Peter Craigie Cup	
Morayshire District Cup	3	Pintaman Trophy	
Morayshire Junior Cup	2	Pompey Cup	
Morayshire Junior League	2	Potts Cup	
Morris Newton Cup	1	Premier Reserve League	
Morrison Trophy	2	Premier Talent Trophy	
Motherwell Charity Cup	3	Prudential Charity Cup	
Munro Cup	3		
Murray Cup	2	R. and B. Fabrications Cup	
Musselburgh Cup	2	R.L. Rae Cup	
Musselburgh Junior League	3	Radio Forth Cup	
		Reid Charity Cup	
Nairn District Cup	3	Reid Sports Cup	
National Drybrough Cup	2	Renfrewshire County Cup	
Nelson Cup	3	Renfrewshire Cup (Senior)	
Ness Cup	1	Renfrewshire Junior Consolation Cup	

Renfrewshire Junior Cup	2
Renfrewshire Junior League	3
Renfrewshire Shield	3
Renfrewshire Victory Cup	3
Renfrewshire-Dunbartonshire Cup	2
Renton Cup	3
Reserve Cup	3
Reserve League	1
Reserve League (East)	1
Reserve League (West)	1
Reserve League Cup	1
Robbie Nicol Cup	2
Robert Lawson Shield	2
Robertson Cup	2
Rollstud Archibald Cup	2
Rosebank C.C. Cup	2
Roseberry Charity Cup	1
Roseberry Cup (Junior)	2
Roseberry Shield	3
Rossshire Cup	3
Rothesay Charity Cup	3
Rothesay-Dunoon Cup	2
Saint Cuthbert's Cup	1
Saint Johnstone Y.M. Cup	2
Saint Michael Cup	2
Saint Mungo Cup	1
Saint Mungo Quaich	1
Saint Vincent de Paul Charity Cup	3
Scottish Alliance	1
Scottish Alliance League	1
Scottish Central Combination	1
Scottish Combined Reserve League	1
Scottish Consolation Cup	1
Scottish Cup	1
Scottish Federation	1
Scottish Football Combination	1
Scottish Junior Cup	2
Scottish Junior League	2
Scottish Junior League – Division 2	3
Scottish Junior League Consolation Cup	3
Scottish Junior League Cup	3
Scottish Junior League Victory Consolation Cup	2
Scottish Junior League Victory Cup	2
Scottish League	1
Scottish League 'C' Division Cup	1
Scottish League Challenge Cup	1
Scottish League Cup	1
Scottish Qualifying Cup	1
Scottish Road Services Cup	2
Scottish Second Eleven Cup	1
Scottish Supplementary Cup	1
Scottish Union	1
Simpson Shield	2
Simpson Sports Cup	3

Sinagoga Cup	3
Smyllum Charity Cup	3
South Ayrshire Cup	3
South Ayrshire Junior League	3
South of Scotland Cup	1
South of Scotland League	1
South of Scotland League Cup	1
South Side Cup	3
Southern Counties Charity Cup	1
Southern Counties Cup	1
Southern League	1
Southern League Cup	1
Stafford Cup	3
Stewart Memorial Cup	2
Stirling and District Junior Cup	2
Stirling Charity Cup	1
Stirlingshire Consolation Cup (Senior)	3
Stirlingshire Cup (Senior)	1
Stirlingshire Jubilee Cup	3
Stirlingshire Junior Charity Cup	3
Stirlingshire Junior Consolation Cup	2
Stirlingshire Junior Cup	2
Stirlingshire Junior League	2
Stirlingshire Junior League – Division 2	3
Stirlingshire Junior League Cup	2
Stirlingshire Victory Cup	3
Summer Cup	1
Swan Cup	3
Taycars Trophy	2
Tayside Cup	3
Tayside Drybrough Cup	2
Tayside Regional League	2
Tayside Regional League Cup	2
Telegraph Cup	2
Thistle Cup	2
Thomson Cup	3
Thornton Shield	2
Thornton Sports Cup	2
Tom Gordon Cup	2
Torrance Cup	3
Tramway Junior Cup	3
Tweedie Cup	1
Upper Nithsdale Charity Cup	1
Usher Cup	2
V.E. Day Commemorative Cup	2
Vernon Trophy	2
Victoria Cup	3
Victory Cup (Senior) (1)	1
Victory Cup (Senior) (2)	1
W.T. Menswear Cup	2
Walker Cup	3

Weekly Record Cup	3	Whyte and MacKay Cup (1)	2
Wemyss Cup	1	Whyte and MacKay Cup (2)	2
West Fife Charity Cup	1	Wick Allan Shield	2
West Fife Cup	2	Wick League Cup	3
West Lothian League	3	Wigtownshire and District Cup	1
West Lothian Millennium Cup	2	Wigtownshire and Kirkcudbrightshire Cup	1
West of Scotland Consolation Cup	2	Wigtownshire Cup	1
West of Scotland Cup	2	Wilkinson Cup	3
Western Cup	3	Williamson Cup	3
Western League (Junior)	2	Wilson Charity Cup	3
Western League (Senior)	1	Wilson Cup	1
Western League Cup	2	Winter Cup	2
Whitbread Cup	2	Wishaw and District Cup	3
Whitbread Trophy	3		
White Horse Cup	2	Zamoyski Challenge Cup	2